陈平语言学文选

LANGUAGE IN A MODERNIZING CHINA

语言与中国的现代化进程

◆ 陈 平 著

商务印书馆
创于1897 The Commercial Press

2017年 · 北京

图书在版编目(CIP)数据

语言与中国的现代化进程/陈平著. —北京:商务印书馆,2017
(陈平语言学文选)
ISBN 978-7-100-13982-3

Ⅰ.①语… Ⅱ.①陈… Ⅲ.①汉语—社会语言学—关系—现代化建设—中国—文集 Ⅳ.①H1-53 ②D61-53

中国版本图书馆 CIP 数据核字(2017)第 114511 号

陈平语言学文选
语言与中国的现代化进程
陈 平 著

商 务 印 书 馆 出 版
(北京王府井大街 36 号 邮政编码 100710)
商 务 印 书 馆 发 行
北 京 冠 中 印 刷 厂 印 刷
ISBN 978-7-100-13982-3

2017 年 7 月第 1 版　开本 787×1092 1/16
2017 年 7 月北京第 1 次印刷　印张 19½

定价:68.00 元

目　　录

Languages in a modernizing China

Abstract As China embarked on the route of modernization in the second half of the nineteenth century, the mainstream consensus in China maintained that the Chinese language and writing system was seriously incompatible with a modernizing China. Modernization reform of Chinese focused on three dimensions of the language—establishment and promotion of a spoken standard, replacement of *wenyanwen* by *baihuawen* as the standard writing style to enhance expressivity of lexicon and grammar, and reform of the traditional Chinese script. The article describes how the current situation in relation to language form and language use in China is the outcome of interaction between spontaneous evolution over hundreds or even thousands of years, and meticulous design and active management since the nineteenth century. It also demonstrates how inherent logic and rules of the Chinese language and script have dictated the success or failure of the efforts at reform and renovation over the century.
Keywords language planning; modernization of China; standard spoken Chinese; standard written Chinese; script reform

1. Introduction

A recent estimate put the number of native speakers of Chinese globally at 1.11 billion in 1995, with English a distant second at 372 million; more significantly, the same estimate put the number of native speakers of Chinese aged 15-24 in 2050 at 166 million, and the number of speakers of English at 65 million, after Hindi/Urdu (73.7 million) and Arabic (72.2 million)[①]. These

① See Graddol (2004).

statistics derive from the fact that Chinese is the official language of the most populous country on earth—China, with a population of 1.3 billion in 2006—and is also used by overseas Chinese communities scattered extensively around the world, with a total population estimated to be in the vicinity of 30-40 million. What we know as Chinese, however, comprises dozens or hundreds of mutually unintelligible dialects. These fall into nine major groups, each of which in turn consists of a number of sub-groups. The names of the major groups of Chinese dialects, their populations and geographical distribution in China are presented in Table 1.

Table 1: Distribution of the Chinese language in China

Name	*Approximate Number of Speakers (million)*	*Major Areas*
Mandarin	660	
Beijing Mandarin		Beijing
Northeastern Mandarin		Heilongjiang, Jilin, Liaoning
Jiao-Liao Mandarin		Shandong, Liaoning
Ji-Lu Mandarin		Hebei, Shandong
Central Plains Mandarin		Henan, Shaanxi, Shandong
Lan-Yin Mandarin		Gansu, Ningxia
Southwestern Mandarin		Sichuan, Yunan, Guizhou
Jiang-Huai Mandarin		Jiangsu, Anhui, Hubei
Jin	45	Shanxi
Wu	70	Shanghai, Southern Jiangsu, Zhejiang
Hui	32	Southern Anhui
Xiang	25	Hunan
Gan	40	Jiangxi
Kejia (Hakka)	40	Guangdong, Fujian, Jiangxi
Yue (Cantonese)	62	Guangdong, Guangxi, Hong Kong
Min	60	Fujian, Guangdong, Hainan, Taiwan

(based on information from Wurm, S. A. et al (eds.), *Language Atlas of China*, Hong Kong, Longman Group (Far East) Ltd., 1987; Li, R. 'Chinese Dialects in China.', in S. A. Wurm et al (eds.), 1987, A-2; and Hou, J (ed.), *Xiandai Hanyu Fangyan Gailun*, Shanghai, Shanghai Jiaoyu Chubanshe, 2002)

As Table 1 shows, Mandarin is by far the largest group of Chinese dialects in terms of population and geographical distribution. All of the other dialects apart from Jin—notably Wu, Cantonese, Min and Hakka—are often referred to as Southern dialects because they are mostly spoken in areas south of the Yangtze River. The origin and path of evolvement of the Chinese dialects is currently a field of robust research in historical linguistics and dialectology, and there are still many unresolved issues and unanswered questions[①]. However, it is generally recognized that the dialectal diversity of Chinese may date back as far as the earliest written record of Chinese civilization. While the base dialect of Chinese originated in the Yellow River region in the north of China thousands of years ago, what later came to be known as Cantonese, Wu and Xiang may have developed in the southeast of China before the Qin Dynasty (221-206 BC), most likely as an outcome of close contact between the Chinese-speaking Han, the largest ethnic group in China, and indigenous people speaking other languages. Affinity varies between the major contemporary Chinese dialect groups, and also between sub-groups within the same group. Cantonese and Min, for instance, are more different from Mandarin than are other dialects, and Cantonese is at least as different from Mandarin as English is from German. Cantonese and Min are also the most heterogeneous of all the dialect groups, each containing a large number of mutually unintelligible dialects.

Modern Standard Chinese is given different names in the major Chinese-speaking communities. It is called *putonghua* (common speech)

① See Norman (1988) and Hou (2002).

in mainland China and Hong Kong, *guoyu* (national language) in Taiwan, and *huayu* (Chinese language) in Singapore. Allowing for some regional variations, all of the Chinese-speaking countries and regions, broadly speaking, look to Beijing Mandarin for norms of pronunciation, and the broader Northern Mandarin for basic vocabulary and grammar. Modern Standard Written Chinese, on the other hand, is by and large the written form of standard spoken Chinese.

The Chinese script is characterized as a logographic writing system, with each basic writing symbol—known as a character—indicating both sound and meaning. This contrasts with a phonographic writing system, in which basic writing symbols typically indicate sound only—a phoneme in the case of an alphabet, and a syllable in the case of a syllabary. Chinese is the only writing system in the world that has been in continuous use for at least 4,000 years. Chinese characters fall into four broad categories according to their graphic formation and composition at the time they first took shape—pictographic, ideographic, compound indicative, and semantic-phonetic compounding. Pictographic characters follow as much as practical the physical shape of the objects they stand for, such as 人 *ren* (person), 山 *shan* (mountain) and 口 *kou* (mouth). Ideographic characters indicate in a diagrammatic manner concepts and objects that do not usually have a physical appearance. Some examples are 一 *yi* (one), 二 *er* (two), 上 *shang* (up) and 下 *xia* (down). Compound indicative characters are formed by joining two or more pictographic or ideographic characters to depict a new concept or object based on the semantics of the components. An example is 休 *xiu* (rest), which consists of a person 人 leaning against a tree 木. Another example is 伐 *fa* (attack), composed of a person 人 and a dagger-axe 戈 *ge*, which originally meant attacking a person with a dagger-axe. Phonetic-semantic compounding characters are composed of two parts, one indicating the phonetic pronunciation and the other the semantic category. Examples are 桐 *tong* (plane tree) and 桃 *tao* (peach [tree]), with the left part 木 'tree' being the semantic indicator, and the right parts 同 and 兆 the phonetic indicator.

The Chinese terms for the Chinese language are *zhongwen* (Chinese writing) and *hanyu* (the language of Han). 'Han' in the second term derives from the name of by far the largest ethnic group in China, the Han. There are 55 other officially recognized ethnic groups in China, usually referred to as *shaoshu minz*u (ethnic minorities). Table 2 shows the genetic affiliation, population of speakers and geographical distribution of the major non-Chinese languages in China:

Table 2: Distribution of non-Chinese languages in China

Genetic Affiliation (major languages)	*Major Areas*
Sino-Tibetan	
Chinese	
Tibeto-Burman (Tibetan, Yi, Bai, Hani, Tujia)	Tibet, Yunnan, Sichuan
Kam-Tai (Zhuang, Dong, Boyei, Dai)	Guangxi, Yunnan, Guizhou
Miao-Yao (Miao, Mian, Bunu)	Hunan, Guangxi, Guizhou, Sichuan
Altaic	
Turkic(Uygur, Kazak, Kirgiz)	Xinjiang
Mongolian (Mongolian, Dongxiang, Daur)	Inner Mongolia, Xinjiang, Gansu
Manchu-Tungus (Xibe, Ewenki)	Xinjiang, Heilongjiang
Austro-Asiatic (Va, Blang, Deang)	Yunnan
Austronesian (Gaoshans)	Taiwan
Indo-European (Tajik, Russian)	Xinjiang, Inner Mongolia
Status undecided (Korean, Jing)	Jilin, Heilongjiang, Liaoning, Guangxi

(based on information from Wurm et al (eds.), *Language Atlas*, and Fu, M and J. Wang, 'Minority languages in China' ; in Wurm et al (eds.), 1987, A-4)

Some ethnic languages, most notably Mongolian, Tibetan and Uyghur, have their own writing system and a time-honoured literary tradition, although many did not have a fully fledged writing system until the second half of the twentieth century①. A few of these ethnic minorities, such as the Huis and Manchurians, have all but abandoned their original native language and adopted Chinese as their mother tongue. Most, however, have maintained their own language and, in some cases and to varying degrees, their own writing system.

2. Chinese language in pre-modern times

Rather than being valued as a symbol of national pride and identity that was important in the formation and advancement of nationalism as was the case in most European nations, the Chinese language was perceived in mainstream intellectual and political circles from the late nineteenth century as grossly inefficient and a serious obstacle to modernization. If China was to become a modern state, it was argued, the Chinese language must undergo drastic and wide-ranging reform②. The following century witnessed an attempt at language reform on a scale unparalleled in human history in terms of the size of population involved and the extent of changes to the way the language was used. Tremendous efforts have been exerted to make the Chinese language more in tune with a modernizing society.

In the eyes of the intellectual and political elites of the time, as well as a considerable proportion of the general public, the Chinese

① See Zhou (2003).

② See Chen (2007) for an in-depth account.

language suffered from three major shortcomings at a time when China embarked on the course of modernization in the late nineteenth century. First, China, with its vast land area, large population and great dialectal diversity, did not have a national spoken standard that would be appropriate for formal purposes and for easy communication across dialects. Secondly, standard written Chinese was essentially based on Old Chinese from the times of Confucius (551?-479? BC), and was completely divorced from the contemporary spoken language. Thirdly, the traditional Chinese script was regarded as a very difficult system to learn and to use, and was considered the main reason for an illiteracy rate as high as 95 percent in China at the turn of the twentieth century. In the remainder of this section, I will examine each of these problems more closely, and also consider initiatives and measures that were proposed and implemented toward their solution.

The Chinese dialects listed in Table 1 display great diversity, most notably in pronunciation but also to a considerable extent in vocabulary and grammar. There was in effect a lingua franca that evolved throughout Chinese history since the earliest times, based mainly on the dialects of the capitals of successive imperial dynasties, mostly in north China. As it was often used by officials, it was called *guanhua* (speech of mandarins), and it is from this that the large group of northern dialects, Mandarin, derived its name.① There is still debate over which regional varieties of Mandarin served as the dialectal base of the lingua franca in pre-modern times. Recent research suggests that it was Nanjing Mandarin, a variety of Jiang-Huai Mandarin, from the beginning of the Ming Dynasty (1368-1644), and Beijing Mandarin from the second half

① *Guan* in guanhua is also interpretable here as 'general public', so *guanhua* can also mean 'speech of the general public'.

of the nineteenth century onward.[1] The lingua franca that was used, as far as we can tell based on the limited evidence available, was an ill-defined hybrid, with speakers in other dialectal areas incorporating any number of features from local dialects into the Mandarin they employed. As could be expected, it did not enjoy the prestige usually associated with a modern standard language, and was even despised by some scholars as only fit for people of lower status such as housemaids. Its use was also highly limited, mostly confined to oral communication between speakers of mutually unintelligible dialects. There was no attempt at codification or standardization of the lingua franca as a standard form of spoken Chinese for the general public. It was not taught at school; nor did it serve as the medium of instruction. The number of people who attained any degree of proficiency in it was minimal in areas of Southern dialects. As a result, dialect diversity posed a huge linguistic barrier to effective oral communication in China.

In a country of such great dialectal diversity, the written language and the writing system in which it was recorded served as the most reliable means of communication, and, combined with other customs and values, played a bonding role for the Chinese as a nation throughout Chinese history until modern times, primarily for the literate but also for other sectors of society. Until the early twentieth century, the standard written Chinese, known as *wenyanwen* (classic literary language), was mainly based on classics in Old Chinese from the period up to the Qin (221-206BC) and Han dynasties (206BC-220) in terms of grammatical and lexical norms. Alongside *wenyanwen*, a new style of written Chinese known as *baihuawen* (vernacular literary language) began to develop from the late Tang dynasty (618-907). This new written form was much

① See Chen (1999).

closer to the contemporaneous vernacular in Mandarin areas in the north of China. Many popular novels such as *Shuihu Zhuan* (*Heroes of the Marshes*) and *Hong Lou Meng* (*The Dream of the Red Chamber*) and dramas were composed in *baihuawen* in the subsequent Song (960-1279), Yuan (1206-1368), Ming (1368-1644) and Qing (1616-1911) dynasties. It was also extensively used for informal purposes such as diary writing and book-keeping. For formal and official functions in education, administration and legal proceedings, however, traditional written Chinese—*wenyanwen*—was the undisputed norm. As it was increasingly divorced from spoken language after the Han dynasty, it took much more time and effort to acquire literacy in *wenyanwen* than in a writing style based on the daily vernacular.

Two features of the Chinese script made it an ideal writing system for the Chinese language for thousands of years. First, it contains a large number of homophonous characters with different graphic shapes to differentiate homophonous words and morphemes, in much the same way as we write *two*, *too* and *to* in English to differentiate words. What makes Chinese substantially different from English in this respect is that the number of homophonous expressions is much larger in Chinese. Take the syllable *ji* for example: when it is pronounced in the first, second, third and fourth tones, which are meaning-distinguishing pitch variations of syllables, it is represented by 47, 33, 12 and 45 distinct characters respectively in the *Modern Chinese Dictionary* (1998), and these encode at least as many different words and morphemes in Modern Chinese. Secondly, the graphic shape of characters does not indicate in a direct and straightforward manner their actual pronunciation in any Chinese dialect. These two features have enabled the Chinese script to be used across times, dialects and even languages, as is the case with Japanese and Korean. On the other hand, the same features are generally regarded as the underlying cause of the considerable difficulty encountered by contemporary learners and users of Chinese script.

In terms of graphic structure, around 90 percent of Chinese characters commonly used in Modern Chinese are the so-called phonetic-semantic compounding characters. While an alphabetic writing system typically has no more than a few dozen letters as its basic units, Chinese has around 1,300 distinct basic symbols that are used as sound-indicating components of characters, and 250 that are meaning-indicating components. As almost all of the characters were first composed more than a thousand years ago, many have undergone considerable change in pronunciation and meaning, so that characters with the same sound-indicating component may now have quite different pronunciations. In addition, the semantic affinity of characters that share the same meaning-indicating component is not always as straightforward as it was when the characters were originally composed. Literacy in Chinese is measured in terms of the number of characters learned. One needs to know at least 1,800 distinct characters as the essential prerequisite to basic reading and writing skills in Modern Chinese, while a primary-school graduate is expected to have learned around 3,000 characters. With the mnemonic value of sound- and meaning-indicating components greatly reduced by historical attrition, literacy acquisition in Chinese demands much more time and effort on the part of learners, at least in the early stages, than phonographic writing systems such as English. A comparative study has found that the reading materials of Chinese schoolchildren up to Grade 4 are only around one-sixth in volume of those at the comparative level in countries that use a phonographic writing system. The reason for the differential is attributed to the much greater amount of time spent on learning the Chinese script in Chinese schools before children can read and write competently in Chinese.

3. Language reform in twentieth-century China

Language reform in China has mainly aimed to address these three problems. Reform started in the late nineteenth century as an integral part of the national drive for modernization, and has focused on three major aspects—the establishment and promotion of a standard spoken language as the national language, reform of the traditional Chinese script through simplification and phonetization, and replacement of *wenyanwen* by a new, modernized *baihuawen* as the base of Modern Written Chinese.

Establishment of a standard national language

The concept of a standard national language for China was borrowed from Japan, which pursued modernization during the Meiji Period (1868-1912) and achieved considerable success in social and political reform, leading to the general advancement of its economic and military strength in comparison to its Asian neighbours. Inspired by Japan's success in promoting the Tokyo dialect as the national language, early Chinese advocates of a national language called for the unification of the Chinese dialects in the form of a national spoken standard, and also for the unification of speech and writing, in the early years of the twentieth century. This was later known as the National Language Movement.

The first issue was to decide which dialect should be taken as the basis for the standard national language. Despite the fanfare surrounding the proposal of a few Southern dialects as possible candidates, Beijing Mandarin was chosen. This came as little surprise, largely because the *guanhua* based on Northern Mandarin had served as a de facto lingua franca for centuries, in spite of its ill-defined nature and relatively small number of fluent speakers in non-Mandarin areas. What language reformers set out to do next was to define precisely the phonological, lexical and grammatical features of the national language, based on Beijing Mandarin, and promote it across the country. Specifically, they needed to decide which features of Beijing Mandarin should be taken as constituents of the national language, which should be left out, and which features of other dialects should be included. The consensus in the first years of the movement was that while the national language was to be based broadly on Beijing Mandarin it should also incorporate features from other dialects. In a resolution on the unification of the national language adopted by the national language planning institution in 1911, it was decided that the constituent features of the national language should be 'correct, elegant, and logical', which opened to the way for heated debate over the exact meaning of these attributes as guiding principles in the codification of the national language.

The standard pronunciation of the national language was defined in terms of the pronunciation of around 6,500 characters that were in common use. Members of a special Commission for Unifying Reading Pronunciation voted in 1913 on the pronunciation of each of these characters, and the results were coded in the *Dictionary of National Pronunciation* published in 1919. This represents what was later called *lao guoyin* (Old National Pronunciation). Whereas around 90 percent of the characters followed their pronunciation in Beijing Mandarin, *lao guoyin* also incorporated features from other Chinese dialects, features from earlier periods of Chinese, and some artificial distinctions not attested to anywhere in actual speech. All of the features that were not part of contemporary Beijing Mandarin were chosen on the grounds of allegedly being 'correct, elegant and logical' and to accommodate speakers of other dialects. The outcome was an artificial, hybrid system that was actually spoken by no-one. Chao Yuan Ren, an eminent Chinese linguist, remarked half jokingly that he and another scholar were the only two people in China who spoke the national language correctly when they were commissioned to make gramophone records of the system for educational purposes.

The artificiality of Old National Pronunciation caused confusion among users and prompted calls for change. The proposal that the pronunciation of the national language be based exclusively on Beijing Mandarin gradually gained widespread support, and finally led to a considerably revised edition of the *Dictionary* being published in 1932. It contains 12,219 characters, with their pronunciation following the general convention in Beijing Mandarin. The system used in the 1932 dictionary was known as *xin guoyin* (New National Pronunciation), which represented the standard pronunciation of the national language of China. In 1956, *putonghua* replaced *guoyu* as the name of the national language of the People's Republic of China, and was defined as follows:

> *Putonghua* is the standard form of Modern Chinese with the Beijing phonological system as its norm of pronunciation, and Northern dialects as its base dialect, and looking to exemplary modern works in *baihuawen* for its grammatical norms.

There are some features of Beijing Mandarin that have not been admitted as part of *putonghua*, as contained in standard reference works such as the *Modern Chinese Dictionary*. They are relatively few in number, and usually of restricted use in Beijing Mandarin. From this perspective, *putonghua*, like other standard languages in the world, is a theoretical abstraction that is not to be equated with any actual linguistic code.

On the other hand, it should also be noted that Beijing Mandarin is by far the closest of all the Chinese dialects to *putonghua*—not only in pronunciation, but also in vocabulary and grammar.

Script reform

The reform of the traditional Chinese script since the late nineteenth century has been the most arduous—and the most controversial—area of language reform in China. Generally speaking, there have been two major approaches to script reform—simplification and phonetization.

Simplification of the traditional Chinese script is achieved mainly through reducing the number of component strokes in characters, and by reducing the number of characters in common use. In the first case, a component of a character is replaced by one with fewer strokes, or a character is replaced by one of its component parts, or by another—usually homophonous—character with fewer strokes. Examples are 氣 → 气, and 臺, 颱, 檯 → 台. In the second case, one of the variant graphic forms of a character is selected as the authorized standard, and all other forms are abolished. Examples are 烟, 煙, 菸 → 烟. Simplified characters have always been popular among users throughout the history of the Chinese script, as they meet the natural inclination towards reduced effort on the part of writers. Historically, however, they have almost always been confined to informal uses and not allowed on formal occasions. Generally speaking, what language planning institutions have done in script simplification is to grant official recognition to the simplified characters that have already been in popular use in handwriting, and to replace complicated characters with their simplified counterparts in school education and in print.

A list of 324 simplified characters was promulgated by the Nationalist government in 1935 for use in schools and publications.

However, it was withdrawn in the same year due to strong opposition from some government officials, which was a striking illustration of the longstanding traditional reverence for Chinese script in Chinese society and the accompanying abhorrence of any attempt to meddle with the official writing system. Script simplification resumed in the 1950s under the new government of the People's Republic of China. The first scheme of simplified characters, promulgated in 1956, comprised 515 simplified characters and 54 basic components of characters. A complete list of 2,236 simplified characters was published in 1964, comprising all of the simplified characters in the first scheme, as well as all characters that have one or more of the simplified characters as their component parts. With some other characters replaced by simpler homophonous ones, a total of 2,264 traditional characters have undergone simplification in this process. The average number of strokes in the traditional characters involved has been reduced from 15.6 to 10.3, which, in the great majority of cases, has made the characters easier for general users to both write and recognize. The simplified script has since replaced the traditional script as the official writing system in mainland China. Singapore adopted the same simplified script as mainland China in 1976, but Taiwan and Hong Kong have retained the traditional script. While this difference may cause some inconvenience to readers from the other areas, it would be an exaggeration to claim it has seriously hindered effective written communication between the two groups. As noted earlier, a large number of simplified characters have long been in widespread use in handwriting in Taiwan and Hong Kong, as well as in mainland China, as part of *caoshu* (cursive style) or *xingshu* (running style), much in the same way as different fonts are used in print and handwriting in English. The choice of the official script in Taiwan stems principally from political considerations of differentiation from the mainland, rather than the technical adequacy of the writing system.[①]

Phonetization involves the design of a new phonographic writing system for writing Chinese. The first phonetic writing in Latin script for Chinese was designed by Jesuit missionaries stationed in China in the late sixteenth century, mainly for the purpose of facilitating Chinese learning by Westerners, but this new way of writing Chinese was destined to extend its function beyond language pedagogy. With more Western missionaries working in China in the second half of the nineteenth century, it was realized that the phonetic writing used by foreigners to learn Chinese could also be used by native Chinese to write their own dialects, and its acquisition usually took only a fraction of the time needed to learn the traditional script. Dozens of schemes in Latin script were designed by Western missionaries to write all the major Chinese dialects and used to translate the Bible and other proselytizing material. The first phonetic scheme designed by a native Chinese was published in 1892 by Lu Zhuangzhang to write his native dialect of Xiamen, a Min dialect. In all, more than a thousand phonetic schemes have been proposed over the past century to write standard Chinese and its various dialectal varieties.

Schemes of phonetic writing for Chinese have been designed to serve one of two major purposes. One is to play an auxiliary or supplementary role to the Chinese script, providing learners and users of Chinese characters with a tool for sound annotation, transcription and indexing. Like the International Phonetic Alphabet, this is not meant to be used as a bona fide writing system. On the other hand, some schemes are designed to function as a fully fledged writing system that may be used as an alternative to the traditional script for those who cannot

① See Chen (2001).

afford the time and effort to learn characters, or that may supersede the traditional script altogether for all functions and purposes.

The first scheme of phonetic writing of Chinese, *zhuyin zimu* (sound-annotating alphabet)—later renamed *zhuyin fuhao* (sound-annotating symbols)—was promulgated in 1918 by the Ministry of Education of the Republic of China for use in annotating the pronunciation of Chinese characters.[①] Instead of adopting Latin script, the basic symbols of *zhuyin zimu* were adapted from simple Chinese characters or character components, much in the same way as *kana* symbols were formed in Japanese. This played a very useful role in facilitating the learning of the standard spoken Chinese in the following decades. It was replaced by *hanyu pinyin* (Chinese phonetic writing)—or shortened as *pinyin*—in mainland China from 1958, but has been in continuous use in Taiwan. The first scheme in Latin script, *guoyu luomazi* (national language romanization), was promulgated by the government in 1928. It superseded other schemes in Latin script, such as the Wade-Giles and Postal systems, as the standard scheme of romanization of Chinese characters to be used in transcription of Chinese names, indexing, and so on. Like *zhuyin zimu*, it has been in continuous use in Taiwan in revised versions, but has been replaced by *hanyu pinyin* on the mainland. In 2001, the Ministry of Education of Taiwan published another phonetic scheme, *tongyong pinyin* (general phonetic writing), which was intended to replace *guoyu luomaz*i as the official phonetic scheme of Chinese in Taiwan, but has not been well received by the general public.[②] In fact, there are several phonetic

① See Chen (1999) for a detailed account of *zhuyin zimu* and other phonetic schemes discussed below.

② This is yet another example that highlights the major consideration on the part of the official language planning institution in Taiwan, which is to differentiate Taiwan from Mainland China as much as possible. Whether ideology will prevail over pragmatism with the general public on language and script schemes in current use in Taiwan, including Wade-Giles, *guoyu luomazi*, *hanyu pinyin* and *tongyong pinyin*. The following are the transliterations of 'Chinese script' in Wade-Giles, *guoyu luomazi*, *hanyu pinyin* and *tongyong pinyin* respectively—*chung kuo wen tzu, jung guo wen tz*, *zhong guo wen zi*, and *jhong guo wun zih*.

The most influential scheme of phonetic writing of Chinese in Latin script is *hanyu pinyin*, which was promulgated by the Chinese government in 1958, and has since been in widespread use in China and elsewhere in the world as the standard phonetic scheme for Chinese. It was designed to represent the pronunciation of Chinese characters in *putonghua*, but has also been adapted for some Southern Chinese dialects such as Cantonese. Like *zhuyin zhumu* and *guoyu luomazi*, *pinyin* was intended to serve an auxiliary role to the conventional writing system. Its main functions include the annotation of the pronunciation of characters to facilitate the learning of *putonghua*, transcription of Chinese names, indexing, and so on. As it is written in Latin script, *pinyin* was also intended to serve as the basis for the design or reform of writing systems of other ethnic languages in China. It has fulfilled all of these functions, and more, successfully in the fifty years since its publication. It has been adopted by many international organizations, including the International Standardization Organization and the United Nations, as well as by a growing number of other institutions such as universities and libraries outside China, as the standard form for the transcription of Chinese names and words. A *pinyin*-based input/output system is also arguably the most popular system for Chinese word processing.

Most designers of phonetic writing schemes for Chinese started with the intention of replacing the traditional Chinese writing system with

---

issues is another matter.

their new design in due course, and this was also the case with *pinyin*. A close reading of the literature on script reform in the early 1950s shows that phonetization of Chinese was firmly on the agenda of the language planning institutions of the new Chinese government. There was debate over the desirability and feasibility of replacing the Chinese script with a new phonographic writing system, and on the technicalities of the various schemes designed to fulfil such a role. Dominant opinions at the beginning, including those of the government leadership, were in favour of introducing a new phonetic scheme that would be used as a fully fledged writing system for Chinese, either to replace the Chinese script as soon as practical, or as an alternative to be used alongside the traditional writing system during a long transitional period. When *pinyin* was finally published, however, there was no mention of its immediate or potential use as a bona fide writing system for Chinese, to the disappointment of many enthusiastic advocates of the phonetization of Chinese.

All of the efforts and attempts to replace the Chinese script with a phonetic writing system have failed so far, not because of lack of enthusiasm on the part of language planners, but due to several seemingly insurmountable linguistic and nonlinguistic obstacles. As noted above, there are large numbers of homophonous words and expressions in Modern Chinese, which are graphically differentiated by different characters, but would assume the same written form in a phonographic system such as *pinyin*. Furthermore, as the only writing system that has been in continuous use for more than 4,000 years, the Chinese script is the written medium of a tremendous amount of literature that has been a defining part of the Chinese civilization. The abolishment of Chinese characters would in effect deny the great majority of Chinese access to their rich literary heritage and deprive them of a good part of what has made them Chinese. The overwhelmingly negative arguments against the Chinese script and many other traditional Chinese values that marked much of the twentieth century have been subjected to more critical scrutiny recently. An increasing number of scholars are of the opinion that quite a few of those views are lop-sided, and at times too radical to be of real benefit for the Chinese nation. With general self-confidence gradually being restored after decades of strong economic growth, it seems that the Chinese are re-examining their own history and cultural heritage, including the Chinese writing system, in a more objective and balanced way.

Reform of modern written Chinese

The replacement of Old Chinese-based *wenyanwen* with a new vernacular-based *baihuawen* as the standard written Chinese has been credited largely to a group of Western-trained scholars in the so-called New Culture Movement of the late 1910s, with Hu Shi (1891-1962) their most visible and eloquent advocate. What happened in China was comparable to similar events in Renaissance Europe, when speakers of English, French and Italian switched from Latin to new literary written languages based on their vernaculars. Citing European examples for the Chinese to emulate, Hu Shi summarized his proposals succinctly in terms of *guoyu de wenxue, wenxue de guoyu* (literature in National Language and a literary National Language), which laid down the basic principles for the development of a new written Chinese based on Modern Chinese, and the development of a national language in a refined literary style. The proposal won widespread support across Chinese society, and within the relatively short period of a decade or two *wenyanwen* was replaced by a new written style in *baihuawen* as the standard written Chinese for the great majority of uses and functions.[1] In present-day China *wenyanwen* as a written style is confined to special circumstances, and texts wholly in *wenyanwen* are rarely composed by contemporary writers.

It would be wrong, however, to assume that *wenyanwen* has totally disappeared from everyday life in China. Old Chinese is still being taught as an important language subject in schools, partly because it is the language of literary heritage, and partly because of the nature of Modern Written Chinese. While based broadly on Beijing Mandarin, Modern Written Chinese has also incorporated a large number of features from other Chinese dialects, foreign languages, and in particular Old Chinese. Many words and expressions in Old Chinese are still in active use, and constitute an indispensable part of the repertoire of Modern Written Chinese because of their stylistic effect of terseness and formality and their special cultural connotations.[2]

4. Language use in present-day Chinese society

The first Chinese law on language and script, the People's Republic of China Common Language and Script Law, was enacted by the National People's Congress of China in 2000, and took effect from January 2001. The law outlines the goals and objectives of language planning in China, and also specifies measures to be taken in implementing the law. What the terms 'common language and script' refer to here

---

① It should be pointed out that as the Modern Standard Written Chinese is based on northern Mandarin, its acquisition is relatively easier for Mandarin speakers than for speakers of southern dialects. Historically, as well as in contemporary China, writing in southern dialects has been rare, despite the large number of speakers of these dialects. For details, see Chen (2007).

② See Hodge and Louie (1998) for an account of social meanings associated with use of expression in Old Chinese and dialects.

are *putonghua* and the simplified script, the use of which is the main focus of management and monitoring by official language planning institutions affiliated with the various government departments. It is also stressed in the opening section of the law that, as a fundamental principle, the use of the common language and script in China should help to safeguard state sovereignty and national dignity, contribute to national unity and ethnic solidarity, and facilitate the material, cultural and moral progress of the socialist society. While providing a general framework for the management of language-related issues in various sectors of the community, the 2000 Law is also an encapsulation of the guiding principles, major targets and achievements of language policy and language planning in China since the late 1950s.

The PRC government has paid much more attention to language policy and language planning, and placed it under tighter government control, than did pre-1949 regimes. An authoritative language planning institution at the national level, the Chinese Script Reform Commission—renamed the State Language and Script Commission in 1985—was established in 1954, and given responsibility for all issues relating to language reform and use in the country. The National Conference on Script Reform convened the following year marked the beginning of an era in which language reform and management were fully integrated into the agenda for the modernization of the nation. Script simplification, design of *hanyu pinyin* and promotion of *putonghua* were identified at the conference as the three major tasks for language planning in China. Apart from the tumultuous years of the "Cultural Revolution" (1966-1976), great efforts have been made to achieve the goals set for each of the three tasks. With the backing of the strong political will and efficient administrative apparatus characteristic of an all-powerful government, considerable success has been achieved since the late 1950s.

Putonghua is now the national standard in all television and radio broadcasting services, and in film and other mass media productions in China. Broadcasting in other major Chinese dialects such as Wu, Min and Cantonese is also available in dialect areas to accommodate people in the older generation, but is normally restricted to several hours a day and local news and weather forecasts. *Putonghua* is stipulated as the standard medium of instruction in school, and it is mandatory for all teachers to pass a proficiency test as part of their qualifications. Compliance, however, varies between regions. As would be expected, school teachers in major cities are much more likely to be proficient in *putonghua* than those in rural and mountainous areas. This difference in terms of the quality of school teachers, combined with a difference in school attendance rates, has had a major impact on the rate of *putonghua* acquisition. The latest survey, in 2004, established that overall 53.05 percent of the population in China speaks *putonghua* with reasonable fluency, with the percentage considerably higher in cities and townships than in the countryside (66.03 percent compared to 45.06 percent). In most non-Beijing Mandarin areas, *putonghua* has become what is known in sociolinguistics as a High Language, fit for use for formal purposes in business, education and public administration, whereas the local dialect is a Low Language, customarily used on informal occasions among family and friends. In some dialect areas, particularly the Wu and Min areas, dialect attrition is becoming a concern. It has been reported that an increasing number of youngsters are less fluent in their local dialect than in *putonghua*, with some losing their dialectal skills altogether. Teenagers in Shanghai tend to use *putonghua* both in and outside the home. A recent study of language use by 6 to 14 year-olds in Jinhua, a large Wu-speaking city in Zhejiang province, found that while all speak *putonghua*, half could no longer speak their local dialect. This has prompted calls for action, with suggestions that a certain number of hours should be set aside at school to teach subject matter in the local dialect as part of measures to preserve the local dialect and culture.

Bilingualism in Chinese and the predominant local ethnic language(s) is the goal of language policy in areas with a sizeable proportion of ethnic minorities such as Inner Mongolia, Xinjiang and Tibet. It has been legislated at the state, provincial and lower levels since the 1950s that ethnic minorities have the right to learn and use their own languages and scripts for various purposes. At the same time, they are encouraged to learn Chinese, while Han people living in these areas are urged to learn the local ethnic languages. Bilingualism is fairly common in Inner Mongolia, Qinghai and Guangxi, where ethnic minorities have been intermingled with the Han for centuries. On the other hand, in Tibet and Xinjiang, around 70 percent of non-Han local residents, mostly farmers and herdsmen, are unable to communicate in *putonghua*. This is because the Tibetans and many ethnic minorities in Xinjiang have a robust tradition of education in their own languages and scripts, and did not come into close contact with the Han until relatively recently. However, the situation is changing. Ethnic minorities in these areas, especially people of the younger generation, are motivated by social mobility and financial advantage to acquire high proficiency in Chinese. It has been reported that the demand for bilingual education in Chinese and ethnic minority languages far outstrips the supply provided by the public education system, and that parents in ethnic minorities use private funding to set up more schools for bilingual education for their children.① It is safe to assume that the accelerating economic development in the provinces with sizeable populations of

① See Chen (2007).

ethnic minorities will be accompanied by a significant increase in the number of bilingual speakers of *putonghua* and local ethnic languages. At the same time, it should also be noted that there has been a steady decline in the number of speakers of certain ethnic languages, some of which are on the verge of extinction. One such example is Tujia, a Tibetan-Burmese language spoken mainly in Sichuan, Hunan and Hubei provinces in China. Among the Tujia population of around 8 million, fewer than 3 percent still speak the Tujia language, with the remainder having switched to Chinese as their first language.

The simplified script has been firmly established as the official standard in China, and has also been increasingly recognized around the world as the most popular, if not the sole standard, script of Chinese. There are occasionally calls for reverting to the traditional complicated script, on the grounds of facilitating written communication with Taiwan and Hong Kong and better access to historical literature. The PRC Common Language and Script Law states that the complicated script may be used, but only for highly restricted functions and purposes such as handwritten shop signs and artistic works. It is very unlikely, however, that the government will revoke the simplification reform and revert to the older script. With the last generation of children who learned the complicated script in primary school now almost 60 years old, the great majority of the Chinese population has grown up in the new writing system that has been in place since the late 1950s. Generally speaking, there is little nostalgia for the complicated Chinese characters in the present-day Chinese community; nor is there any enthusiasm for a new fully fledged phonographic writing system for Chinese, except perhaps among a tiny number of calligraphers, academics and professional language planners. So firmly entrenched has the current writing system become in China that, in all likelihood, it will remain relatively stable for the foreseeable future.

5. Conclusion

The development of an efficient, supra-local means of oral and written communication for all regions and areas of the country and mass literacy for the population are integral to the multi-faceted process of national modernization. In a developing and modernizing society such as China has been since the late nineteenth century, when people leave the rural villages to which the elder generations had been confined for hundreds of years, they tend to find dialectical diversity a serious impediment to communication with people from other parts of the country, and feel an urgent need for an overarching standard in which they can communicate with others with ease and efficiency. Mass literacy, on the other hand, is indispensable to any country aspiring to the ranks of industrialized modern nations. Broadly speaking, all the efforts of language reform and language planning in China over the past century or so have aimed at these two major objectives—a national spoken and written standard to facilitate communication, and an improved writing system to facilitate mass literacy.

The current situation in relation to language form and language use in China, as described in this chapter, is both the outcome of spontaneous evolvement over hundreds or even thousands of years, and, more significantly, the effect of meticulous design and active management as part of the unremitting endeavour for national modernization since the late nineteenth century. A de facto lingua franca across dialectal barriers evolved largely on the basis of the dialect of the capital cities of successive imperial dynasties in Mandarin areas before modern times. Through the process of codification and standardization, it developed into a national standard language that has been effectively promoted and extensively used in China since the first half of the twentieth century. Similarly, a vernacular style of writing, *baihuawen*, which was confined to casual uses before the twentieth century, has replaced the formal written language of *wenyanwen* as the basis of standard modern written Chinese as a result of the New Culture Movement of the late 1910s. The current Chinese writing system is likewise a hybrid of tradition, reform and innovation. Broadly speaking, simplification of the traditional Chinese script is nothing more than official recognition and standardization of the simplified forms of characters that had been in widespread use in handwriting over hundreds of years. Phonetization of Chinese, on the other hand, was initiated by Western Jesuits in China in the late sixteenth century and has greatly facilitated the acquisition and use of Chinese characters in China and elsewhere, although it has not achieved the objective entertained by some language reformers of providing a fully fledged alternative writing system for the language.

References

Chen, Ping. 1999. *Modern Chinese: History and Sociolinguistics*, Cambridge, Cambridge University Press.

Chen, Ping. 2001. Policy on the selection and implementation of a standard language as a source of conflict in Taiwan, In: Nanette Gottlieb and Ping Chen, eds., *Language Planning and Language Policy: East Asian Perspectives*, London, Curzon, 2001, Pp. 95-110.

Chen, Ping. 2007. China, In: Andrew Simpson, ed., *Language and National Identity in Asia*, Oxford University Press, 2007, Chapter 7, 139-167.

Fu, Maoji and Jun Wang. 1987. Minority languages in China, In: Wurm et al., eds., A-4.

Gradol, David. 2004. The future of language, *Science* 303 (2004), 1329-1331.

Hodge, Bob and Kam Louie. 1998. *The Politics of Chinese Language and Culture*:

The Art of Reading Dragons, London and New York, Routledge.

Hou, Jingyi. ed. 2002. *Xiandai Hanyu Fangyan Gailun* [*Introduction to Modern Chinese Dialects*], Shanghai: Shanghai Jiaoyu Chubanshe [Shanghai Educational Publishing House].

Li, Rong. 1987. Chinese dialects in China, In: Wurm et al., eds., A-2.

Norman, Jerry. 1988. *Chinese*, Cambridge, Cambridge University Press.

Wurm, Steven A. et al. eds. 1987. *Language Atlas of China*, Hong Kong, Longman Group (Far East) Ltd, 1987.

Zhou, Minglang. 2003. *Multilingualism in China: The Politics of Writing Reforms for Minority Languages 1949-2002*, Berlin and New York, Mouton de Gruyter.

语言与中国的现代化

提　要　中国自 19 世纪下半叶开始踏上现代化进程。当时及 20 世纪上半叶的社会主流意见普遍认为，汉语语言文字的现状，同国家现代化的要求严重地不相适应，必须加以彻底的改造。 汉语语言文字的现代化改造主要围绕三个方面进行：一是确立和推广全民族的共同语；二是用接近当代口语的白话文取代文言文，并丰富它在词汇和语法等方面的表现力，使之发展成为通用的现代汉语标准书面语；三是文字改革。本文分析 100 多年来汉语规划在这些方面取得的进步，并探讨其中的内在规律。本文认为，汉语和汉字的发展现状，是历史和传统以及改革和创新这两股主要力量交互影响、交互作用的结果，汉语和汉字在改革和创新方面的成功举措，都遵循了汉语语言文字发展的内在逻辑和规律。

关键词　语言规划　中国现代化进程　汉语标准口语　汉语标准书面语　文字改革

（This article was first published in *The Cambridge Companion to Modern Chinese Culture* edited by Kam Louie, Cambridge University Press, pp.198-217, in 2008. Permission by Cambridge University Press to reprint the article in the present volume is gratefully acknowledged.）

Language, nationalism, regional and ethnic identity in China

Abstract There have been two potentially conflicting views on the relationship between language and nationalism, regional and ethnic identity in China over the past 150 years. The predominating view among scholars and educators, particularly before the 1930s, was that, instead of being a sacrosanct symbol of Chinese-ness, the Chinese language was a hindrance to the modernization of the country and should undergo drastic reform, presumably because it was too difficult to learn and use. A pragmatic approach was pursued to make the language a better tool in practical linguistic terms with little attention paid to ideology. On the other hand, there has been a strong view that the Chinese language, particularly its script and the standard written form, has contributed profoundly to the integrity of the nation by virtue of its bonding role in the vast and populous land through millennia. It has been held that China has never disintegrated into various states along dialectal or linguistic lines largely due to the integrating role of the logographic script and the standard written language encoded in the script used across dialects and times. How to reform the language so that it would better suit a modernizing China without at the same time weakening its presumed unifying function has been a central theme in language planning and language policy in China. In this article, I will elaborate on the development of this theme since the mid nineteenth century, with special reference to representative and influential views and initiatives from the general public, scholars and educators, and language planning institutions under the successive Chinese governments.

Keywords nationalism; regional identity; ethnic identity; language and script reform; dialect

1. Introduction

The People's Republic of China (PRC) currently contains the world's largest, single country population, with over 1.3 billion Chinese citizens distributed over an area approximately three times the size of western Europe. As a modern nation-state, China is comparatively young, having emerged during a twentieth century filled with tremendous internal turmoil and social change. As a civilization populated and maintained by a single dominant ethnic group sharing a common culture, however, China has a vast history with a writing system dating back as far as 1,700 B.C. This paper examines issues relating to language and the establishment and support of national identity in modern, post-imperial China, and how language use is presently directed in contemporary China. In doing so, I will make important reference to a distinction between "ideological" versus "utilitarian" views of language in relation to the development of modern nation-states, and to the value of languages as markers of the national, regional and ethnic identity of their speakers.

A significant ideological/utilitarian distinction can be argued to underlie the design and implementation of differing types of language planning and language policy in different countries, and also provides a key to a sound understanding of varying attitudes toward issues such as multilingualism, language standardization, language maintenance and attrition. The ideological view is best represented in the philosophy developed by German scholars such as J. G. Herder (1744-1803), J.G. Fichte (1762-1814), and W. Humboldt (1767-1835), who saw language as a defining characteristic, or essence/Geist, of a nation. Language, according to this view, naturally serves as a unifying force for nationalist movements attempting to secure statehood, and then continues to function as a highly important symbol of the identity of nation-states once established (and can also serve as an identifying symbol of groups of speakers of other sub-state sizes). The utilitarian view, on the other hand, sees language as nothing more than a practical tool, whose value is determined mainly in terms of its efficiency, perceived or real, in facilitating oral and written communication for its speakers in their educational, political, social and economic activities. A native language or dialect, from this perspective, may or should undergo substantial reform, or even be abandoned in favour of another language or dialect, if and when this is deemed to serve the communicative needs of the people more effectively.

With such a difference in approach to language in mind, I will examine perceptions of Chinese during the late nineteenth and early twentieth century periods of strong nationalist support for the modernization of China as an independent, progressive nation-state. It will be shown that during this time, the ideological view of language was weak and sometimes simply absent from the mainstream intellectual and political discourse, and that perceptions of the "national" language on the part of the elite of Chinese society were in fact very negative, in a way that is both striking and quite uncommon among nationalist movements. I will then discuss the bi-dialectalism in China which has arisen as a result of the promotion of a standard form of Chinese in the country, and note that certain major dialects now seem to be in clear decline in terms of population of speakers and domains of use. Accompanying this is the attrition of regional identity which has local dialect as its most differentiating marker. Finally, I discuss the status of non-Chinese minority languages and the evolving patterns of bilingualism which exist among the communities associated with these languages.

2. A Linguistic Sketch of China

2.1 Chinese and its Dialects

The term "Chinese" as a designation for a single language is commonly used to refer to a grouping of regional dialects spread throughout the area of China which are clearly related in various ways. In accordance with the latest, and also the most generally accepted classification, Chinese is composed of nine major dialects. Their names, approximate population of speakers, and locations in terms of geographical area in China are summarized in Table 1. As can be seen from the figures in Table 1, the northern dialect known as "Mandarin" in English is spoken by a huge population covering most of north, north-east, and parts of south-west China, and greatly outnumbers the total number of speakers of other Chinese dialects (660 million vs. 374 million).

Table 1: Distribution of the Chinese Language in China

Name	*Approximate Number of Speakers (million)*	*Major Areas*
Mandarin	660	
Beijing Mandarin		Beijing
Northeastern Mandarin		Heilongjiang, Jilin, Liaoning
Jiao-Liao Mandarin		Shandong, Liaoning
Ji-Lu Mandarin		Hebei, Shandong
Central Plains Mandarin		Henan, Shaanxi, Shandong
Lan-Yin Mandarin		Gansu, Ningxia
Southwestern Mandarin		Sichuan, Yunan, Guizhou
Jiang-Huai Mandarin		Jiangsu, Anhui, Hubei
Jin	45	Shanxi
Wu	70	Shanghai, Southern Jiangsu,

续表

Name	*Approximate Number of Speakers (million)*	*Major Areas*
		Zhejiang
Hui	32	Southern Anhui
Xiang	25	Hunan
Gan	40	Jiangxi
Kejia (Hakka)	40	Guangdong, Fujian, Jiangxi
Yue (Cantonese)	62	Guangdong, Guangxi, Hong Kong
Min	60	Fujian, Guangdong, Hainan, Taiwan

(based on information from Wurm 1987, Li 1987, and Hou 2002)

The nine major regional dialects differ from each other to a considerable extent in their pronunciation, and to a lesser extent in their lexicon and grammar. Principally as a result of the former phonological variation, the dialects are in fact mutually unintelligible, and the linguistic distance between, for example, Beijing Mandarin and Cantonese can be likened to that separating French from Italian. Many of the dialects can furthermore be broken down into numerous sub-dialects which themselves may be mutually unintelligible, and so it is actually more accurate to refer to the nine major dialects as 'dialect groups'. Due to the fact that speech from (and even within) the various regional dialect groups cannot be mutually understood, it has also sometimes been suggested (e.g. Bloomfield 1961) that Mandarin, Jin, Wu, Min etc should be classified as separate Chinese languages rather than just dialects. However, whether linguistically correct or not, such a separation into distinct languages does not accord with speakers' perceptions of the varieties they have as mother tongues, and within China the term *fangyan* 'dialect' is always used to refer to varieties such as Cantonese and Hakka, and never replaced with the term *yuyan* 'language'. There is, therefore, a widespread belief that the various forms of regional speech present in China are varieties of a single language, Chinese.① This perception is further buttressed by the important fact that speakers of all regional varieties of Chinese are connected in the use of a single, standardized written form of Chinese, and by a long commonly-shared literary history.②

Exactly when and how the regional varieties of Chinese took their earliest shape and evolved throughout history is still not very well known. In spite of many unsettled issues in the history of Chinese, however, most researchers agree that the existence of an original standard form of Chinese can be traced back to well over two thousand years ago. In the era of Confucius (551-479 BC) this was known as *yayan* ‘elegant language’, and served as the base of written Chinese and also (it is believed) as a standard spoken form for those with (mostly official) dealings across dialect boundaries. Significantly later on, from the beginning of the Ming Dynasty (1368-1644), the shared standard was called *guanhua* ‘mandarin’ or ‘speech of officials’, a term which remained in popular use until the end of the nineteenth century when it was replaced by the new nationalist-related term *guoyu* ‘national language’.③ The geographical base of the de facto administrative

① Just as, for example, speakers of "English" from Aberdeen in Scotland and Louisiana would feel that they are speaking the same underlying language, even though they might not be able to understand each other's speech.

② The relation of the regional dialects of Chinese to written Chinese is therefore not unlike the relation of regional forms of spoken Arabic to written Arabic. Though speakers of Levantine and Gulf Arabic may not be able to understand each other when they speak their regional dialects, they are linked by a common written form which is understood by all.

③ The term *guoyu* was actually used before modern times to refer to the native language of the ruling class, which may not have been Chinese, as in the case of the early emperors of the Qing Dynasty (1616-1911), who spoke Manchu. *Guoyu* in the modern sense of national language was borrowed from Japanese, which combined two Chinese characters (meaning ‘country’ and ‘language’) to refer to the new concept of national language borrowed from the Europeans during the Meiji Period (1868-1912). Since the late nineteenth century up until the mid 1950s, *guoyu* was used to refer to a newly codified standard form of Chinese also switched several times in history. In the Sui (581-618) and the Tang (618-907) Dynasty, it was based on the local dialect of present-day Xi'an. In the Northern Song Dynasty (960-1127) the base switched to present-day Kaifeng and Luoyang, and then to Nanjing in the Ming and early Qing Dynasty. It was not until the mid nineteenth century that Beijing Mandarin subsequently replaced the Nanjing dialect as the base of this shared, official lingua franca.

The second half of the nineteenth century also marked the arousal of nationalism in China, and the beginning of a process of the modernization of China as a nation state, to a large extent as a reaction to the successive invasion and military defeats of China by Western powers since the First Opium War (1840-1842), causing a gradual, worrying erosion of its sovereignty. The specific concept of a national language was introduced into Chinese discourse from Japan in the late nineteenth century, following Japan's own rapid modernization. Before this period, the concept of standard language in China was mainly applicable to written Chinese, specifying, among other things, the proper graphic shape of Chinese characters and their pronunciation. Concerning the latter, in traditional dictionaries this was indicated in terms of the phonological categories that Chinese logographic characters belonged to in earlier periods of historical development, rather than their actual pronunciation in any contemporary vernacular. The dictionaries were of principal use for writers who needed to select words with appropriate sounds for rhyming purposes in poem composition, and facilitated the continued production of high literature in a classical writing style known as *wenyanwen*. In addition to works written in *wenyanwen*, there was also the occasional use of a written form close to genuine, contemporary speech,

standard form of Chinese as the national language of China.

known as *baihuawen* or ‘vernacular literary literature’. However, prior to the twentieth century, use of *baihuawen* was much more restricted and less common than the formal standard.

The National Language Movement which became increasingly active during the beginning of the twentieth century set out to officially establish and promote a standard language across the whole of China, and to replace the written standard based on Old Chinese with one that was closer to the contemporary vernacular. Together with the creation of a phonetic representation of Chinese as an ancillary aid for the learning of character-based written Chinese, the development of a new standard form of written and spoken Chinese constitute an important part of the modernization of China as a nation state in the twentieth century. In attempting to reach an accepted codification of the national language, it was hotly debated for more than a decade through into the 1920s whether standard Chinese should be based predominantly on the Beijing dialect of Mandarin Chinese, or alternatively incorporate phonological features from other dialects, such as the Nanjing dialect. The former approach eventually prevailed, and 1932 saw the publication of *Guoyin Changyong Zihui* (*A Glossary of Frequently Used Characters in National Pronunciation*), which set the phonetic values of words in the new standard spoken Chinese as predominantly those of Beijing Mandarin. Somewhat later on, in the early 1950s, the Chinese appellation of this standard was changed from *guoyu* ‘national language’ to *putonghua* ‘common language’, being officially defined by the government as follows:

> ‘*Putonghua* is the standard form of Modern Chinese with the Beijing phonological system as its norm of pronunciation, and Northern dialects as its base dialect, and looking to exemplary modern works in *baihua* ‘vernacular literary language’ for its grammatical norms.’

Putonghua, as described above, and perhaps like many standard languages, is an abstraction, and is not the native language of any real set of individuals. In pronunciation, it is mainly based on Beijing Mandarin; in vocabulary and grammar, it is the spoken form of the vernacular literary language commonly written by contemporary Chinese writers. This generally excludes specific localisms of Beijing dialect and has also incorporated a large number of words, phrases, and grammatical features from other sources, mainly other Chinese dialects, Old Chinese and foreign languages (for details, see Chen 1999)[①]. *Putonghua* is consequently not fully equivalent to Beijing Mandarin. Nevertheless, as a form of Mandarin does comprise the dominant and major component of the base of *putonghua* (and *putonghua* is commonly rendered in English as 'Mandarin' [②]), speakers of Mandarin dialects throughout the north and southwest of China find the acquisition of *putonghua* and its written form relatively straightforward, whereas speakers of other dialects are at a disadvantage both in the learning of *putonghua* itself and in the acquisition of literacy in general, as this is now mastery of a standardized written equivalent of *putonghua*. Non-Mandarin speakers are accordingly faced with the task of having to learn to read and write in a linguistic code which is markedly different from their

① Although there was the official adoption of lexical items from various dialects in the initial creation of *putonghua*, in the current production of vernacular written language writers from non-Mandarin dialect areas tend to avoid the use of expressions which are still peculiar to their own dialects, so as to ensure a wide, national readership. Since the mid-1950s, the avoidance of dialectalisms in writing has indeed been held to be an important aspect of the standardization of the language, in tandem with the promotion of *putonghua* as a spoken standard across the country, and can even be noted as a common practise earlier in the twentieth century when *baihuawen* came to replace *wenyanwen* as the base of modern standard written Chinese. In contemporary Chinese fiction, it is usually very difficult to tell the dialectal background of writers, unless they make a conscious effort to display their regional and dialectal identities in their writing, which is rarely the case.

② Hence courses in *putonghua* offered in schools and universities in the west are regularly referred to as teaching Mandarin or Mandarin Chinese.

native, regional form of speech. In order to assist in the acquisition of general literary skills, speakers of southern, non-Mandarin dialects are therefore regularly drawn to first learn the spoken standard, and then convert this knowledge of *putonghua* into a competence in reading and writing standard written Chinese. The use that *putonghua* has here in facilitating literacy skills is, as a result, considered to be one of the most important motivating factors in the promotion of *putonghua* among dialect speakers. How *putonghua* has been successfully spread among the population, and the effects of this for the regional dialects, will be returned to later in section 4.

2.2 Non-Chinese Languages in China

In addition to the Han Chinese[①] population in China, there are 55 other officially recognized ethnic groups in the country, generally known as *shaoshu minzu* 'ethnic minorities'. According to the 1990 census, the ethnic minorities account for 8% of the total population in China, and are distributed over 60% of the country. The Zhuang, with a population of 16 million, are the most populous ethnic group after the Han. Following this, the Manchu, Hui, Miao. Uygur, Yi, and Tujia each have a population of between 5 to 10 million, and the Mongolian, Tibetan and Korean, 1 to 5 million. Table 2 lists the major geographical areas where the ethnic minorities are predominantly settled:

---

① The term 'Han' refers to all those members of the Chinese population who have a form of Chinese as their mother tongue and who are also ethnically Chinese by ancestry and culture—hence all the dialects groups identified in table 1, both in the north and south of the country. A common cover term for Chinese, including all its dialects, based on the word Han is *hanyu* 'Han language', and gives rise to the associated terms *hanwen* 'written Chinese' and *hanzi* 'Chinese character/script'. A further, more recent way of referring to Chinese in general, which is fully neutral in terms of ethnicity but somewhat more restricted in the way it can be used, is the term *zhongwen* 'Chinese language'.

Table 2: Major Geographical Areas of Ethnic Minority Groups in China

Major areas	*Percentage of ethnic minority population per province*
Tibet	96%
Xinjiang	62%
Qinghai	42%
Guangxi	39%
Guizhou	35%
Yunnan	33%
Ningxia	33%
Inner Mongolia	19%

Ethnic minority communities are granted a certain degree of autonomy in government, education and other aspects of social-economic life by the Constitution of the PRC. It is stated in the 1999 Constitution of the PRC that 'regional autonomy is practised in areas where people of minority nationalities live in compact communities. In these areas organs of self-government are established for the exercise of the right of autonomy' . Currently there are five autonomous regions on the provincial level, namely Tibet, Xinjiang, Guangxi, Ningxia, and Inner Mongolia. On lower tiers of administration, there are 30 autonomous prefectures, 120 autonomous counties, and hundreds of autonomous villages. The government and legislative bodies in the autonomous areas have the power to pass laws and issue executive regulations that are adopted for special local circumstances so long as these do not violate state laws and regulations (cf. Y. Chen 2001).

Language is not an indispensable marker of ethnicity in China. Among the 55 ethnic minority groups, the Manchu and the Hui are native speakers of Chinese, and do not have their own languages.① Other ethnic minorities may speak more than one language. The Yao,

① More precisely, there are less than 100 Manchu people who still speak Manchu, out of a population of 10 million.

for example, speak at least three different languages, Mian, Bunu and Lakkia. In total, about 72 non-Chinese languages are spoken by 53 ethnic minority groups, and these belong to the non-Sinitic branch of Sino-Tibetan, and other language families including Altaic, Austro-asiatic, Austronesian, and Indo-European, as presented in Table 3.

Table 3: Distribution of Non-Chinese Languages in China

Genetic Affiliation (major languages)	*Major Areas*
Sino-Tibetan	
Chinese	
Tibeto-Burman (Tibetan, Yi, Bai, Hani, Tujia)	Tibet, Yunnan, Sichuan
Kam-Tai (Zhuang, Dong, Boyei, Dai)	Guangxi, Yunnan, Guizhou
Miao-Yao (Miao, Mian, Bunu)	Hunan, Guangxi, Guizhou, Sichuan
Altaic	
Turkic(Uygur, Kazak, Kirgiz)	Xinjiang
Mongolian (Mongolian, Dongxiang, Daur)	Inner Mongolia, Xinjiang, Gansu
Manchu-Tungus (Xibe, Ewenki)	Xinjiang, Heilongjiang
Austro-Asiatic (Va, Blang, Deang)	Yunnan
Austronesian (Gaoshans)	Taiwan
Indo-European (Tajik, Russian)	Xinjiang, Inner Mongolia
Status undecided (Korean, Jing)	Jilin, Heilongjiang, Liaoning, Guangxi

(based on information from Wurm 1987 and Fu & Wang 1987)

Some minority languages, such as Mongolian, Tibctan, and Uygur have a well-established literary tradition. Before 1949 when the PRC was founded, 21 minority languages had their own writing systems. After 1949, under the auspices of the central government, new writing systems in roman script were devised for some of the languages that did not have their own standard writing, and certain old scripts underwent reform or refinement. A total of 54 writing systems for 29 minority languages are now in current use, with some languages having more than one writing system to accommodate dialectal diversity. All the documents of the annual sessions of the National People's Congress and the Chinese People's Political Consultative Conference are published in Mongolian, Tibetan, Uygur, Kazak, Korean, Yi and Zhuang in addition to Chinese, and there are newspapers, journals, television and radio services regularly provided in a range of the minority languages.

3. Perceptions of Language and Nationalism in Modern China

3.1 The Role of Linguistic Nationalism in Modern China

Three major shifts in political power have occurred in China over the past century. In 1911, the imperial Qing dynasty was overthrown and the Republic of China was founded the following year. In 1927, the Nationalist Government, with its capital in Nanjing, defeated the Northern Warlords and for the first time after the 1911 Revolution assumed administrative authority over the whole country in the role of a central government, and in 1949, the Nationalist government was replaced by the government of the PRC with its capital in Beijing. It is generally agreed by Chinese historians that nationalism was the primary motivating force behind all three historical events.

After a series of humiliating military defeats, first at the hands of the British in the Opium Wars, then by the Japanese in the Sino-Japanese War of 1894-1895, and finally by the Allied Forces in 1900, China found itself in danger of sharing the same fate as neighbouring countries such as Korea and Vietnam, which had been turned into colonies by the Japanese and the French respectively. The full-scale invasion of China by Japan in the Anti-Japanese War starting from 1937 intensified the sense of crisis in the collective psyche of the Chinese people, and from the mid-nineteenth century onwards, national independence clearly became the most ardent political aspiration of the Chinese as a nation.

Modernization of the Chinese language then came to be an important part of the nationalist movement in China, and synchronous with the development of China as a modern nation-state. Dialectal diversity was considered to be a serious problem in oral communication in China before the movement to establish and promote a national standard began at the turn of the twentieth century, and written Chinese was also perceived to be highly problematic. As discussed in section 2.1, standard written Chinese at the time, *wenyanwen*, was based on the norms of Old Chinese, which were completely divorced from the contemporary spoken language. In addition to this, there was a vernacular literary language, *baihuawen*, but *baihuawen* had only been used for informal and low culture functions such as the writing of popular novels, scripts for folk stories and plays, and diaries. The standard writing system was furthermore one which allowed for little variation when employed in its regular formal functions such as state examination and official documentation, and therefore seemed ill-suited for expansion into other domains.

Contrary to the pattern attested in Europe where language has repeatedly played an important ideological and political role in the formation of nation-states, during the nationalist period in China the Chinese language seldom, if ever, served as a symbol of national identity. In fact one could even say that the nationalist sentiment for national independence and social progress in China was as strong as the sentiment against its language, particularly the written language used in printed materials. Far from enjoying a sacrosanct aura, the

Chinese language was blamed as one of the fundamental causes of the backwardness of the country. It was targeted as an object for drastic reform, and some argued it should actually be abandoned in favour of another language if attempts at reform turned out to be unsuccessful.

In the mainstream intellectual and political discourse for more than a century following the Opium Wars, the worrisome plight of China was attributed mainly to a lack of proper education among the majority of the population, which in turn was attributed to the perceived low efficiency of the language, in particular the written language and its complicated character-based script. The acquisition of literacy in Chinese, it was argued, was a very time consuming burden that not many people could undertake. Lu Zhuangzhang, the first native Chinese who designed a phonetic writing system for his Southern Min dialect, summarized a common view in the preface to his book published in 1892:

> 'Chinese characters are probably the most difficult script to learn in the world... I believe that the strength and prosperity of our country depends upon the physical sciences, which can grow and flourish only if all people—men and women, young and old—are eager to learn and be knowledgeable. If people are to be eager to learn, then the script needs to be phoneticized in such a way that, after they have acquired the alphabet and rules of spelling, they will know how to read without further instruction. Speech and writing also need to use the same language, so that what is said by the mouth will be understood by the mind.' (Lu Zhuangzhang 1892:2-3)

In terms of its call for an alignment of spoken and written forms of Chinese and a simplification of the script (possibly by a shift to a different, alphabetic representation of Chinese), Lu expressed a very general feeling among those anxious for reform (for further discussion, see Chen 1999:165). Subsequently, the establishment and promotion of a new spoken standard, the reform of the written language and the simplification of the traditional writing system occurred as the three major components in the modernization of Chinese during the nationalist movement's drive towards an independent, modern state of China.

In one sense, then, a very classic pattern of linguistic nationalism may have appeared to be at work in China's new 'awakening' from the late nineteenth century onwards. Hobsbawm (1990:160) remarks that the common path of linguistic nationalism sees a dialect develop into "a new all-purpose standard 'national' literary language, which will then become official". However, what makes the case with Chinese drastically different from the situation with most European languages during their associated nationalist movements is the perception that the Chinese and European language reformers had with regard to their respective languages.

3.2 Perceptions of the Chinese Language during the Nationalist Movement

Consider first the following quotation about French by Rivarol in 1784 (from Judge 2000:73-4):

> 'There has never been a language in which it has been possible to write in a purer and clearer manner than ours, a language which has been so opposed to ambiguity and all kinds of obscurity, a language more sober and yet more gentle, more adapted to all kinds of style, a language more chaste in its expressions, more judicious in its figures, a language which, while loving elegance and ornamentation, is most opposed to affectation.'

In stark contrast to Rivarol's eulogy of his native language, French, the following are comments and proposals in relation to Chinese that were made in the early part of the twentieth century by some of the most prominent intellectual and political figures in China of the time:

> 'If we don't want China to perish, and if we want it to be a civilized nation in the twentieth century, the best thing to do would be to abandon Confucianism and Daoism, and the simplest way toward this end would be to abandon written Chinese, in which the Confucian doctrines and Daoist fallacies were recorded. After written Chinese is abandoned,... we should adopt Esperanto, an artificial language that is concise in grammar, uniform in pronunciation, and elegant in its word roots.' (Qian Xuantong 1918:144)
>
> 'In the period of transition (before the Chinese language is abandoned), we need to first abolish the Chinese script. The Chinese language may be maintained for the time being, but should be written in roman script.' (Chen Duxiu 1918:146)
>
> 'I completely agree with Mr. Chen Duxiu on his proposal to abolish the Chinese script while maintaining the Chinese language for the present. I believe China should have a phonetic writing system in the future.' (Hu Shi 1918:146)
>
> 'There are many impediments to the dissemination of knowledge among the Chinese. Two of them have been disastrous. The first is having living human beings use the language of the dead; the second is the continued maintenance in modern life of a script that is both primitive and clumsy... The origin of the Chinese script is extremely uncivilised, and its graphic shape very bizarre. It is extraordinarily difficult to learn, and uneconomical to use. Indeed, it is the clumsy, coarse script of monsters and demons, and the most inconvenient tool in the world.' (Fu Sinian

1919:147)

'The Chinese script is certainly an effective tool of obscurantist policy... and the tuberculosis of the labouring masses. If we don't get rid of these insidious germs, we will end up dead ourselves.' (Lu Xun 1929:160)

'Chinese characters are like the filthiest, most abominable, most wicked, medieval night soil cesspit.' (Qu Qiubai 1931:690)

Considerable space has been used here to present these views in order to highlight two points (cf. Gao 2003 for more of similar views). First, all of the above writers were clearly filled with very strong negative feelings towards written Chinese, and in particular the use of traditional Chinese characters. With some of them, the negative feelings extended to the Chinese language per se. Second, these very negative perceptions of the Chinese language, in particular of *wenyanwen* and the script, were not the idiosyncratic ravings of a few eccentric professors. All of these writers belonged to, and indeed constituted, the intellectual elite of Chinese society in the first half of the twentieth century, wielding tremendous influence upon their contemporaries and following generations. Hu Shi (1891-1962), Chen Duxiu (1879-1942), and Fu Sinian (1896-1950) were leaders in the May 4th New Culture Movement in 1919, which marked the beginning of Modern China. Hu Shi and Fu Sinian were also both presidents of the prestigious Peking University. Lu Xun (1881-1936) was generally recognized as the most prominent writer and thinker of his time. Chen Duxiu was the founding General Secretary of the Chinese Communist Party from 1921, and Qu Qiubai (1899-1935) held the same position in 1927. More importantly, language planning and language policy in the successive governments was mainly in the charge of these people and their like-minded colleagues. Qian Xuantong (1887-1939) was the designer of the first scheme of simplification of the

Chinese script, which was promulgated by the Nationalist government in 1936. The founding chair of the first official language planning institution of the People's Republic of China, the Association of the Reform of Chinese Script, was Wu Yuzhang (1978-1966), a close ally of Qu Qiubai on language reform, and Wu and Qu, together with certain Soviet linguists, were the engineers of the design of an influential phonetic writing system for Chinese, *Ladinxua Sin Wenz* 'Latinized New Script', the precursor to *Hanyu pinyin* 'Chinese Phonetic Writing' (which is still in current use in various functions). It is largely thanks to the successful efforts and failures of these individuals in initiatives in language planning that the Chinese language, in respect of the spoken and written standard and its writing system, is what it is now.

All of these prominent figures in twentieth century China held sincere and strong nationalist sentiments, and in their respective ways played important and highly commendable roles in the nationalist movement working for modernization of the country. On the other hand, as demonstrated in the above quotations, they held minimal respect for the Chinese language, and the Herderian ideological view of language as the treasured essence of a nation and its people was completely absent among them. To the extent that they did take a keen interest in language, and participated actively in the reform of the Chinese language, they were putting into practice a fully utilitarian view of language that had no place for the ideological value of Chinese in the national identity. Indeed, perhaps at no other point in modern history has the intellectual and political elite of a major emerging nation seemed to hold its mother tongue in such apparent abhorrence, and used such strong depreciatory language in condemnation of the language. There were, to be sure, certain dissenting voices defending the Chinese language, but these were generally weak and few and far between, at least in the first half of the twentieth century, and the views presented above prevailed in the mainstream discourse on language in China from the late nineteenth century well into the first half of the twentieth century, and to some extent, have even persisted to the present time.

How should we now explain this rather unique situation in which highly negative perceptions of the Chinese language, and particularly of written Chinese and the Chinese script, dominated mainstream thinking and discussion in modern China? Broadly, it can be suggested that there were three principal factors contributing to such a situation, the first of these having to do with the historical development of China and how this may have been different from the development of nations elsewhere.

With regards to Europe, it is well documented that language played an important ideological and political role in the formation of its nation-states, and particularly in Central and Eastern Europe, serving to arouse the self-awareness of speakers as groups distinct from neighbouring peoples speaking other languages. As observed by Anderson (1983:66), the Herderian concept of the nation being linked to language as a private-property ‘had wide influence in nineteenth century Europe and, more narrowly, on subsequent theorizing about the nature of nationalism.’ ‘National print-languages’, Anderson also remarks (1983:71), ‘were of central ideological and political importance’ in the formation of nationalism in Europe between 1820 and 1920. Linguistic nationalism, embodied in the publication of important works in a vernacular, standardization of the vernacular, and its promotion to the state of being a language fit for all formal and official functions, was an integral part of nation-state building. Language and nationalist movements in Europe were felt to be very closely linked in many cases, so that (for example) the birth of Hungarian nationalism was considered to be an event which occurred in 1772 with the publication of certain works of literature in the Hungarian language.

Unlike the European nation-states, however, China as a civilization, and as a nation in a pre-modern sense, had been a historical given for millennia. Before the advent of modern times it had been a country with a central government, and had used a common written language since the imperial Qin Dynasty (221-206 BC). The series of events occurring since the mid nineteenth century certainly developed a sense of crisis over the survival of the nation in the face of foreign invasion, but the existence of the Chinese as a nation, in the traditional and the modern sense, was taken for granted. Consequently there was no real need for language to serve as a symbol of identity or a bonding force in the national awareness of the Chinese people.

Secondly there was a political factor. Although prior to the twentieth century China was ruled for three hundred years by foreign Manchu emperors in the Qing Dynasty, language was seldom a politicized issue during this time and not part of the tension that existed between the ruling Manchu and their mostly Han subjects. This was for the simple reason that the foreign rulers abandoned their own language and adopted Chinese. During the conquest of China proper by Manchu troops, Han Chinese men were sometimes executed for refusing to wear their hair in braids of the same special style as the Manchu, but were never pressurized to learn Manchurian, and continued to speak and write in Chinese just as in previous times. As language consequently played no significant political role in the three hundred years of rule by a non-Han dynasty, it could not, and did not, serve as a symbol of identity for the non-Manchu subjects in the first nationalist movement that led to the overthrow of the dynasty in 1911. Such a situation then remained more or less the same in the following decades in China as nationalism grew stronger, and language was not focused as a symbol of the nation's identity.

A third factor relates to certain key linguistic features characterising China before the National Language Movement. As discussed in section 2.1, a large proportion of the Chinese population spoke mutually unintelligible dialects prior to the spread of *putonghua*. To most regional dialectal speakers, the lingua franca that did exist at the time in a restricted fashion (*guanhua*) was actually of low prestige, and often referred to with a derogatory tone. In the face of both severe dialectal diversity, and the low status of *guanhua*, no spoken vernacular was available to serve as a strong and proud symbol of the Chinese nation.

The striking lack of the use of language as a positive symbol to mobilize citizens during the nationalist movement in China can therefore be explained as having multiple, converging causes, and in the absence of positive properties being associated with Chinese at this time, those responsible for the linguistic development of China as an emerging, modern nation-state came to focus on the inefficiencies that they perceived in especially the written form of the language, these being seen as critically holding the common people back from developing as a modern nation.

If one is, however, to try to be objective and find positive effects of the Chinese language on the cohesion of China as a single nation-like unit, even though not highlighted by observers at the time of nationalist growth, somewhat ironically it is the traditional writing system of Chinese with its complicated script which is likely to have served as the strongest connecting bond among the Chinese people otherwise largely separated in communication by the existence of mutually unintelligible dialects. As observed in Chen (1999:128), 'in spite of the remarkable differences between dialects, the fact that there has been a single written standard makes the Chinese language less of a disintegrating force than would otherwise be the case.' Before the establishment and promotion of a spoken standard, which attained some success only in the second half of the twentieth century, it was in fact the print language that embodied a common Chinese-ness with regard to the linguistic aspect of the national identity. Chinese people shared the same written language and script across time and distance for so long that it became taken for granted, and was, in the words of Hobsbawm (1990:57) 'not so much a group criterion as something that all people have, like legs.' Though such a point was not appreciated and made use of during the nationalist development of China, it is nevertheless an important covert fact about the unifying effect of Chinese writing for much of the history of the country and its huge population.

4. Language Reform, *Putonghua*, and the Regional Dialects

The Chinese language, ultimately, was not abandoned, but it has now undergone significant reform with regard to its standard spoken and written forms, and its writing system.

Reform of the style and conventions of language used in written Chinese was a complete success. *Baihuawen* replaced *wenyanwen* as the base of a new written standard and eliminated the earlier significant distance between written and spoken forms of Chinese, increasing access to reading and writing and the potential use of written Chinese by common people.① Concerning the actual orthographic representation

① In certain quarters it was claimed that the syntactic reforms of written Chinese also brought the written language closer to that of various European languages such as English. Wang Li, an eminent Chinese linguist, observed in 1954 that, as a result of much development of Chinese in its grammatical of written Chinese which had caused such heated discussion during the nationalist movement, attempts to replace Chinese logographic characters with a phonographic, alphabetic writing system were not successful, despite decades of effort on the part of language planners whose theoretical assumptions were based on strong negative perceptions of the Chinese script. Importantly there was no lack of political support for such a change, as evidenced by repeated calls from the national language planning institution and the senior leadership in the 1950s to move in the direction of phonetization. The cause of the failure was instead a simple linguistic one. Considerable dialectal diversity, and the existence of over-many homophonous morphemes and words in contemporary Chinese makes the phonetic, alphabetic writing of Chinese for everyday use an unfeasible option. What did happen to the script, however, is that it underwent a thorough simplification process in which many of the complex, traditional characters had their shapes converted into new simplified characters requiring fewer strokes. Although this did not reduce the overall, large number of characters to be learned for written Chinese, it endeavoured to make the characters easier to memorize and reproduce as a way to facilitate the acquisition of reading and writing. The traditional script was thus given a new appearance in the utilitarian interests of improving literacy in the country, just as the classical style of written Chinese, *wenyanwen*, was abandoned and replaced by a more colloquial style that was easier to master.①

---

structure, articles in newspapers and magazines could be translated into English and other similar European languages almost in a word-for-word manner without substantial alteration of the structure (Wang 1954; Chen 1999:86). Objections were occasionally raised to this perceived "Europeanization" of Chinese, but did not have much effect on changes occurring in Chinese, which continue to occur in the present.

① The simplification of Chinese characters in mainland China resulted in a system of writing

The vocabulary of standard spoken and written Chinese was also considerably expanded during the period of reform and modernisation, so that a shared, standard form of the language would be available for use in speech and in writing in all domains of life, including those relating to science, education, government and modern administration. The particular way that nations undertake this kind of expansion of standard languages is often interesting to observe and may frequently be informative about attitudes towards language as a national symbol. "Philological nationalism" and the insistence on the linguistic purity of a national language's vocabulary can be noted to have occurred in many instances where new nations are being constructed, or established nations are being defended against foreign cultural influences. In the area of vocabulary and the importation of loanwords, nationalist views considering language an important symbol of the identity of a nation may apply pressure for the translation of loanwords into equivalent morphemes and words in the national language rather than the direct adoption of foreign words and their pronunciation (see, for example, the protectionist policies against *franglais* adopted by the French Academy, or Hobsbawm 1990 on German). Resistance to the general introduction of foreign loanwords has been rather weak in Chinese. The period before and after the Sino-Japanese War in 1894-1895 saw an influx of loanwords from Japanese into Chinese on an unprecedented scale, and the process of borrowing words from other languages, particularly European languages, accelerated strongly after that. However, it has frequently been observed that there is a strong

---

that has become visually distinct in many of its common characters from that used in other Chinese communities, such as Taiwan, Hong Kong, and overseas Chinese communities in southeast Asia, north America and Europe, where traditional characters continue to occur (though these are used to write in a modern style that is close to spoken Chinese, as in mainland China).

preference to translate foreign words into Chinese,[①] rather than just adapt foreign pronunciations to the phonology of Chinese. In Wang Li (1954) it is suggested that this kind of semantic translation, rather than phonetic transliteration, reveals the national self-esteem of the Chinese speaking people and a protective instinct towards the national language. If so, this would seem to be an instance where ideological issues do affect language policy with regard to Chinese, and attribute an important nationalist symbolic power to the language. Such a conclusion is actually not justified, though, and there are good reasons to believe that the preference for the semantic translation of loanwords into Chinese has more to do with the nature of the Chinese writing system than with national self-esteem. In the overwhelming majority of Chinese words, each logophoric character is also an independent morpheme, resulting in a common one-character-one-meaning correspondence in the language. Speakers of Chinese are so used to this correspondence that a string of characters used to represent the pronunciation of a foreign word with no regard for the inherent meanings of the characters used to capture this pronunciation does not fit well with their reading habits, and hence is widely dispreferred (see Chen 1999 for further discussion).

In tandem with the reform and development of written Chinese, the promotion of *putonghua* in mainland China came into full swing in 1955. With the exception of the chaotic decade of the "Cultural Revolution" (1966-1976), it has continually been a major task of language planning institutions of the central government, and a series of executive directives and regulations have been issued by government institutions at various levels that relate specifically to its promotion. Over time, *putonghua* has steadily expanded in domains of use, and

① An exception to this is the case of loanwords from Japanese which are already written in Chinese characters and hence very easy to make use of without the need for further translation.

increasingly specific standards have been set on the proficiency levels of those who are required to speak *putonghua* in their work. A directive by the Ministry of Education in 1989 stipulates that, except in ethnic minority areas, *putonghua* is to be used as the medium of instruction in classrooms from kindergartens through primary schools to lower middle schools across the country. It was further announced by the Ministry of Education in 2003 that all teachers, television and radio broadcasters, actors and actresses, public servants, and normal school graduates must pass a test in *putonghua* proficiency to meet their job qualifications. Attempting to enforce such a directive, it was reported in Shanghai that public servants who fail to meet a certain proficiency level of *putonghua* will furthermore lose their jobs.

Generally speaking, the promotion of *putonghua* as a national language has been very successful. Within the all important area of education, an overwhelming majority of urban schools in the regional dialect areas have adopted *putonghua* in all of their school activities. For example, in the province of Guangdong, where Cantonese is the dominant local dialect, *putonghua* is generally used in more than 83% of primary schools in the capital city of the province, Guangzhou. The percentage of schools which commonly use *putonghua* for all purposes is even higher in the areas of certain other dialects such as the Min and Wu dialects. In rural areas, however, the situation is somewhat different, and particularly so in poor rural areas, where qualified teachers are more difficult to find and retain. In rural areas of Guangdong, for example, it is reported that *putonghua* is used in only 50% of primary schools. Given the widespread use of *putonghua* in teaching, as the medium of instruction, and in other activities in school, a person's competence in *putonghua* correlates quite closely with the length and quality of education that s/he has received. Those who have received nine years of schooling or more can normally be expected to understand and speak *putonghua* reasonably well. The increasingly widespread outreach of television and radio broadcasting by national stations based in Beijing, which almost exclusively use *putonghua*, has also greatly facilitated the popularization of standard spoken Chinese across the country. As discussed in Chen (1999), as much as 90% of the Chinese speaking population has now acquired comprehension proficiency in *putonghua*, and more than half of the population can speak it with varying degrees of fluency.

As a result of the spread of *putonghua*, a situation of diglossia now obtains in regional dialect areas in China where members of the population are proficient in both *putonghua* and a local dialect of Chinese. In such areas, *putonghua* occurs as the High/H language, normally used in education, mass media, government, public service and for all formal purposes. It is generally perceived as the linguistic code of prestige and upward social mobility, representing good education, high culture, intelligence and all the other trappings of elitism. Among university professors, government officials, and company managers, it has been observed that use of *putonghua* has come to be the norm, even if such people can also fluently speak a local dialect. Local dialects, by way of contrast, function as the Low/L languages, and are mainly used among family members and friends, and in informal environments. While dialects, as markers of regional identity, are normally associated with folksiness, familiarity and friendliness, they may also sometimes be taken as markers of vulgarity, at least in some parts of the country like Shanghai, according to the observations of certain sociolinguists.

In policy as well as in practice, bi-dialectalism in *putonghua* and a local dialect has been a goal of language planning in China since the mid 1950s. Whereas much effort has gone into the promotion of *putonghua*, generally speaking no harsh measures have been taken against the use of regional dialects.[①] Except in radio and television broadcasting and film making where the use of dialects is strictly regulated and restricted to certain types of programs, for a long period of time it has been practically up to individuals whether they use *putonghua* or local dialect in their everyday activities. Consequently, it is not uncommon to find people, particularly those beyond middle age, using local dialects on occasions where *putonghua* is normally expected, such as in formal official or business functions. Language selection here is more or less open to personal choice, much in the same way that individuals exhibit different preferences in food and clothing.

As perhaps might be expected, the increasingly popular use of *putonghua* has also been accompanied by attrition of other dialects in terms of population of speakers and domains of use, particularly among the younger generation. The pace and the extent of attrition varies with regard to the different regional dialects. Of the three major southern dialects, Yue, Wu, and Min, Yue (Cantonese) is relatively stable, but the latter two have shown signs of decline over the past decade. Generally speaking, the attrition of regional dialects is most evident in two kinds of physical environment. The first is large cities which have sizeable migrant populations. The second is areas in the countryside with a wide spread of different local dialects. The conurbation of Shanghai is a good example of the former, while the latter is best illustrated by Min-speaking areas such as Fujian province in the southeast part of China.

Considering the situation in Shanghai first, the dominant local dialect of the city is a Wu dialect which has been a high-prestige dialect in the wider Wu speaking areas over the past century. In spite of its

---

① This contrasts with the situation in Taiwan and its promotion of *guoyu* from 1945 through to the late 1980s (see Chen 2001; Simpson 2007).

higher sociolinguistic status in comparison with other Wu dialects, the Shanghai dialect has shrunk considerably in its population of speakers and domains of use. For example, it has been reported that dozens of verbs which are peculiar to the Shanghai dialect and do not exist in *putonghua* are now no longer used by native Shanghai university students, and the use of the Shanghainese among younger generations has been confined to the description of activities involved in daily life, such as eating, work and participation in family life. For topics of a more serious nature, *putonghua* is used. In addition to this, people of the younger generation, particularly those who were born in or after the 1990s of parents with good education, tend to adopt *putonghua*, rather than the Shanghai dialect, as their first language, using it at home as well as in school. Similar dialect attrition is also evident in other Wu-speaking areas. It is reported that in Jinhua, a Wu dialect city in Zhejiang province, all children from 6 to 14 years old are able to speak *putonghua*, whereas only 23% of them speak the local Jinhua dialect fluently, and a significant 52% cannot speak the local dialect at all.

A related situation of attrition has been observed among the young in Min dialect speaking areas. *Putonghua* is now reportedly the only language used by many children in kindergartens and primary schools and at a higher level of education, it is found that a large number of local university students are no longer able to speak the Min dialect with any fluency, and do not understand idioms and colloquial expressions in local dialect.

The occurrence of dialect attrition in the country did not attract attention until quite recently. During the past few years, the first voices of concern over the decline, and possible eventual death of certain of the dialects have begun to be heard, and it has been suggested that measures should be taken to halt this decline. Specifically, it has been proposed that more airtime should be given to television and radio programs in local dialects, and that school children should have some hours of their weekly schooling taught in the local dialect instead of *putonghua*. However, in the main it is a very small number of linguists which has shown concern over the weakening of dialects in the face of an increasingly dominant *putonghua*. Ordinary people in the dialect areas display little interest in such issues, and do not seem to care about the decline of dialects. In fact, as pointed out recently by a journalist in Shanghai, students and parents now appear to be much more enthusiastic about enhancing their proficiency in English than maintaining the local dialect.

In Edwards (1985:71) it is observed quite generally that 'bilingualism is often only a temporary phenomenon, [later] replaced with dominant-language monolingualism.' Nevertheless, it can also be noted out that two languages or two dialects can in fact co-exist for a long period of time if their maintenance is backed by political (and sometimes also financial) support from the government of a country, and where there exist important domains of use for each language or dialect, and special values attached to each. Turning to consider China's official government policy and position on the regional dialects and their relation to *putonghua*, in 1955 the *People's Daily*, the official mouthpiece of the central government in Beijing, editorialized that:

> '*Putonghua* serves the whole population and dialects serve the needs of people in their own regions. Promoting *Putonghua* does not mean that dialects would be abolished. It is only intended to gradually narrow the scope of uses of the dialects, which is in conformity with objective laws of social progress. Dialects should, and will co-exist with *putonghua* for a considerably long period of time.' (*People' Daily* Editorial October 26, 1955)

At the same time, two prominent scholars in the national language planning institution, Luo Changpei and Lü Shuxiang, maintained that:

> 'The national common language, in the course of its development, will absorb nutrients from other dialects. The national common language will take from dialects all the elements which are full of vitality and essential to its development, leaving out those which have synonymous expressions in the national language. Dialects will have less and less to contribute to the national common language, and they will gradually dwindle and eventually die out as a result of the effect of the national common language. However, this will be a very long process. The formation of the national common language is not conditional on the extinction of the dialects. The former simply precedes the latter.' (Luo & Lü 1955: 88)

Obviously, while dialects are allowed to co-exist with *putonghua*, there has been little effort, if at all, on the part of language planning institutions to actively support or promote regional dialects. As just one example of such lack of support, it can be noted that all applications in the 1990s from non-Beijing Mandarin areas for permission to launch TV and radio broadcasting services and newspapers in local dialects were rejected by the central authorities.

On the other hand, it is instructed that folk arts unique to regions of the country, such as local operas, story telling, comic dialogues, etc. must be performed in local dialect, and this is still an area of language use where local dialects hold on strongly. However, it is unlikely that folk art forms, in and of themselves, contribute significantly to the maintenance of the local dialects, as they have long lost their appeal to people of younger generations in the competition against other forms of entertainment such as cinema, sports and television.

The only important remaining factor that may stimulate long-term maintenance of local dialects in the face of the much more powerful *putonghua* is the unique, high value that speakers may attach to their local dialect, their "language loyalty" . In this regard, the regional dialects appear to differ to certain degrees. For example, T'sou and You (2001:260) suggest that Cantonese commands a higher degree of loyalty than the Wu or the Min dialects do. In most areas which do not feature high loyalty to local dialects, it is essentially on the basis of pragmatic considerations that individuals decide which language to make use of. In this respect, *putonghua* is usually considered to be of much higher instrumental utility than the regional dialects. Even among Cantonese speakers, pragmatic motivations often override language loyalty, and Pan (2000) observes a clear increasing trend over the past decade among native salespeople in Guangzhou to switch to *putonghua* in order to attract customers and facilitate business transactions. Generally speaking, *putonghua* and the regional dialects in present-day China are each associated with distinct levels of socio-economic status. Urban, well-educated, young people in regional areas are more likely than other members of the population to be proficient in *putonghua*, and are more likely to use this in their work and everyday life. On the other hand, rural, poorly educated, and elderly people are more likely to be mono-dialectal, or poor speakers of *putonghua*. If young people find little appeal in a local dialect in the face of another much stronger language, that dialect will certainly be in jeopardy. It seems that an increasing number of people of the younger generation in China have decided that the high prestige of *putonghua*, and its usefulness as the base of standard written Chinese outweigh any positive feelings of attachment to a regional identity embodied by the local dialect. With some speakers, such a regional identity is in fact not something to be valued in the first place. The decline of various major Chinese dialects is consequently already a reality, and the death of many of the dialects in the not too distant future is something which would seem to be distinctly likely.

5. Ethnic minority languages

The relationship between the Chinese nation and the various ethnic groups in China, in the dominant view, is characterized in terms of the notion *duoyuan yiti* 'pluralistic integrity', which was proposed by the eminent Chinese anthropologist Fei Xiaotong in 1989, and has since been extensively accepted by the mainstream academic community and the government in China. In this view, the Chinese nation is a structure composed of two levels: on the lower level is a pluralistic base composed of more than fifty distinctive ethnic groups, and these groups together constitute an integral whole on the upper level. It is maintained that the Chinese nation has been in existence since ancient times, but its identity awareness has awakened and developed only in modern times during the course of confrontation with Western powers in China beginning in the nineteenth century (Fei 1999:3). Accordingly, citizens of China may have two basic group-oriented identities, one as a member of the Chinese nation, and a second as a member of a particular ethnic group. For the Han, the Chinese language is a marker of both of their identities, but for the ethnic minorities, their ethnic language, if they have one, is first and foremost a marker of their ethnic identity.

When the PRC was first established, the official policy of the new state towards ethnic minorities within its borders was that all ethnic minorities should have the freedom to make use of their own languages and scripts, though also be encouraged and helped to acquire

Chinese. In the first decade after 1949, an accommodative approach was subsequently adopted toward the use of indigenous ethnic languages in government, education, and other social, cultural, and economic activities in areas where ethnic minorities had a significant presence. Under the auspices of the central government in Beijing, new writing systems were designed for some minority languages which did not have a standard script and old writing systems underwent reform so that ethnic minority children could receive primary and secondary education in their own language. This policy was, however, disrupted during the period of 1958-1977, when a more heavily assimilative approach toward the minority languages prevailed. It then became advocated that it would be more useful for ethnic minorities to learn Chinese than their minority languages, and Chinese should consequently be adopted as the medium of instruction in schools in the minority regions. With the end of the "Cultural Revolution" in the mid-1970s, and a redirection of government thinking, since 1977 the central government has once again basically switched back to its pre-1957 accommodative approach towards the minorities languages. More recently, issues relating to the use of languages in ethnic minority areas have been highlighted in certain laws, policy statements, and executive regulations issued by the central government (Zhou 2003). The 1999 Constitution of the PRC reaffirms the freedom of ethnic groups on language issues in a range of articles partially quoted below. It should be noted that in the common English translation of these and other related official documents, the word 'nationality' often occurs where 'ethnic group/minority' might be expected to occur. This relates directly to the idea of 'pluralistic integrity' referred to above, and the view that the Chinese nation may be comprised of a set of many (lower level) nationalities. It also results, in part, from the fact that in Chinese there is no specific word for 'nation' that is distinct from 'ethnic group', and the word *minzu* is used to refer to groupings of both types. Because of this, the translation of *minzu* as 'nationality' when actually referring to sub-national ethnic groups is both common and not seen to conflict with the notion of China as a higher order nation/*minzu* encompassing various 'ethnic' *minzu*/nationalities.[①]

> Article 4: ...The people of all nationalities (ethnic groups) have the freedom to use and develop their own spoken and written languages, and to preserve or reform their own ways and customs.
>
> Article 121: In performing their functions, the organs of self-government of the national autonomous areas, in accordance with the autonomy regulations of the respective areas, employ the spoken and written language or languages in common use in the locality.
>
> Article 134: Citizens of all nationalities have the right to use the spoken or written languages of their own nationalities in court proceedings. The people's courts and people's procurators should provide translation for any party to the court proceedings who is not familiar with the spoken and written languages in common use in the locality.

More concrete measures have been initiated in several other laws and executive regulations that followed the 1999 constitution, such as the PRC Law on the National Common Language and Script, and the Law on Regional Autonomy for Minority Ethnic Groups in the PRC, both

① This ambiguity (or wider coverage) of the Chinese word *minzu* is, to some extent, similar to the situation with the English word *nation* about a century ago. The word *nation* originated in Latin and was borrowed into English from French. The present concept of 'nation', used in its political sense, is a relatively recent phenomenon in English. As observed in Hobsbawm (1990:18) 'the *New English Dictionary* pointed out in 1908 that the old meaning of the word envisaged mainly the ethnic unit, but recent usage rather stressed the notion of political unity and independence.' The concept of *minzu* in Chinese differs from that of *nation* in English in that it is hard to tell which of the two senses of *minzu* is more common in modern Chinese, 'nation' or 'ethnic group'.

passed at the national level in 2001. Autonomous regions, prefectures and counties have also passed local laws and regulations specifically relating to the use of languages and scripts along the same lines as the constitution and other state laws, and these now facilitate the implementation of the official policy on language use in ethnic minority communities.

At the same time, it has to be noted that it has always been official policy to promote *putonghua* nationwide, and ethnic minority communities are not exempted from this. Competence in Chinese in addition to local minority languages has been actively encouraged among minority people, and so has competence in minority languages on the part of the Han working in minority areas. Bilingualism in a minority language and Chinese is in fact a major goal of language planning in minority areas. According to the relevant regulations, efforts should be made to ensure as much as possible that both minority languages and Chinese are used in education, government, mass media, and other major socio-economic activities in ethnic minority communities, and minority languages can be considered as the principal languages in areas with a predominantly ethnic minority population. Schools consisting mainly of minority students should use textbooks in minority languages and adopt minority languages in the classroom, and Chinese should be taught starting from the upper years of primary school or from lower middle school.

If we now consider how general linguistic pressures have affected the speech patterns of China's ethnic minorities, these can be classed as falling into three major groups with regard to the bilingualism of their speakers in both a minority language and Chinese, mainly depending on whether the groups have had a long history of close contact with Chinese, and whether they have an established literary history (Dob 1992, Zhou 1992).

The first group is composed of ethnic minorities such as the Tibetans, the Uygurs, and the Kazaks. These peoples each have an established literary tradition in their own ethnic language, and have a spoken form which is generally accepted as a standard language and extensively used in their own community for various socio-economic, educational and administrative purposes. The languages of these minorities have furthermore all served as important markers of the ethnic identity of the groups which speak them. Historically they have generally not had much close contact with the Han Chinese in their everyday life. As a result of these factors, the number of bilingual speakers of a minority language and Chinese in these communities is relatively low.

Ethnic minorities in the second group include the Mongolians, the Zhuang, the Yi and the Miao. Many of these minorities have lived in mixed communities with Han Chinese. Some, such as the Mongolians, may have a long literary tradition in their own language, but many of the other minorities in this group do not. The use of traditional Zhuang and Yi writing, for example, was considerably limited, and commonly confined to informal purposes such as the recording of folk literature and book keeping, etc. For high level, formal purposes, the Zhuang and the Yi mostly used Chinese. In these minority groups, the proportion of bilingual speakers is now quite high. More than half of the Miao and the Yi, for instance, speak Chinese in addition to their ethnic language (Li Rong 1987), and about 22% of the Miao people and 14% of the Mongolian have actually switched to Chinese altogether, fully losing their competence in Miao/Mongolian.

In the third group there are relatively small ethnic minorities like the Qiang, Bai, Dongxiang, Mulam, and Maonan. These either do not have their own writing system, or have no established literary tradition. They have been in regular, close contact with the Han, and most of them are bilingual in their ethnic language and Chinese, with a high percentage of them having adopted Chinese or some other larger minority language as their first language. A considerable number of China's ethnic minorities belong to this third, more assimilated group.

Quite generally, it can be noted that in almost all the ethnic minority communities in the country, the number of bilingual speakers of a minority language and Chinese has been growing rapidly over the past decades, and in some regions there is a growing shift from minority languages toward Chinese among the people of the younger generation.

Further illustration of the degree of variation that exists in bilingualism in ethnic minority communities can be given from a brief comparison of three sizeable minority areas in different parts of the PRC. First of all, in the far northeast of China, in Inner Mongolia, it is found that Mongolian and Chinese are used side by side as two equal languages on more than 95% of occasions in government, public service and businesses, and 90% of printed materials are produced in both languages. In education, students are free to choose between Mongolian language, Chinese language and bilingual schools, and an increasingly high proportion of the Mongolians in the region can now speak and read Chinese as well as Mongolian.

In the northwest of China, the vast area of Xinjiang (three times the size of France) is characterized by much higher linguistic diversity. Generally speaking, Chinese is the common language used in public, except in certain cities where a single ethnic minority may be numerically dominant. *Putonghua* is the working language of the government in the capital city of the province, as well as in other major cities and towns. It is also the norm in schools at all levels and in public service, and is commonly used as a lingua franca by people of different ethnic minority groups. Most of the ethnic minority people living in major cities and towns speak *putonghua*, with proficiency levels varying greatly according to their age and educational background. Some of the minority people in townships and villages speak their own ethnic language only, particularly the elderly and those with little education.

In comparison with the strong inroads of Chinese into Inner Mongolia and Xinjiang, the mountainous area of Tibet in the southwest of China is a region where the locally dominant ethnic language (Tibetan) has been holding on particularly strongly in the face of the spread of *putonghua*. Tibetan is the major language of administration, law and public service in Tibet, and while Chinese is also used in such domains, it is second to Tibetan in importance. Tibetan is furthermore the medium of instruction in primary and secondary schools for local children, with Chinese being taught from the upper grades of primary schools. Currently more than 80% of the Tibetans speak only Tibetan, resulting in Tibet having a much smaller bilingual population than Inner Mongolia, Xinjiang and other minority areas.

Where bilingualism exists in ethnic minority communities, this is commonly seen as an important bridge between communities, allowing in particular for connections between monolingual minority language speakers and monolingual Chinese speakers. Because of this function, it has the support of the central and local government, and, generally speaking, is embraced with enthusiasm by minority language speakers as well, especially those who are in close contact with the Han and eager to participate in the economic, social and political life of the majority Han society. With many minority languages, particularly those in the first (Tibetan/Uygur/Kazak) group discussed above, bilingualism, once in place, is expected to be a long and stable process. With certain other minority languages, such as those in the third group, bilingualism seems to be more of a transitional process that is relatively short and unstable. Overall, it is currently estimated that about half of the minority languages are in decline in terms of population of speakers and domains of use, mostly in favour of Chinese and in a few cases in favour of another stronger minority language. Quite a few minority languages are also now on the verge of extinction, for example, Hezhe presently has only about a dozen remaining speakers, all of whom are more than 60 years old. Two other languages which are clearly endangered are She and Tujia. In the 1980s it was reported that just 1000 of the She, which had a population of 368,000, still spoke the She language, and the rest spoke Chinese or another minority language, and similarly that only 6% of the Tujia spoke their ethnic language and the rest Chinese (cf. Fu & Wang 1987). The number of minority language speakers in these two communities is likely to have shrunk further over the past two decades, so it seems fairly clear that the She, the Tujia and the Hezhe are following the Manchu and the Hui in abandoning their own languages.[①] Although no reliable nationwide investigation into the issue has been conducted so far, it is a safe assumption that in many minority communities, particularly those in the third group discussed above with close contacts to the Han Chinese, language shift toward Chinese is in steady progress, and may lead to the significant endangerment of many of China's minority languages.

As in the case with regional dialects of Chinese, economic and pragmatic motives have been the most potent forces directing language use in ethnic minority areas. With the expansion of *putonghua* into all parts of China, Chinese now is a very strong language in many minority

① Another similar case is that of the Jino, who have recently abandoned bilingual education in Jino and Chinese, and decided to adopt Chinese as the exclusive medium of instruction in schools.

areas, and for ethnic minority people, competence in oral and written Chinese is very helpful to upward mobility and economic progress, opening up many opportunities which are not available to those who speak only their ethnic languages only. Consequently, even in areas where there may be a close connection between minority language and ethnic identity, such as in Xinjiang with its Uygur and other Turkic muslim groups, it is reported that ethnic minorities are very eager to send their children to Chinese language kindergartens or Chinese language schools. Since there are more applicants for admission than the schools can accommodate, ethnic minority business people are now using private funds to set up Chinese language kindergartens and schools to meet the increasing demand, and some ethnic minority primary schools, at the request of parents and students, are even offering Chinese as a subject from the first grade, instead of from the third grade as stipulated by the government.

6. Conclusions

Examining the recent history of China and the relation of language to national identity, this chapter began by emphasizing that language has in fact seldom played a positive ideological role in fostering the consciousness of the national identity in China and in mustering loyalty to the nation. In stark contrast with the situation in various European nations, in mainstream intellectual and political discourse in China from the late nineteenth century onward there has been relatively little nationalist passion in China for the Chinese language as a possible symbol of national identity. On the contrary, the perceptions of Chinese on the part of the elite of Chinese society were in general very negative during the important period of nation-building in the early half of the twentieth century, and rather than being viewed as a sacrosanct symbol representing the essence of the Chinese nation, the Chinese language was instead seen as an instrumental utility, and perceived to be a very inefficient one.

More or less the same utilitarian view has been taken toward regional dialects of Chinese in relation to the new standard form *putonghua*. While an overwhelming majority of the population in dialect areas speak and comprehend *putonghua* in addition to their dialects, there has been a clear shift toward *putonghua* in certain major dialect areas such as the Wu and Min, particularly among the people of the younger generation in urban areas. In these areas, bi-dialectalism now seems to be leading to monolingualism. Local dialects of Chinese are without question the most important markers of regional identity in China, but factors other than utilitarian ones seem to be unable to halt the decline of the dialects in these areas. While the promotion of *putonghua* by language planning institutions since the 1950s has definitely played an important role in the decline of certain regional dialects, the most important factors causing changing patterns of language use and maintenance are pragmatic and economic.

The situation with ethnic minority languages is similar to that with regional dialects of Chinese in that they too have come into contact with a much stronger language. An important difference between the two cases is that while bi-dialectalism (i.e. competence in *putonghua* and a regional dialect of Chinese) is just tolerated, to some extent, by language planning institutions, considerable efforts have been exerted by government at all levels to effect and support bilingualism in the ethnic minority areas. Partially as a result of government encouragement of the maintenance of minority languages, it appears that bilingualism in some ethnic minority areas may remain quite stable—at least more stable than bi-dialectalism in various of the Chinese dialect areas. Meanwhile, it has to be re-emphasized that there has also been a shift toward Chinese in other ethnic minority communities; the process has been complete with some minorities, and is still in progress with certain others.

Whereas the ethnic identity of non-Han minorities is perhaps likely to survive the loss of their ethnic languages (at least for a certain time), as in the case of the Manchu and the Hui, one can be less optimistic about the continuity of regional Chinese identities if the local dialects are abandoned. The situation with regional dialects of Chinese and, to some extent, ethnic minority languages, in China can be summarized in the words of Edwards (1985:163): 'Economic success and communicative efficiency militate against the viability of "small" languages in contact with powerful ones. These are factors of great weight, accompanying social processes like urbanisation, modernisation and social access which are very difficult to combat (even if this were generally desired, which it is not).' What can be added here is that where a utilitarian rather than an ideological view of language prevails, as is the case in modern China, the maintenance of such smaller languages and dialects is set to be even more difficult.

References

Anderson, Benedict. 1983. *Imagined Communities: Reflections on the Origin and Spread of Nationalism*, London & New York: Verso.

Atlas. 1987. *Language Atlas of China*, Steven A Wurm et al., eds., Hong Kong: Longman Group (Far East) Ltd.

Barbour, Stephen. 2000. Nationalism, language, Europe, In: Barbour & Carmichael, eds., 1-17.

Barbour, Stephen and Cathie Carmichael. eds. 2000. *Language and Nationalism in Europe*, Oxford University Press.

Bloomfield, Leonard. 1961. *Language*, New York: Holt, Rinehart and Winston.

Chen, Duxiu. 1918. Fu zhu, In: Shi Hu, ed., 1935, 146.

Chen, Ping. 1999. *Modern Chinese: History and Sociolinguistics*, Cambridge: Cambridge University Press.

Chen, Ping. 2001. Policy on the selection and implementation of a standard language as a source of conflict in Taiwan, In: Gottlieb & Chen, eds., 95-110.

Chen, Yunsheng. 2001. *Zhongguo Minzu Quyu Zizhi Zhidu*, Beijing: Press of Economics and Management.

Dob, White. 1992. The position and role of minority languages and their writing systems in China, *International Journal of the Sociology of Language* 97, 47-57.

Edwards, John. 1985. *Language, Society and Identity*, Oxford: Blackwell.

Fei, Xiaotong. ed. 1999. *Zhonghua Minzu Duoyuan Yiti Geju*, revised ed., Beijing: Central University of Nationalities Press.

Fu, Maoji and Jun Wang. 1987. Minority languages in China, In: Atlas, A-4.

Fu, Sinian. 1919. Hanyu gai yong pinyin wenzi de chubu tan, In: Shi Hu, ed., 1935, 147-164.

Gao, Yuanbao. 2003. Tongyi yuchayi: Zhongguo xiandai zhishifenzi de yuyan guannian zhi wu, *Shanghai Wenxue* 10/2003, 76-88.

Gellner, Ernest. 1983. *Nations and Nationalism*, Oxford: Basil Blackwell.

Gottlieb, Nanette and Ping Chen. eds. 2001. *Language Planning and Language Policy: East Asian Perspectives*, London: Curzon.

Hobsbawm, Eric J. 1990. *Nations and Nationalism since 1780: Programme, Myth, Reality*, Cambridge: Cambridge University Press.

Hou, Jingyi. ed. 2002. *Xiandai Hanyu Fangyan Gailun*, Shanghai: Shanghai Jiaoyu Chubanshe.

Hu, Shi. 1918. Fuzhu, In: Shi Hu, ed., 1935, 146.

Hu, Shi. ed. 1935. *Zhongguo Xinwenxue Daxi*. Vol. 1, *Jianshe Lilun Ji*, Shanghai: Liangyou Tushu Yinshua Gongsi.

Hu, Yushu. ed. 1980. *Xiandai Hanyu Cankao Ziliao,* Shanghai: Shanghai Jiaoyu Chubanshe.

Judge, Anne. 2000. France: ‘One state, one nation, one language?’ In: Barbour and Carmichael, eds., 44-82.

Li, Rong. 1987. Chinese dialects in China, In: Atlas, A-2.

Luo, Changpei and Shuxiang Lü. 1955. Xiandai Hanyu guifan wenti [Standardization of Modern Chinese], In: Hu, ed., 1980, 81-106.

Lu, Xun. 1934. Guanyu xin wenzi, In: *Lu Xun Quanji*. Vol. 6. (printed in 1973), Beijing: Renmin Wenxue Chubanshe.

Lu, Zhuangzhang. 1892. *Yimuliaoran Chujie: Zhongguo Qieyun Xin Zi Xia Qiang* [*First Steps in Complete Understanding at a Glance: A New Chinese Script for the Xiamen Dialect*], (reprinted in 1956). Beijing: Wenzi Gaige Chubanshe.

Pan, Yuling. 2000. Code-switching and social change in Guangzhou and Hong Kong, *International Journal of the Sociology of Language* 146, 21-41.

Qian, Xuantong. 1918. Zhongguo jinhou zhi wenzi wenti, In: Shi Hu, ed., 1935, 141-146.

Qu, Qiubai. 1931. Putong Zhongguohua de ziyan de yanjiu, In: *Qu Qiubai Wenji*, Vol. 2. (printed in 1953), Beijing: Renmin Wenxue Chubanshe, 683-693.

Simpson, Andrew. 2007. Taiwan, In: Andrew Simpson, ed., *Language and National Identity in Asia*, Oxford University Press, 235-259.

Smith, Anthony. 1991. *National Identity*, Reno, Las Vegas & London: University of Nevada.

T'sou, Benjamin K.Y. and Rujie You. 2003. *Hanyu yu Huaren Shehui* [*Chinese Language and Society*], HK: City University of Hong Kong Press.

Zhou, Minglang. 2003. *Multilingualism in China*: *The Politics of Writing Reforms for Minority Languages 1949-2002*, Berlin & New York: Mouton de Gruyter.

Zhou, Yaowen. 1992. Bilingualism and bilingual education, *International Journal of the Sociology of Language* 97, 37-45.

中国的语言、民族主义与地区及族群认同

提　要　本文全面探讨汉语在中国现代化进程中所起的作用以及自身的演变特点，以欧洲国家为参照系，侧重考察汉语与中国的民族主义和地区 / 族群认同之间的关系，并比较汉语和欧洲语言在有关方面的异同。语言民族主义以语言为手段，凝聚和强化本民族的民族意识，增强民族成员之间的认同感，并以此为基础建立或巩固以本民族为主体的现代民族国家。本文指出，从 18 到 20 世纪，语言民族主义是许多国家立国强国根基的重要组成部分，语言在近代欧洲语言与民族主义关系密切，是国家和民族认同的主要标记之一，同大多数欧洲国家相比，中国近代和现代语言规划工作强调最多的是如何改进汉语、汉字和汉文，为国家和民族的现代化进程服务，主要着眼点不在于语言作为民族认同的标记功能，而是语言作为交际手段的工具价值和实用效率。

关键词　民族主义　地区认同　族群认同　语言文字改革　方言

(This article was first published in *Language and National Identity in Asia* edited by Andrew Simpson, Oxford University Press, as Chapter 7 "China", pp.141-167, in 2007. Permission by Oxford University Press to reprint the article in the present volume is gratefully acknowledged.)

Modern Written Chinese in development

Abstract As a case study in the formation of a new written language in a speech community moving from diglossia toward a "standard-with-dialects", this article analyzes the development of M[odern] W[ritten] C[hinese] during the past 80 years. After a brief account of the historical background, the article discusses the sources and avenues of influence on the development of MWC, then examines the emergent grammatical and lexical norms, and investigates the variations displayed by the four main Chinese communities: mainland China, China's Taiwan and Hong Kong, and Singapore. The role of language planning is also explored. The similarities and differences between China and Western Europe, in their progress from diglossic to non-diglossic communities, are discussed.
Keywords language planning; modernization of Chinese; bilingualism; diglossia; standard-with-dialects; Modern Written Chinese, standardization

1. Introduction

Around 400 years ago, Western Europe went through a process whereby vernacular languages such as English, French, Italian etc. replaced Latin as the standard written media for literary and scholarly purposes. A similar process took place in China 300 years later, under different circumstances and with somewhat different outcomes. As a case study in the development of a standard written language in a modernizing society in the 20th century—involving language change, language variation, and language planning—this article describes and analyzes the evolution of Modern Written Chinese (MWC) since the turn of the century, along with the variations among the major Chinese communities and the role of language planning in the process. China was traumatically defeated 150 years ago in the Opium War (1840-1842); for the first time, the Chinese were forced to recognize that the Middle Kingdom, for all its past glories, had lagged behind the Western powers since the Industrial Revolution. Since that time, tremendous efforts have been exerted to revitalize or modernize the country. As one of the factors to bear the blame for the backwardness of the country, the Chinese language was picked as one of the most important targets for reform: It was considered largely responsible for wide-spread illiteracy, because it was too difficult to learn and use. Specifically, three aspects of the Chinese language were identified as reform targets in this drive for modernization: (a) promotion of a lingua franca among mutually unintelligible dialects, (b) establishment of a new type of standard written language, and (c) reform of the character script. Although reform in each of the three areas can be traced back to earlier times, it is only in the past 150 years, especially in the context of drastic nationwide socio-political changes during the past 80 years or so, that considerable achievements have been realized in all these areas. This article is concerned with the development of MWC during the past 80 years. After a brief discussion of the historical background, I examine the evolution of MWC during this period, focusing on the major sources and avenues of influence on the formation of its grammatical and vocabulary norms. Then, on the assumption that MWC takes Northern Mandarin as its base dialect, I discuss how the norms actually observed in MWC today deviate from those of Northern Mandarin as a result of developments during the past 80 years. In this regard, I investigate the current situation with MWC in Mainland China, China's Taiwan and Hong Kong, and Singapore, where Chinese is used as the official language or one of the official languages. I also explore the effect of language planning activities on the development of MWC. At the same time, I discuss briefly the similarities and differences between China and Western Europe on the relevant issues.

2. Definition of terms

***Hanyu* 'Han language'**

What is currently called the "Chinese people" is actually composed of dozens of ethnic groups, among which the *Han* is by far the largest in number. *Hanyu* (*yu* 'speech') is the name for the language of this major ethnic group, which is at the same time taken as representative of the Chinese as a whole.

***Zhongwen* 'Chinese language'**

Zhong is here the abbreviated form of *Zhongguo* 'China' ; *wen* also means 'language' , being derived from the more specialized meaning of 'script' .

***Huayu* 'Chinese language'**

Huayu means the language of the *Hua* 'the Chinese' . This is the normal term used in Singapore, Malaysia, and other Southeast Asian areas for the Chinese language. It is also used in mainland China, Taiwan, and Hong Kong, but is usually confined to collocations such as *Huayu guangbo* 'Chinese broadcasting' .

***Wenyan* 'classical literary language'**

refers to a specific type of written Chinese that was the norm for literary, scholarly, and official functions for about 2,000 years prior to the May 4th Movement in 1919. Its grammar and vocabulary are almost exclusively based on Classical Chinese from before the Qin Dynasty (221-206 BCE) to the Wei-Jin period (CE 220-420). It is generally believed that, during its formative period (pre-Qin through the Han Dynasties, 206 BCE to CE 220), *wenyan* as a refined writing style was closely connected to the spoken language then prevalent. Later, the *wenyan* of this period became a model for the writing of literati. It deviated more and more from actual speech, which never stopped changing throughout the years.

***Baihua* 'vernacular literary language'**

Baihua was a new type of written language, developed toward the end of the Tang Dynasty (CE 618-907), which was much closer to the contemporary vernacular. While *wenyan* remained supreme as the standard written language, *baihua* served all low-culture functions such as transcriptions of Buddhist admonitions, scripts for folk stories, and plays; by their nature, these required a written language that accurately reflected the way texts were actually pronounced among less literate people. *Baihua* gained currency from the end of the Tang Dynasty, providing the medium for many literary works that represented the cultural attainments of the periods, e.g. *qu* 'verse' in the Yuan Dynasty (1271-1368) and novels in the Ming (1368-1644) and Qing (1644-1911) Dynasties. For a long period, there were actually two types of written Chinese, *wenyan* and *baihua*. Because of the conservatism prevalent among the ruling class and scholars, *wenyan* was considered refined and elegant, thus ideal for high-culture functions, while *baihua* was despised as coarse and vulgar, suitable only for low-culture functions. The language used in popular writings during the Ming and Qing Dynasties such as *Jin Ping Mei* (*The Golden Lotus*), *Shuihu Zhuan* (*Heroes of the Marshes*), *Ernü Yingxiong Zhuan* (*Heroic Sons and Daughters*), and *Hong Lou Meng* (*The Dream of the Red Chamber*) is usually referred to as the traditional *baihua*, as distinct from the modern *baihua* that developed after 1910.

***Guanhua* 'Mandarin'**

Hua here means 'speech' . *Guanhua* has two interpretations, 'public' or 'official' (cf. J. Li 1934:13). *Guanhua* thus means the spoken language of the public or of officials; it is known in the Western world as 'Mandarin' . The term *guanhua* in Chinese linguistics has two interrelated uses. First, it refers to a spoken language that was used as a lingua franca among speakers of mutually unintelligible dialects. Second, it refers to a dialect of Chinese that is the native tongue of the majority of the Chinese population. *Guanhua* in the second sense provided the basis for *guanhua* in the first sense. The dialectal diversity of the Chinese language was reported as much as 2,000 years ago (Xu & Zhan 1988). There is ample literature in the Chinese classics that demonstrates how differences among the dialects attracted the attention of educators, scholars, and diplomats. Although no one can tell for sure the exact period when a lingua franca emerged, used for oral communication across dialect barriers, it is generally believed that its emergence could not have been later than the 14th century. This language was known by the name *guanhua* in the 16th century. Judging from the written records representative of this *guanhua*, we can conclude with some certainty that it was based on the pronunciation of the Beijing dialect. In other words, the Beijing dialect has been the basis for a lingua franca for at least 600 years. This *guanhua* is the forerunner of what was later called *guoyu* and *putonghua*.

***Guoyu* 'national language'**

Guo means 'national' ; the combination *guoyu* was adopted from Japanese, in which it refers to the Japanese language. During the last few years of the Qing Dynasty, it was first proposed that the term *guanhua* should be replaced by the more inclusive *guoyu*, used to contrast with dialects as regards grammar and vocabulary as well as pronunciation. After the 1911 revolution that founded the Republic of China, *guoyu* became the formal term for what was taken to be the standard Chinese language, although the defining features of this language were not agreed upon until later. It is still the name for the standard Chinese used in Taiwan and in many overseas Chinese communities.

***Putonghua* 'common speech'**

Putonghua came into use in the late Qing Dynasty, referring to approximate, impure versions of *guanhua* (*putong* literally means 'ordinary' or 'average', with the implication of being non-sophisticated).① However, the term acquired a specialized meaning when it was officially adopted in mainland China in 1955 as the name for Modern Standard Chinese; the component *putong* was reinterpreted as meaning 'widespread, collective'. Essentially, *putonghua* refers to the same thing as *guoyu*, but the term *guoyu* was discarded in mainland China in favor of *putonghua*. It was felt that calling the national language *Hanyu*, the language of the Han people, might sound chauvinistic—ignoring or downplaying the fact that, in addition to Chinese, more than 80 other languages are spoken by ethnic minorities in the country.

The official definition of *putonghua* was laid down in the "Directive concerning popularization of *putonghua*," issued by the State Council in mainland China in 1956: "*Putonghua* is the Common Speech or Language of the Han people, which adopts the Beijing sound system as its standard of pronunciation, Northern Mandarin as its base dialect, and the exemplary works of modern *baihua* literature as its grammatical model." The Constitution of the People's Republic of China in its

① The term *putonghua* first appeared in Zhu Wenxiong's *Jiangsu Xin Zimu* [*New Alphabet of Jiangsu*], published in 1906 (cf. X. LI 1985:23).

1982 revised version stipulates for the first time that *putonghua* is to be promoted across the country.

3. Sources and avenues of influence on development of MWC

3.1 Replacement of *wenyan* with *baihua* as the base of MWC

The linguistic situation in China in 1910-1920 exemplifies what is characterized as "diglossia" by Ferguson (1959).[①] As defined by him, diglossia refers to the situation in which a language has two grammatically and lexically distinct varieties, one "high" and one "low", which are stable in a community. The low variety is usually the primary dialect, used for ordinary everyday transactions; the high variety is usually the vehicle for a large and respected body of written literature, is the only variety taught in school, and is used for literary, scholarly, and other formal functions. For centuries there were two written varieties of Chinese, *wenyan* and *baihua*, of which the high *wenyan* was the seldom challenged written standard. The low *baihua* was despised by the literate elite, and was confined to low-culture functions until the New Culture Movement began just before 1920. Against the background of increasingly influential modern Western ideas and awakening nationalism, the movement had three major themes—the Literary Revolution, democracy, and science—which, when combined,

---

① For some defining examples of diglossia, cf. Ferguson 1959. Norman (1988:250) holds a similar view on the diglossic situation in China before 1910.

aimed at creating a culture more consonant with modern times and the common people. The initiators of the movement (mainly Western-trained intellectuals like Hu Shi, Chen Duxiu, and Lu Xun) advocated democracy and science as the only correct prescription for a strong and prosperous China. For democracy and science to take root in China, the masses needed easy access to education. Since the standard written *wenyan* was divorced from actual speech, it stood as the main obstacle to a higher literacy rate. A major goal of the Literary Revolution, therefore, was to replace *wenyan* with a variety that was much closer to the daily vernacular, so that learning and using the written language would become easier for the masses. *Baihua* was chosen as the replacement; it was meant to serve as the base for a standard written language for all functions, including the literary, scholarly, and official.

Although similar proposals were made at least two decades earlier, it was only because of enthusiastic and effective promotion by people like Hu Shi, Chen Duxiu, and Lu Xun, and in the context of rapid social changes, that the proposal gained support. In 1919, the May 4th Movement broke out in protest at the injustice toward China on the part of a few Western powers at the end of World War I. The movement imparted a sense of urgency to the need for radical domestic reforms. Against the background of this wide-spread mood for change and reform, so characteristic of China at that time, the proposal to replace *wenyan* with *baihua* achieved amazing success within a couple of years, winning support from both the intellectual community and the government. A few years later, the Ministry of Education of the central government declared that *guoyu* was to be taught in all primary and secondary schools. A large number of articles appeared in journals and newspapers, promoting the new status of *baihua* as the standard for all purposes and occasions. Teaching aids and materials such as textbooks, dictionaries, grammars, and gramophone records became available. Within less than a decade, *baihua* won out over *wenyan* as the basis of a normal written language for Chinese in the practical sense of the word.

As the written counterpart of *guanhua*, the new *baihua* was based on Northern Mandarin, with the Beijing dialect as most prestigious representative. It is generally true that a written language should have more grammatical and lexical apparatus at its disposal than the spoken counterpart, so as to compensate for the lack of prosodic features and extralinguistic means (such as gestures and facial expressions) that usually accompany speech. However, because of the long confinement of *baihua* to limited functions, the traditional variety was not sophisticated enough to satisfy the demands of the standard written language in a rapidly modernizing society. As *baihua* was extended to new functions, its resources had to be expanded. Since shortly after 1910, MWC has been undergoing considerable enrichment in its linguistic repertoire. With respect to the norms of grammar and vocabulary, the variety used in the early 1920s is remarkably different from that of today. The formation of the norms for MWC on the basis of the traditional *baihua* has been a process of absorbing features from three major sources: non-Northern Mandarin dialects, Classical Chinese, and foreign languages.

3.2 Sources and avenues of influence on MWC

Non-Northern Mandarin dialects

Recent research in Chinese dialectology shows that there are seven major dialects, or more precisely dialect groups, in Chinese; these are differentiated mainly in terms of distinctive sets of phonological features that have evolved since Classical Chinese. They are Mandarin, Wu, Xiang, Hakka, Gan, Min and Cantonese; the non-Mandarin groups are called the Southern dialects. Mandarin itself is composed of four varieties: Northern, Northwestern, Southwestern, and Jiang-Huai (cf. Xu & Zhan 1988).① For convenience, I refer to each of the dialects as a unit, understanding that they are all actually dialect groups that can be further divided when required by a higher degree of analytical refinement.

Phonological distinctions among Chinese dialects stand out most conspicuously; but the diversity in grammar and vocabulary is also considerable, though it has not been accorded due attention until recently (cf. P. Chen 1992, Hashimoto 1988, Zhu 1985). As mentioned earlier, *baihua* was used from the Tang Dynasty onward as the written language for informal functions. Judging by the writings handed down from that period, the *baihua* of the time was mainly based on Northern Mandarin, with the Beijing dialect at its core. This is true not only for writers from the Northern Mandarin area, but also for those from the other dialect areas. However, features peculiar to their own dialects were also used by writers from non-Northern Mandarin background; this was only to be expected when these writers adopted varieties closer to their spoken vernaculars than *wenyan*. Dialect features in grammar and vocabulary are taken as important evidence in identifying the authors of some *baihua* writings.②

---

① Scholars of Chinese linguistics may differ on the grouping and subgrouping of dialects. For instance, the *Language Atlas of China* (Atlas 1987) has adopted a somewhat different scheme of subgrouping for Mandarin, according to which there are eight subgroups: Northeastern, Beijing, Beifang (Jilu), Jiaoliao, Zhongyuan, Lanyin, Southwestern, and Jianghuai.

② For instance, it is observed that traditional Northern Mandarin differs from the Southern dialects with respect to yes/no questions. Of the following patterns, (a)-(b) are used in the former, and (c) in the latter:

(a) VP + *bu* 'not' + VP

(b) VP + *meiyou* 'have-not'

(c) adverb + VP

In the traditional *baihua* literature, as expected, (a) and (b) are normally found; but (c) is also used occasionally, presumably by writers from the Southern dialect areas. The choice between (a)-(b), on the one hand, and (c) on the other, has been cited as evidence in ascertaining the identity of the author of *Jin Ping Mei* (cf. Hashimoto 1988, Zhu 1985).

The major goal of written language reform between 1910 and 1920 was to eliminate, or at least reduce, the gap between writing and speech. Indeed, among the most popular slogans for the reform was *wo shou xie wo kou* 'My hand writes down what I say with my mouth' . If put into practice literally, the proposal could have given rise to serious problems when the spoken lingua franca was still far from being extensively mastered among writers. It could have brought about problems with native speakers of non-Northern Mandarin dialects, especially the Southern dialects, given the fact that only a tiny proportion of them spoke reasonably good *guanhua*. Written texts exclusively based on the Southern dialects are hardly intelligible to readers unfamiliar with these varieties.

Many factors prevented MWC from diversifying into several distinct languages, each based on a vernacular dialect. The most important was the strong influence of the exemplary *baihua* literary works mentioned earlier, which had been familiar to all literates at that time. Speakers of dialects other than Northern Mandarin had to conform to the grammatical and vocabulary norms of the traditional *baihua* as much as possible if they intended their writings to reach a readership across dialect barriers. For them, the norms they followed in writing were acquired not via speech, but from exemplary written works based on a dialect they had not yet learned how to speak. This illustrates the importance of the role played by written texts in the formative process of standard written Chinese.

However, the situation was like that which affected *baihua* writers in earlier centuries. Regardless of the normative force of exemplary works, the influences of dialects other than Northern Mandarin could not be eradicated from the writings of native speakers of the other dialects, especially in a period when *baihua* was felt to need improvement because of the all-purpose function imposed upon it for the first time in history. As the concept of standardizing MWC was not raised until later, writers of non-Northern Mandarin background in the early days of the Literary Revolution, as well as in the 1920s and 1930s, were actually quite free in their choice of grammatical and lexical devices, constrained only by the concern that they should not adversely affect their intelligibility for a wide range of readership. A substantial proportion of the most influential writers in the 1920s and 1930s were native speakers of the Wu dialect, such as Hu Shi, Lu Xun, Zhou Zuoren, Yu Dafu, Xu Zhimo, Mao Dun, and Ye Shengtao.① In their writings, all of them displayed features characteristic of the grammar and vocabulary of their native tongue. Because of the popularity of these writers, many Wu features subsequently became part of established MWC norms.

While basically following the norms formed in mainland China from 1910 to the late 1940s, MWC in Taiwan, Hong Kong, and Singapore has also been under the influence of local dialects—mainly Min in Taiwan and Singapore, and Cantonese in Hong Kong. As a result, the grammatical and lexical norms of MWC differ somewhat among the four major Chinese communities. We return to this point later.

Classical Chinese

Classical Chinese constitutes another major source of influence on the formation of the norms of MWC. The situation with Chinese in the 20th century is usually assumed to be similar to what happened to Western European languages four centuries ago: The range of functions of a written vernacular was extended to include that of the high culture, which until then had been served by another literary written language,

---

① As stated in Davies (1992:203), the regional dialect background of 213 writers who were active from the early 20th century onward is as follows: Beijing 2%, other Northern Mandarin 14%, Southwestern Mandarin 22%, Jiang-Huai Mandarin 11%, Wu 40%, Cantonese 6%, and Min 5%.

namely Latin in Western Europe and *wenyan* in China. However, Chinese differs remarkably from the European languages in that, whereas Latin was virtually a dead language after being replaced by the Modern European languages, *wenyan* is still alive in MWC in a way that is not paralleled in Europe.①

As mentioned earlier, *wenyan* is based on Classical Chinese, while *baihua* is close to the contemporary vernacular. As regards the relationship between Classical Chinese and the Northern Mandarin vernacular in MWC, it is better to view them as two poles along the parameter of formality in styles; the former is suitable for extremely formal and frozen texts, the latter for casual or informal occasions. Between them, many intermediate positions may exist, combining features from Classical Chinese and the vernacular in various proportions. Most writings taken to be models of MWC are closer to the vernacular end, but quite a few are closer to the other end. The syntactic, morphological, and lexical features of Classical Chinese are extensively preserved in words, phrases, and sentence patterns that have been actively used in MWC. This situation can be ascribed to the merits of Classical Chinese that are unmatched by the vernacular-based traditional *baihua*. First, because of its continuous use for more than two millennia, *wenyan* had accumulated a richer repertoire of morphemes, words, and expressions than what was available in *baihua* at the beginning of this century. As a result, writers of MWC regularly turn to Classical Chinese

① Journalism is the field where *wenyan* holds on most tenaciously. Until the end of the 1940s, almost 20 years after the movement to promote *baihua*, a large portion of editorials and news reports were still written in *wenyan* instead of *baihua*. The situation has changed somewhat since then; but still, expressions characteristic of Classical Chinese are ubiquitous in Chinese newspapers and journals published in every Chinese community, especially for titles. I examined at random the front page of the February 25 (1992) issue of *Renmin Ribao* [*People's Daily*] from mainland China: Of the 11 titles on the page, 5 contain words and expressions that are distinctively *wenyan*.

as a fountainhead of linguistic resources. Second, *wenyan* is superior to *baihua* in terms of compactness and terseness; it is capable of conveying more information than the latter in the same space, often resulting in a highly refined style. Finally, the remoteness of *wenyan* from actual speech, and its function as the medium used in the Chinese classics, help to impart a tone of formality, and derivatively an aura of authority,to the present-day readers. By virtue of these merits, features of Classical Chinese constitute an essential part of the norms of MWC, characteristic of the styles that indicate qualities like succinctness, refinement, and formality. As a matter of fact, *wenyan* writings still make up from one-third to one-half of the content in high school textbooks of Chinese in mainland China, Taiwan, Hong Kong, and Singapore. A good knowledge of Classical Chinese is considered vital for mastering the whole range of styles in MWC.

Therefore, in spite of the passionate calls since 1910 to eradicate all traces of Classical Chinese from the new vernacular-based MWC, *wenyan* seems to die hard. Aside from the merits that make *wenyan* functionally useful, it is the continuous use of the logographic script that makes it possible for words and expressions from Classical Chinese to be extensively employed in the MWC. Classical Chinese is basically a monosyllabic language; each word is represented by a single syllable in the form of a single character in the overwhelming majority of cases. But the inventory of syllables was drastically reduced as Classical Chinese evolved into Modern Chinese.① With syllables becoming less and less differentiated, many monosyllabic words which were pronounced differently in Classical Chinese later became homonymous

---

① There is ample evidence that the inventory of basic syllables in Chinese as spoken in the 8th century was reduced by half as compared with what was represented in *Qieyun* (compiled in 601). It was further reduced by at least another half in the 14th century, as shown in *Zhongyuan Yinyun* (compiled in 1324). For a detailed account, see L. Wang 1980.

in speech. As a compensating mechanism for this phonetic attrition, many words of two or more syllables were formed, substantially reducing the number of homonyms that could bring about ambiguity in speech.① At the same time, although the presence of a large number of homonymous monosyllables makes it rather difficult to understand wenyan in speech, those homonyms are much easier to process in the written language, where they are represented by characters with differentiating graphic shapes. That, in my view, is the fundamental reason words and expressions of Classical Chinese occur much more frequently in MWC than in speech. If Chinese characters are ever abolished in favor of a romanized script, as has been advocated for more than a century, it would be extremely difficult, or even impossible, to use features of Classical Chinese as freely and extensively as is currently done in MWC.②

Foreign languages

Foreign languages stand as the most important source of influence on the evolution of MWC norms. To meet the demand for new terms in the fast-growing fields of humanities, social sciences, and modern science and technology, Chinese borrowed many words—first mainly from Japanese, then from European languages. The process of lexical borrowing on a large scale started in the mid-1800s, and accelerated around 1900. First used in *wenyan*, the borrowed words continued to be used in

---

① According to the latest statistics (cf. Beijing 1986), the average length of words in MWC is 1.48 syllables. In the fields of social and natural sciences, bi- and multisyllabic words make up to 51 % of the vocabulary in texts.

② Chao (1968, 1977) illustrated this point in an insightful manner when he composed two short stories using *wenyan* words which are pronounced exactly the same except for the tone in some cases, but are represented by different characters. The texts do not make any sense if transcribed into a romanized system.

baihua after it replaced *wenyan* as the base of the written language.

Aside from being sources of new terms, foreign languages—especially European languages like English, French, and Russian—have also exerted an important influence on the evolution of the grammatical norms of MWC since 1910. The most remarkable difference between present-day MWC and traditional *baihua* lies in the grammatical norms, which are much more Europeanized today than 80 years ago. Discussing the Europeanization of MWC, L. Wang (1954) observed that, as a result of the notable change of Chinese in its overall grammatical structure, well-written articles in present-day newspapers and magazines can be translated into Russian or English almost in a word-for-word manner, without substantial alternation in the structure. This tendency toward Europeanization of MWC has been growing since the 1950s, with no sign of decline.

The process of rapid Europeanization of the grammatical norms of MWC can be ascribed to three major factors. First, the expressiveness of the traditional *baihua* left much to be desired, especially as regards the accuracy or explicitness required in scholarly and scientific writings. Second, the great majority of the intellectual elite that led the New Culture Revolution held the traditional Chinese culture in abhorrence in all its major aspects—including the character script, and consequently the Chinese language. The extreme radicals among them advocated that the Chinese language should be replaced *in toto* by another language, such as Esperanto or English, in order to modernize the whole nation. Failing that, they argued, modern *baihua* should at least be Europeanized as much as possible.[①] In translating from European languages into

① These people succeeded to some extent. In addition to the examples to be discussed later, a well-known example of their achievements is the introduction into MWC of the distinct 3rd person pronouns for masculine, feminine, and neuter gender. Three different characters are now used for this purpose, although there is no difference in actual pronunciation.

Chinese, they proposed as a matter of principle that the structure of the original text should be followed as closely as possible, and this viewpoint has been taken as the distinctive feature of the so-called school of direct translation. Third, a large number of translated works have been pre-pared by people who were, strictly speaking, unqualified for the task. It is certainly easier for them to follow the syntax of the source language dogmatically, resulting in a highly Europeanized Chinese rendition, than to bring the product more in line with idiomatic usage in traditional *baihua*. These sloppy translators and the adherents of the direct-translation school have combined to create what has been referred to as "translationese" , a highly Europeanized Chinese style.

Given the aspirations for Western ideas that have permeated intellectual circles—and through them, all of Chinese society during the past 150 years—the influence of such translationese on the shaping of MWC norms cannot be underestimated. In fact, most leading scholars in all disciplines in China since 1900 were once engaged in translating from Western languages or Japanese as part of their academic activities. It is almost impossible for an educated Chinese to avoid translated works in his or her daily intellectual life.

During two periods, translated works constituted an especially important part of the daily reading of the educated Chinese. First, in the 1920s and 1930s, translated works provided the main source of information for those interested in fresh Western ideas as distinct from traditional Chinese scholarship. The second period started during the 1950s, when the teachings of Marx, Lenin, and Stalin were revered as the guiding ideology in mainland China. It was advocated and sometimes stipulated by the government that political writings by the Communist ideologists, often in very poor translationese, were to be read by every literate Chinese. For decades it was the vogue in mainland China, as in the Soviet Union and the Eastern European countries, for political leaders and mass media writers to cite these coarsely translated political writings in their directives, articles, and books; and these were in turn studied and quoted by the masses. The language used in these writings, which is typically very Europeanized in grammar and vocabulary, has played a modeling role that is imitated by the writers of MWC.

Overt he 80 years since *wenyan* was replaced by *baihua* as the base of a new written language, MWC has developed into a more or less standard written language with its own grammatical and lexical norms. By this process, Chinese has moved away from diglossia toward what is described as a "standard with dialects" situation: The standard is similar to a variety of the language that is used in ordinary conversation, more or less naturally in some places, and is used as a superposed variety in other places (cf. Ferguson [19591 1964:435).[①] While still based on Northern Mandarin for its core grammar and vocabulary, however, MWC has been under strong remolding influence from three major sources: Classical Chinese, non-Northern Mandarin dialects, and foreign languages. These have been responsible for the emergence of a large number of new grammatical and lexical norms in MWC that were not normally used in the base dialect. We now turn to some of these features that have emerged in MWC during the past 80 years, and examine the variations displayed by the four Chinese communities in the use of MWC.

4. Norms and variation in present-day MWC

As a result of influence from the three major sources, a large number

① Strictly speaking, diglossia continues among native speakers of non-Mandarin dialects who have not acquired native or near-native proficiency in Mandarin. How much extra effort is needed before they learn how to read and write in MWC—and what educational, social, and political implications this has—are rewarding topics for further research.

of new grammatical and lexical norms have emerged in MWC since 1910-1920; these were previously absent in traditional *baihua* and the spoken vernacular of Northern Mandarin. While still based on Northern Mandarin for its core grammar and vocabulary, present-day MWC contains a large number of features that are characteristic of non-Northern Mandarin dialects, or of foreign languages, particularly European languages. Features which might have raised objections decades ago, as being substandard or non-Chinese, are now generally accepted or extensively used. Furthermore, the norms of MWC vary depending on geographical areas. The four Chinese-speaking countries and regions, while sharing the major norms of MWC, have each developed their own regional features, mainly because of the influence of other local dialects or languages.

As stated earlier, texts in MWC may contain features of Classical Chinese in various proportions, depending on the styles or genres of the writing; hence it would be futile, as in some writings on the topic, to list the specific features of Classical Chinese that have been incorporated into the norms of MWC. I now concentrate on the new grammatical and lexical norms in MWC that can be ascribed to influence from non-Northern Mandarin dialects or foreign languages. Then I examine how the four major Chinese communities vary with regard to the norms of MWC.

4.1 Grammar

4.1.1 Newly developed norms

Features of non-Northern Mandarin dialects in MWC. Some of the new grammatical norms in MWC originated in dialects other than Northern Mandarin. As a large proportion of such features are characteristic of several non-Northern Mandarin dialects, it is often impossible to pin down their origin in terms of a particular dialect. Thus patterns 1-2 are both used for yes-no questions, as in sentences 3-4.[①]

(1) *you meiyou* + VP

(2) VP + *meiyou*

(3) a. *Nimen you meiyou kanjian ta chuqu*?

You have not-have see he out

b. *Nimen kanjian ta chuqu meiyou*?

'Did you see him go out?'

(4) a. *Ta houlai you meiyou huilai*?

he later have not-have return

b. *Ta houlai huilai le meiyou*?

he later return PFV not-have

'Did he come back later?'

Pattern 1 was originally confined to dialects in the Southern areas, mainly Wu, Min, and Cantonese; it was not found in Northern Mandarin, which normally uses Pattern 2. In MWC, however, 1 has been extensively used as a freely interchangeable alternative to 2.

Pattern 6 represents a usage in the traditional *baihua*, where the normal position for the place of destination in relation to verbs of movement is in a prepositional phrase in front of the verb, as in 7b and 8b. The Southern dialects normally use Pattern 5, where the place of destination follows the verb, as in 7a and 8a. In MWC, both patterns have been accepted equally as normal.

(5) *lai/qu* 'come/go' + place of destination

(6) *dao/shang* 'to' + place of destination + *lai/qu*

(7) a. *Ni zuotian lai zher le ma*?

---

① Abbreviations used in this article basically follow the practice in Li & Thompson 1981: DUR = durative aspect; PFV = perfective aspect; Q = question; CL = classifier.

you yesterday come here PFV Q

b. *Ni zuotian dao/shang zher lai le ma?*

you yesterday to here come PFV Q

'Did you come here yesterday?'

(8)a. *Ta qu youju ji yi feng xin.*

he go post-office mail one CL letter

b. *Ta dao/shang youju qu ji yi feng xin.*

'He went to the post office to mail a letter.'

Another feature involves extension of the verbal measure word *yixia* 'a bit'. In traditional *baihua*, this word was used only with a small number of verbs, usually those related to the meaning of hitting. Now, following the usage of Southern dialects, the use of *yixia* has been extended to other verbs in MWC, such as *kan* 'look' and *shi* 'try', as in 9a and 10a. More specialized measure words, *yi yan* 'one eye' for *kan*, and *yi shi* 'one try' for *shi*, would be required in Northern Mandarin, as in 9b and 10b (cf. J. Chen 1989:148).

(9) a. *Rang wo lai kan yixia.*

let me come look a-bit

b. *Rang wo lai kan yi yan.*

'Let me have a look.'

(10) a. *Qing ni shi yixia.*

please you try a-bit

b. *Qing ni shi yi shi.*

'Please have a try.'

As has been widely reported in the literature, some of the features originating in the Southern dialects, like those discussed earlier, have found their way not only into MWC, but also increasingly into the speech of native speakers of Northern Mandarin. These speakers use them just as naturally as the indigenous forms, without being aware that such expressions would have grated on the ears of their grandparents in the 1910-1920 period. The situation is undoubtedly ascribed to the extensive presence of such features first in MWC, which in turn exerts strong influence on the speech of its readership, whatever their dialect background may be.

Europeanization of MWC grammar

Some of the newly emerged grammatical norms in MWC are clearly outcomes of the Europeanization process that has been in progress since 1910. One of these is the extension of use of *bei* as a passive marker. In traditional *baihua*, this marker was only used for undesirable events.

(11) *Lao Wang zuotian bei laoban xun le yi dun.*
LW yesterday BEI boss scold PFV one CL
'LW was scolded by the boss yesterday.'

(12) *Xiao Li laoshi bu jiao fangzu, jieguo bei fangdong*
XL always not submit rent finally BEI landlord
gan le chulai.
throw PFV out
'XL never paid rent, and in the end was thrown out by the landlord.'

Since 1910, however, the usage has been extended beyond undesirable to neutral or desirables situations, more or less like a pure grammatical marker for passive voice.

(13) *Wo changchang bei pai dao ne ge diqu qiu*
I often BEI assign to that CL district go
jiancha gongzuo.
inspect work
'I am often assigned to that district for work inspection.'

(14) *Ta bei dajia guangrongde xuan wei daibiao.*
he BEI all honorably elect as representative

'As an honor, he was elected by all as the representative.'

Such extension of the use of *bei* was first considered a distinctive feature of translationese, motivated by imitation of passive markers in European languages. Gradually, it made its way into the norms of MWC, and is now extensively used by writers.

Another feature involves lengthy and complicated modifiers. Traditional *baihua* tends to have short sentences, because of its resemblance in style to actual speech; this also reflects the intrinsic restraint against lengthy constructions that was characteristic of Chinese at various phases of development prior to its close contact with European languages. In present-day written Chinese, however, lengthy sentences are very common, especially in texts of expository or argumentative genres; most examples involve long, complex prenominal modifiers that are connected to the head noun by the function word *de*. As reported by J. Chen(1989:145), a 4,500-character article by Mao Zedong, whose writings are taken as exemplary of MWC in mainland China, contains *de* 123 times, introducing various kinds of pre-nominal modifiers that result in lengthy and convoluted constructions. In contrast, in a 5,520-character speech by a worker, only 43 tokens of *de* are recorded. The marked discrepancy between the written and spoken mode shows the influence of foreign languages on MWC via translationese, one characteristic feature of which is locating all modifiers of nouns at the front of the modified, strung together with the aid of *de*. The following example is from Mao (1969:1151).

(15) *Xin-minzhuzhuyi guojia shouli you-zhe cong guanliao*
New-democratic state hand-in have-DUR from bureaucrat
zichan-jieji jieshou guolai de kongzhi quang guo
capitalist-class take over DE control whole country

jingji mingmai de juda de guojia qiye, you you
economy lifeline DE huge DE state enterprise also have
cong fengjian zhidu jiefang chulai, suize zai
from feudalist system liberate out although in
yi ge po chang shijian nei zai jibenshang
one CL quite long time within in basically
renran shi fensan de geti de, danshi zai
still be scatter DE individual DE but in
jianglai keyi zhubude yin xiang hezuoshe
future can gradually lead toward cooperative
fangxiang fazhan de nongye jingji.
direction develop DE agriculture economy
'The new democratic state will possess huge state enterprises taken over from the bureaucrat-capitalist class and controlling the economic lifelines of the country, and there will be an agricultural economy liberated from feudalism which, though it will remain basically scattered and individual for a fairly long time, can later be led to develop, step by step, in the direction of cooperatives.'

The two object NPs, *guojia qiye* 'state enterprises' and *nongye jingji* 'agricultural economy', each have lengthy and complex modifiers in front of them, bound to the head by *de*. For all their seeming clumsiness, constructions of this type, while never found in the traditional *baihua* or contemporary vernacular, abound in MWC-especially in scientific, political, and journalistic writings. The extensive acceptance of such constructions in MWC is facilitated by the functional contribution they have made to the expressive power of the language. In traditional *baihua*, attributes to nominals usually follow the head noun, unless they are quite short, as in the following.

(16) *Ta mai le yi liang hongse de paoche, 1991*
he buy PFV one CL red DE sports-car 1991
nian chuchang de.
year produce DE
'He bought a red sports car, which was made in 1991.'

Lengthy prenominal modifiers, although grammatical, were actually very seldom used. The functional deficiency involved here is that postnominal modifiers, like *1991 nian chuchang de*, are normally subject to the non-restrictive interpretation only. In translating restrictive relative clauses of European languages into Chinese, there was often little choice but to put the modifiers in front of the head noun, so as to distinguish them from those of the non-restrictive interpretation. Since restrictive clauses in European languages can be lengthy and complicated, so are the corresponding prenominal constituents in Chinese translation. Such usage has spread very rapidly since the 1920s. Now, in contrast to the short, mostly postnominal modifiers typically used in the traditional *baihua* and present-day vernacular, constructions involving long and complicated prenominal modifiers have become the norm in MWC for sentences that have modifiers in restrictive use. This is a welcome development: The pattern certainly enhances the explicitness and precision of the text, making MWC a better tool in a modern society.

Finally, we find proliferation of affix-like morphemes. Since 1910, a group of morphemes has emerged in MWC that serve functions like those of prefixes and suffixes in European languages, e.g. English non-, -ness, -tion, -ical, and -ize. Imitating the use of such European affixes, the MWC morphemes are attached to other words, modifying their meanings and changing their parts of speech. Among the most commonly used are *fei-* 'non-', *-xing* '-ness ', '-tion', *-hua* ' -ize':

(17) *fei* 'non-' + *huiyuan* 'member' > *fei-huiyuan* 'non-member'

(18) *lilun* 'theory' + *xing* '-ness, -tion' > *lilun-xing* 'theoreticality'

(19) *quanwei* 'authority' + *xing* > *quanwei-xing* 'authoritative'

(20) *xiandai* 'modern' + *hua* '-ize' > *xiandai-hua* 'modernize'

(21) *jixie* 'machine' + *hua* > *jixie-hua* 'mechanize'

Morphemes used in this way are still increasing in number, and tend to match all the important affixes in European languages, particularly English. The emergence and proliferation of these affix-like morphemes in Chinese, especially in MWC, is another important feature that has developed since 1910 under the influence of European languages.

4.1.2 Regional variations in grammatical norms of MWC

What were discussed earlier as newly emerged norms in MWC are established not only in mainland China, but also in the other three principal Chinese communities: Taiwan, Hong Kong, and Singapore. As speakers in these areas usually turn to mainland China for the standard of *putonghua* (or *guoyu, huayu*), especially in terms of pronunciation and grammar, their MWC has inherited almost all the grammatical features that developed in mainland China since 1910. At the same time, however, each place has also developed its own norms.

China's Taiwan

About 71 % of the population in Taiwan speak a Min dialect as their native language (Huang 1988), and 12% speak Hakka. *Guoyu* has been promoted in Taiwan since the island was returned to China in 1945, 50 years after it was ceded to Japan in 1895. A well planned educational program, carried out with stern and efficient administrative measures, has led to outstanding achievements in the popularization of *guoyu* on the island. It is generally believed that the percentage of Mandarin-speaking population is much higher in Taiwan than in mainland China.

As the majority of the population are bilingual speakers of *guoyu* and Min, it is inevitable that some Min features have entered MWC grammar and vocabulary, constituting a subset of norms that is not attested in the MWC of mainland China. With regard to deviances from the grammatical norms in mainland China, the most noteworthy is the use of *you* and *meiyou*.

You and *meiyou* function as verbs in Modern Chinese. In addition, *meiyou* is used as the negative counterpart of the perfective aspect marker *le*, indicating the non-completion of an action. However, the two verbs fulfill more functions in MWC of Taiwan than in mainland China: Both can also be used as markers to indicate the occurrence or non-occurrence of an action, or to indicate the existence or nonexistence of a situation.

(22) Q: *Ni you meiyou qu kan ta?*
you have not-have go see he
'Did you go to see him?'
A: *Wo you qu kan ta.*
I have go see he
'I went to see him.'

You in the answer is used as the affirmative counterpart of *meiyou*, indicating the occurrence of the action. This usage is very common in MWC in Taiwan, but is not allowed in mainland China, where *le* is normally used for such purposes (ex. 23). Consider also (24-26).

(23) *Wo qu kan le ta*
I go see PFV he
'I went to see him.'

(24) *Wo zaoshang you zai jia.*
I morning have at home
'I was at home in the morning.'

(25) *Lao Luo nianji you da yidian, danshi ye bu tai lao.*
LL age have old a-bit but yet not too aged
'LL is a bit too old, but not much too old yet.'

(26) *women xianzai dou shi xuesheng, meiyou zhuanqian.*
we now all be student not-have earn-money
'At present we are all students, and don't have any income.'
(cited from Kubler 1985:140)

Here *you* and *meiyou* are used to stress the existence or nonexistence of a situation. Such use is not accepted in the MWC of mainland China, where there is no corresponding expression to serve such semantic functions. This is a typical example of the influence of the Min dialect on MWC in Taiwan. According to R. L. Cheng (1985, 1990), two words *u* and *bo* in the Min dialect are used for the functions served by *you* and *meiyou* in (22)-(26). When native speakers of the Min dialect speak or write in *guoyu*, they tend to express cognitive/semantic content in terms of their native dialect. As *u* and *bo* are distinctively non-Mandarin, *you* and *meiyou* have been chosen as the formal substitutes (cf. also Huang 1988, C. Li 1983).

Hong Kong

Hong Kong is different from the other communities in that Cantonese, not Mandarin, is the language used by over 98% of the Chinese population. Only a very small number of the local residents can speak *putonghua*—

although learners have been growing rapidly in number in anticipation of 1997, when the Crown Colony will be returned to mainland China (cf. Tian 1992, P. Wang 1989). The written Chinese of Hong Kong, however, is supposedly based on Northern Mandarin, in conformity with the standard in mainland China. Given the role of Cantonese as the lingua franca among local Chinese (and also given the fact that English has long been the language for high-level administrative, commercial, legal, and educational purposes), MWC norms in Hong Kong inevitably deviate somewhat from those in mainland China. Although the most remarkable differences lie in the vocabulary, there are also some variances in grammatical norms. Compare the word order of the verb and the adverb *duo* 'more' in the following sentences.

(27) a. *Ta hui zai zher zhu duo ji tian.*
he will in here live more several day
b. *Ta hui zai zher duo zhu ji tian.*
'He will live here for a few more days.'

The adverb *duo* precedes the verb in Northern Mandarin, but follows it in Cantonese. Under the influence of Cantonese, both word orders are frequently attested in the MWC of Hong Kong.

Singapore

The linguistic situation in Singapore is similar to that in Taiwan: Of the ethnic Chinese who comprise 76% of the nation's population, more than 47% speak varieties of Min as their native language. Min also functioned formerly as the lingua franca among Chinese Singaporeans (Kuo 1985). In 1979 the government launched a *Huayu* Promotion Campaign, which aimed to replace the Min dialect with *huayu* as the lingua franca of the Chinese population, and in the long term as the native language of all ethnic Chinese. With the efficiency characteristic of Lee Kuan Yew's administration, the campaign achieved great success (see Newman 1988, Platt 1985). According to a 1987 survey, 87% of Chinese Singaporeans above age 12 speak fluent Mandarin (cf. H. Wang 1990:347).

As in Taiwan, the MWC of Singapore inevitably comes under the influence of the locally predominant Min dialect. As observed in several research reports (C. Chen 1986, Lock 1989, Wu 1990, Zhou 1989), almost all the grammatical features generally accepted as the norm in the MWC of Taiwan, but not of mainland China, are also extensively used in Singapore.

4.2 Vocabulary

4.2.1 Newly emerged lexical norms

Along with grammar, the vocabulary of MWC also underwent a process of elaboration from 1910 onward. New words and expressions have entered MWC from three major sources, namely Classical Chinese, non-Northern Mandarin dialects, and foreign languages. We are concerned here with the last two.

Borrowings from non-Northern Mandarin dialects

While based on Northern Mandarin for the core vocabulary, MWC has borrowed many words from other dialects. Such borrowings either fill lexical gaps, expressing notions that had no names in Northern Mandarin that could be appropriately used in MWC; or they provide the users of MWC with alternative expressions that encode more or less the same kind of semantic notions, but differ as regards stylistic nuances. For instance, the word for 'rubbish' in Northern Mandarin, as represented by the Beijing dialect, is *zang-tu* 'dirty soil'. If the word were used in MWC, readers who do not speak Northern Mandarin would probably interpret it in terms of the literal meaning of the component characters, which is quite different than the specialized meaning of the expression in the spoken vernacular. The Wu dialect word *laji* nicely fills the gap. By contrast, the word *baxi* 'acrobatics, trick', which was also borrowed from the Wu dialect, is now used in MWC, with a deprecatory connotation, side by side with words from Northern Mandarin like *zaji* 'acrobatics' and *huazhao* 'trick'. Other common examples include *ganga* 'awkward', *mosheng* 'unfamiliar', *biejiao* 'shoddy', *mingtang* 'what lies behind something, result', and *gao* 'to do'. These are mostly from the Wu dialect, further testifying to the influence of the large number of prominent Wu writers on the evolution of MWC during the most formative periods of the 1920s and 1930s (see earlier discussion).

Translations or borrowings from foreign languages

The most important source of new words in MWC is from other languages. During the past 150 years, Chinese has translated or borrowed heavily from European languages. A large portion entered Chinese via Japanese. Ahead of the Chinese in introducing novel ideas from the West, the Japanese coined many new words by using kanji, the Chinese characters. Broadly speaking, these new words in Japanese fall into two groups. The first is composed of words that were used earlier in the Chinese classics, but were now assigned a new, though often somewhat related meaning so as to serve as Japanese equivalents of European expressions. Examples are *jing-ji* (Ja. *keizai*) and *bao-xian* (Ja. *hoken*). Used in the Chinese classics for more than a millennium, the two words mean 'to govern and to help', and 'to safeguard places that are strategically located and difficult of access', respectively. During the Meiji period (1868-1912), the Japanese used these two words to translate 'economy' and 'insurance', thus assigning new meanings to the old forms.

The second group contains words that were newly coined by the Japanese, with the component characters often used in the meanings of Classical Chinese. Examples include *du-cai* 'alone-decide' (Ja. *dokusai*) for 'dictatorship', and *zhe-xue* 'wisdom-study' (Ja. *tetsugaku*) for 'philosophy' (for a detailed account, cf. Coulmas 1989, Wang 1980). A large number of these kanji words were later borrowed into Chinese, constituting an important proportion of the new words and expressions that have appeared since the end of the 19th century. Many have been assimilated into the basic vocabulary of Modern Chinese, including such frequent words as the following:

(28)

JAPANESE	ENGLISH	CHINESE
fukumu	service	*fuwu*
kakumei	revolution	*geming*
kankyo	environment	*huanjing*
gutai	concrete	*juti*
mokuteki	goal	*mudi*
tetsuzuki	procedure	*shouxu*
joken	condition	*tiaojian*
shihon	capital	*ziben*

Few Chinese today realize that these expressions were actually borrowings from Japanese.

Since 1910, Chinese has increasingly translated and borrowed words directly from European languages, mainly English. The trend continues to the present day. Since Chinese has a logographic script, words in romanized script must be transformed into expressions in Chinese characters when they are introduced into Chinese. Generally speaking, there are five possible methods to introduce a new notion from the European languages.

(a) Loan translation: The foreign term is translated in a literal way, with a morpheme-for-morpheme match between the two languages. This method is most frequently used in translating compounds or phrases.

(29)	*mi-yue*	'honeymoon'
	ma-li	'horse power'
	lan-qiu	'basketball'
	shengming-xian	'lifeline'

(b) Semantic translation: A new Chinese word is coined, using indigenous morphemes in a way that attempts to capture the most characteristic feature of the foreign concept. The literal meaning of the Chinese words may not match that of the original, as can be observed in these examples.

(30)	*qi-che*	(steam vehicle)	'car'
	gang-qin	(steel musical instrument)	'piano'
	you-piao	(postal coupon)	'stamp'
	da-zi-ji	(strike character machine)	'typewriter'

(c) Phonetic transcription: By this method, words are directly borrowed from the source languages, with Chinese characters used to simulate their original pronunciation.

(31)	*shafa*	'sofa'
	mada	'motor'
	tanke	'tank'
	qiaokeli	'chocolate'

(d) Juxtaposition of (b) and (c): A Chinese morpheme is added to the transliterated word to indicate the semantic category, thus facilitating the intelligibility of the new lexical item.

(32)	*che-tai*	(car-)	'tire'
	jiu-ba	(liquor-)	'bar'

balei-wu (-dance) 'ballet'
pi-jiu (-liquor) 'beer'

(e) Combination of (b) and (c): While matching the sound of the original word as in transliteration, the combination of the characters also has its own semantic meaning, intended to be indicative of the semantic content of the foreign word.

(33) *mi-ni* (enchanting you) 'mini'
ai-zi (generated by love) 'AIDS'
lei-da (thunder arrive) 'radar'
wei-ta-ming (safeguard his life) 'vitamin'

Throughout the evolution of MWC, vocabulary is the domain where norms differ most remarkably in terms of times and places. There was a period, mainly in the 1920s and 1930s, when it was common for a single notion from the West to be given two or more names in Chinese, frequently as a result of different methods used to introduce the term into Chinese. Furthermore, dialect areas may differ as to the preferred form, even when the same method of translation or borrowing is used. Following are some examples (letters in parentheses indicate the methods used in coining the word).

(34) 'microphone' *hua-tong* (speech tube) (b)
mai-ke-feng (c)

(35) 'engine' *fadong-ji* (launch machine) (b)
yin-qing (draw lift) (e)

(36) 'cement' *shui-men-ting* (c)
yang-hui (foreign dust) (b)—prevalent in the Wu dialect area
shui-ni ((water mud) (b)—prevalent in the Northern Mandarin area

(37) 'rifle' *bu-qiang* (footstep gun) (b)

laifu-qiang (-gun) (d)

(38) 'vitamin' *wei-ta-ming* (safeguard his life) (e)
wei-sheng-su (safeguard life element) mainly (c), except for the first character, which reflects (e)

As a rule, the situation in which functionally undifferentiated terms for the same referent coexist in the same language community will not last long. Competition has been under way among the alternatives for the status of MWC norm. Generally speaking, two principles are at work throughout the evolution of norms among competing items.

First, preference is given to loan translation and semantic translation over transliteration. For instance, with regard to the examples just given, the standard names for 'microphone' , 'engine' , 'rifle' , and 'vitamin' are *huatong*, *fadongji*, *buqiang*, and *weishengsu*, respectively.

Second, preference is given to the name prevalent in Northern Mandarin areas over other areas. Thus, for 'cement' , *shuini* (rather than *yanghui* or *shuimenting*) has been established as the norm

The explanation for the resistance to transliteration lies in the logographic nature of Chinese script, and the traditional importance attached to reading rather than speaking in the Chinese world. In addition to their sound value, most Chinese characters used in texts have their own semantic content as well. Chinese readers tend to pay more attention to the meaning conveyed by the graphic forms of the characters than to their phonetic values; it is not uncommon for Chinese readers to recognize the semantic content of characters without being able to pronounce them. Although much controversy still surrounds the cognitive mechanisms underlying the processing of texts in Chinese characters, most researchers seem to believe that the Chinese script indicates meaning more directly than do alphabetic or syllabic scripts, which are connected to the meaning completely via sound (cf. Hoosain 1991 for details). Since characters in transliteration are used for their sound value only, the string of characters for a word does not make much sense as regards the inherent meaning of the graphic forms, and thus requires more processing effort on the part of readers. When alternatives exist, Chinese readers who tend to read meaning into the graphic forms of a text would prefer words in which each character makes sense, as opposed to those coined purely through transliteration.

Table 1: Lexical variations in the Chinese of mainland China, Taiwan, Hong Kong, and Singapore

English	China			Singapore
	Mainland	Taiwan	Hong Kong	
'taxi'	*chuzu qiche*	*jichengche*	*dishi*	*deshi*
'gasoline'	*qiyou*	*qiyou*	*dianyou*	*dianyou*
'folk dance'	*minjianwu*	*tufengwu*	*tufengwu*	*tufengwu or minjianwu*
'film'	*jiaojuan*	*jiaojuan*	*feilin*	*jiaojuan or feilin*
'motorcycle'	*motuoche*	*jiche*	*diandanche*	*motuoxika* (or any of the other three)
'disabled'	*canji*	*canzhang*	*shangcan*	*canque* (or any of the other three)

4.2.2 Regional variations in lexical norms of MWC

As lexical norms vary with time, they also vary with place. Indeed, the four Chinese communities differ considerably with regard to MWC vocabulary. Such variations constitute a main source of difficulty or misunderstanding when Chinese read publications from the other areas (cf. Hsu 1979, Huang 1988, C. Li 1983, Lui 1990, H. Wang 1990, Zhou 1989). Table 1 presents some examples.

Variation is at its greatest with the transcription of proper names from European languages. Very often the same referent assumes different Chinese names in the four Chinese communities, composed of different characters that have the same or similar pronunciations. It is reported that Mrs. Thatcher's name appeared in 27 different forms of transcription in Chinese publications (Ho 1989).

Mainland China and China's Taiwan

Discrepancies between these two areas can be ascribed to three factors. First, because of the long period of separation, the two areas have developed separate lexical norms, although the lexical terms involved are all constructed from indigenous sources in Northern Mandarin, as exemplified by the following expressions:

(39) MAINLAND CHINA	TAIWAN	ENGLISH
chuzu qiche	*jichdngche*	'taxi'
minjianwu	*tuifengwia*	'folk dance'
canji	*canzhang*	'disabled'
chubei	*cundi*	'reserve'
lijiaoqiao	*jiaoliudao*	'overpass'
yuhangyuan	*taikongren*	'astronaut'

Second, nearly half a century's rule of Taiwan by the Japanese had an effect on the MWC used there. Some borrowings from Japanese that became the norm in Taiwan, but not in mainland China, are the following:

(40) TAIWAN	JAPANESE	MAINLAND CHINA	ENGLISH
biandang	*bento*	*hefan*	'meal in a box'
fuzhi	*fukushi*	*fuli*	'welfare'
chezhang	*shasho*	*shoupiaoyuan*	'conductor'

Third, some expressions from the local Min dialect have acquired the status of MWC norms in Taiwan, as follows:

(41) TAIWAN	MAINLAND CHINA	ENGLISH
fansu	*baisu*	'sweet potato'

baibai	*jibai*	‘hold a memorial ceremony for’
shuai	*daomei*	‘doomed’

China’s Hong Kong

Distinctive characteristics of Hong Kong mainly result from the fact that Hong Kong MWC is under strong influence from English and Cantonese. The vocabulary of Hong Kong MWC contains a larger number of borrowings from English than in either mainland China or Taiwan, as exemplified in Table 1. Furthermore, as Cantonese is the predominant spoken language among the Chinese residents there, many Cantonese words have entered MWC as the norm over their Mandarin counterparts. For example, Hong Kong MWC normally uses the Cantonese-derived words *huichun* ‘New Year couplets’, *suochi* ‘key’, and *xuegui* ‘refrigerator’, instead of the corresponding *chunlian*, *yaoshi*, and *bingxiang* used in mainland China and Taiwan.

Singapore

Singapore is unique in that the lexical norms in the MWC used there are not as well established as in the other three places, displaying more variation within the community. In many cases, variant forms from mainland China, Taiwan, and Hong Kong show stable coexistence in Singapore, with the frequency of use differing from case to case. The situation is also illustrated in Table 1: Whereas each of the other three communities has a single normal term for each of the notions, Singapore often has several alternatives. As remarked by H. Wang (1990:356), it seems that Singaporeans have not made up their mind yet whether to establish a set of distinct standards for their own community, with regard to MWC grammar and vocabulary, or to adhere to the set of standards adopted in mainland China or Taiwan.

Tendency toward reducing variation in lexical norms. For several decades the MWC vocabulary in mainland China was so different from that in Taiwan, Hong Kong, and other overseas Chinese communities that it was easy to identify the source of a publication on the basis of words used in the text. The situation has changed somewhat since the end of the 1970s, when mainland China started adopting an "open door" policy: This has caused some changes in MWC lexical norms. On the one hand, a large number of new expressions have rushed into mainland China through the open door. For example, *piliwu* 'break dancing' and *chao youyu* 'to fire', 'to sack' have been adopted from Hong Kong MWC, and *gongshi* 'consensus', *xintai* 'mentality', *gouxiang* 'idea' from Taiwan. Such words have gained currency in mainland China, sometimes used side by side with the traditional norms, such as *guandao* (vs. *qudao*) 'channel', and *shuizhun* (vs. *shuiping*) 'level'. On the other hand, closer contacts between the Chinese communities have also introduced certain expressions, formerly peculiar to mainland China, into Taiwan, Hong Kong, Singapore, and other overseas Chinese communities. Words such as *cujin* 'promote, accelerate', *jinzhang* 'in short supply', and *guashuai* 'be in command', which were rarely heard outside mainland China decades ago, are becoming increasingly popular in newspapers and magazines in the entire Chinese world.

5. Efforts of language planning for the development of MWC

Language planning is definable as "an explicit and systematic effort to resolve language problems and achieve related goals through institutionally organized intervention in the use and usage of languages"

(Christian 1988:197). Two types are recognized in the literature: status planning, which refers to the allocation of languages or language varieties to given functions (e.g. medium of instruction, official language, or vehicle of mass communication), vs. corpus planning, which refers to activities that aim to develop a single language or variety of a language in some way, such as coining new terms, reforming spelling, or adopting a new script (cf. also Cooper 1989:32).

5.1 Status planning

What happened to the traditional *baihua* in the period 1910-1920 is a typical case of status planning: A vernacular-based written variety of Chinese was promoted for all literary and scholarly purposes, replacing the established *wenyan* that was based on Classical Chinese. As we have seen, it has achieved remarkable success, but in a way notably different from the case with Latin as regards the motivation of the activity and the status of the replaced language.

In Western Europe, the replacement of Latin by vernacular languages was a direct reflection of the raising of national consciousness; in China, however, the replacement of *wenyan* was first and foremost prompted by the desire to reduce widespread illiteracy, as an integral part of the drive to modernize the whole country. China at the turn of the century was characterized by surging nationalism, just as Western Europe was approximately three hundred years earlier. But instead of being looked upon as a sacred symbol of nationalism or statehood, the Chinese language as a whole was treated more as a culprit that should be held responsible for the misery of the nation. *Baihua* finally won over *wenyan* as the basis of MWC, not because it was a better symbol of the nationalism or statehood, but mainly because it was easier to learn and to use.

Furthermore, when Latin gave way to the modern European languages, it essentially became a dead language; but in China, although *wenyan* gave way to *baihua*, it still plays an important role in MWC, providing for special stylistic effects that otherwise could not be obtained. In other words, MWC is not exclusively based on the traditional *baihua* (or its base dialect, Northern Mandarin), as advocated since 1910. According to the official definition, MWC should look to *baihua* as the model for its lexical and grammatical norms. However, as Cooper(1989:134-5) observes, people may often agree that an all-purpose model exists, and yet not use it for all the purposes for which they feel it appropriate, if in fact they use it at all. One reason for this is that we have to move from style to style or from variety to variety to suit our communicative context—casual or formal, sacred or secular, etc.—as well as to suit our communicative content: "Because the style or variety we employ is itself part of the meaning we convey, we cannot restrict ourselves to a single style without restricting our ability to implement our communicating content" (Cooper 1989:135).

As a style indicative of formality, terseness and refinement, *wenyan* is still alive and well in MWC. To the extent that *wenyan* represents a tradition that was venerated for more than two millennia, the present status of *wenyan* in MWC indicates the strength of traditionalism in the Chinese world.

5.2 Corpus planning

Ferguson (1968) describes three basic types of corpus planning. *Graphization* refers to activities which establish and/or refine the writing system of a language. *Modernization* refers to efforts to expand the resources of a language, particularly its vocabulary, to meet the new functional demands placed upon it in the modern world. *Standardization* means development of a norm which overrides regional and social dialects. All three aspects of corpus planning have been involved in the development of the Chinese language during the past 80 years. As graphization does not concern us in this article, I discuss the other two aspects in relation to the development of MWC.

In the exercise of corpus planning, modernization is usually accompanied by standardization. This process, according to Rubin (1977), is composed of six interrelated parts. The first three are (a) isolation of a norm, (b) evaluation of the norm by some significant group as “correct” or “preferred”, and (c) prescription of the norm for specified contexts or functions. For standardization to take effect, the prescribed norm must then (d) be accepted,(e) be used, and (f) remain in effect until another norm replaces it. As observed by Haugen (1983:271) and Cooper (1989:144), a common, if not absolutely essential, feature of this process is codification, the explicit statement of a norm.

As mentioned earlier, the expansion of the Chinese vocabulary started after the Opium War in 1840, and accelerated after the turn of the century to accommodate the fast-growing number of new notions in a rapidly changing and modernizing society. An official institution, the National Bureau of Compilation and Translation, was established in Nanjing in 1932. One of its major functions was to set up standard terminologies in all educational and academic institutions, in a way similar to that of the Hebrew Language Council as reported by Cooper (1989:123). This institution has been in operation since 1932 both in mainland China and Taiwan, although under other names in mainland China since 1949 (cf. Liu 1986, Tse 1986). At the same time, semi-official translation institutions, publishing houses, and individuals have also been coining new words and expressions, mainly in translations from foreign languages, with a varying extent of acceptance by the wider community. Alternative names may still be found for the same notion in MWC, especially in the domains of the humanities and social sciences.

The first serious attempt to standardize MWC in a comprehensive way was launched in mainland China by Lü & Zhu (1952), which was originally serialized from June 6 to December 5, 1951, in *Renmin Ribao* [*People's Daily*], the most important newspaper in mainland China. Targeted at what was described as a chaotic situation with regard to the use of MWC in its grammatical, lexical, and stylistic aspects, the work analyzed major types of "wrong and ungrammatical usages" as exemplified by a large number of sentences collected from contemporary publications; and it prescribed appropriate forms. It is interesting to note that, of the emerging features that originated in non-Northern Mandarin dialects and foreign languages, very few were labeled as substandard. Most of the errors pointed out were ascribable to negligence or incoherence in matters of grammar and logic. The work was greeted with great enthusiasm across the country, and served as the standard "writer's manual" for many years to come. However, not all its admonitions and suggestions have been accepted. For instance, the use of morphemes like *-xing* and *-hua*, as the Chinese equivalent of the Western suffixes -ness and -ize, seems to have become more popular during the past decades, in spite of the objection raised in Lü & Zhu (1952).

The first explicit statement of the Modern Chinese standard was made at the First National Conference on Writing Reform, convened in Beijing in 1955. This resulted in the Directive Concerning Popularization of *Putonghua*, issued by the State Council in 1956. Before that, considerable consensus existed with regard to the standard of pronunciation of Modern Chinese, after heated debates on the issue in the early 1920s (cf. J. Li 1934); but opinions still differed as to standards of vocabulary and grammar. Some maintained that not only pronunciation, but also vocabulary and grammar, should be based exclusively on the Beijing dialect; given the historical fact that the dialectal basis of *baihua* extends beyond the Beijing dialect, some believed that the vocabulary and grammar of *putonghua* should also be built on a wider dialectal basis. In the end, the latter viewpoint prevailed, as demonstrated by the final definition of *putonghua*. Following the conference, a campaign to standardize Modern Chinese was launched in mainland China—together with the other two stated tasks of language reform, promoting the speaking of *putonghua* and reforming the script system (cf. Barnes 1974, 1983, C. Cheng 1979).

The Conference on the Standardization of the Modern Chinese Language, held in Beijing in 1955, set forth several tasks that had to be accomplished in the endeavor to standardize Modern Chinese; among them was the compilation of a standard reference grammar and an authoritative dictionary of Modern Chinese. Efforts toward the latter goal have culminated in *Xiandai Hanyu Cidian* [*Modern Chinese Dictionary*], a medium-sized dictionary containing around 56,000 words and phrases, published in 1979; however, the grammar project has not yet started.

Generally speaking, the following principles have been invoked in establishing lexical norms among alternative expressions for MWC in mainland China:

(a) Words that were confined to the local Beijing dialect were rejected in favor of equivalent expressions of wider circulation in the Northern Mandarin area. For example, *bangwan* ‘dusk’ and *koushui* ‘saliva’ , rather than the Beijing localisms *caheir* and *halazi*, were chosen as norms.

(b) Words peculiar to the non-Northern Mandarin areas gave way to the corresponding expressions in the Northern Mandarin area. Some examples illustrating the point have been given earlier.

(c) With regard to translations or borrowings from other languages, when there were alternatives, transliterations gave way to words formed by other methods, preferably by the method of semantic translation. As the eminent Chinese linguist L. Wang put it (1954), semantic (rather than phonetic) translation reflects the national self-esteem of the Chinese-speaking people.

Proper names should be transliterated with combinations of characters which do not convey any connotation that might arise out of the inherent meanings of the characters used. A good example is the Chinese transliteration of Mozambique. It was *Mo-san-bi-gei* (not-three-nose-give) in the 1950s, which was later replaced by *Mo-sang-bi-ke* (not-mulberry-than-can). Obviously, the combination of the four characters in the first name has an undesirable meaning, whereas it is not the case with the second name. A corresponding list of English sounds and Chinese characters was promulgated by the official Xinhua News Agency in the 1950s, followed by a handbook that contained the standard translations of the most frequently used proper names.

The effort to standardize the lexical norms in MWC according to the listed principles has been quite successful in mainland China. Actually, few people in the 1990s understand the meaning of phonetically transcribed words that were prevalent before the 1940s, such as the following:

(42) EARLIER FORMS	ENGLISH	LATER FORMS
yanshipilicun	'inspiration'	*linggan*
demokelaxi	'democracy'	*minzhu*

puluo	'proletariat'	*wuchanjie*
buerqiaoya	'bourgeois'	*zichanjieji*
yinde	'index'	*suoyin*

In addition, many natives in Beijing, especially the youngsters, do not even understand such former local expressions as *qudengr* for *huocai* 'match' or *yizi* for *feizao* 'soap', let alone use them in writing.

However, little has been achieved in the way of ridding MWC of the elements of Classical Chinese, as has been advocated by some language planners since 1910. So long as the character script is still used as the written system of Chinese, such proposals may well continue to prove fruitless.

In contrast to the considerable success with the MWC lexicon, there is far less consensus with regard to which grammatical features in MWC should be granted "standard" status, and which should be labeled "substandard," especially when dialect features are involved. The official documents of the National Conference on Language that was convened in January 1986, as well as articles in journals of language planning, make little mention of standardization for the grammatical norms of MWC. Actually, grammatical features that deviate from the vernacular Northern Mandarin are much less obtrusive to the general readership of MWC than lexical deviance, and thus much more likely to be incorporated into the norms of MWC.

China's Taiwan and Hong Kong, and Singapore

A similar situation exists in Taiwan. Standardization efforts have concentrated on the vocabulary of MWC, especially with regard to translated terms, and little attention has been paid to the grammatical aspect. Up to 1974, according to Tse (1986:29), 66 lists of scientific and technical terms had been authorized by the Ministry of Education through the National

Bureau of Compilation and Translation. With increasing contact between mainland China and Taiwan, calls arise on both sides to reduce the terminological discrepancies, especially in the fields of modern sciences and technology.[①] Whether this will materialize seems to hinge upon the political relationship between the two sides in the future.

Corpus planning of MWC has been less active in Hong Kong than in mainland China and Taiwan, largely because, until 1970, English was the sole written language for almost all formal occasions in Hong Kong (including government administration, tertiary instruction, court proceedings, and commercial transactions); written Chinese was relegated to marginal status, used mainly for informal purposes among local Chinese. The situation changed somewhat in 1974 when the Official Language Ordinance was promulgated, for the first time declaring English and Chinese to be official languages of Hong Kong. In dealing with the ensuing tremendous amount of translation of government documents and laws from English to Chinese, government agencies have compiled handbooks to standardize the terminologies involved, usually from English to Chinese. Curiously, these manuals are circulated only within a small circle, and are not easily available to the public (cf. Ho 1989). As matters stand, lexical terms and grammatical usages are not very consistent in the MWC in Hong Kong; they are dependent on the personal language background or preference of writers, and little effort has been exerted on the part of the official institution to set up grammatical or lexical norms.

Officially speaking, Singapore looks to mainland China for the standard form of *huayu* in its phonological, grammatical, and lexical

---

① It is reported that a working group has been set up in Taiwan under government auspices to reduce terminological discrepancies between Taiwan and mainland China (*Zhongyang Ribao* [*Central Daily News*], International Edition, May 30, 1992, p. 7).

aspects. However, the influence of local Chinese dialects and other languages on the evolution of MWC norms is obvious. There is a Panel for Standard Chinese Vocabulary under the Ministry of Education, which monitors the actual use of lexical items in Singapore, but it has not yet promulgated a list of standard lexical items for general consideration (Lu 1990). With regard to the grammatical standard, it has been observed by Wu (1990) that a large proportion of teachers and students can recognize grammatical patterns that deviate from those of Beijing, and in some cases brand them as substandard; however, they use these patterns regularly. What we see is a typical case of an attitudinal rather than behavioral classification of the assumed grammatical norms. No local language planning agency has taken a stand on grammatical features of this kind.

6. Conclusion

China was in a typical diglossic situation when *baihua* replaced *wenyan* as the base of MWC in the late 1910-1920 period. Over the past 80 years, MWC has developed into a written language with fairly consistent norms in grammar and vocabulary. During this period, MWC has assimilated many grammatical and lexical features from non-Northern Mandarin dialects and from foreign languages, particularly European languages. Furthermore, it has incorporated features of Classical Chinese into its norms of usage, to meet the functional needs of specific styles. While still based on Northern Mandarin for its core grammar and vocabulary, MWC is characterized by a linguistic repertoire that is much richer than that found in traditional *baihua* or in the current vernacular. Mainland China, Taiwan, Hong Kong, and Singapore differ slightly with respect to norms in grammar and vocabulary, mainly because of influence from local dialects and languages. Efforts in language planning have succeeded in elevating the status of *baihua*, and, to a certain extent, in standardizing the lexical norms of MWC. However, the grammatical norms in MWC, as observed today, have been by and large the natural outcome of spontaneous evolution over the past 80 years.

Chinese originally may have represented diglossia on the largest scale of any attested instance (Ferguson[1959]1964:426). The development of MWC represents the process by which Chinese has been moving way from the traditional diglossia that characterized the Chinese world in 1910. As MWC is based on Northern Mandarin for its core grammar and vocabulary, we conclude that Chinese has been progressing toward a "standard and dialects" status with respect to writing. However, to the extent that a large number of features from Classical Chinese, non-Northern Mandarin dialects, and foreign languages are incorporated into MWC norms—which may not appear regularly in ordinary usage—Chinese has not developed as far away from the traditional diglossia as Modern European languages have done.

References

Atlas. 1987. *Language Atlas of China*, Hong Kong: Longman Group (Far East) Ltd., for the Australian Academy of Humanities and the Chinese Academy of Social Sciences.

Barnes, Dayle. 1974. Language planning in Mainland China: Standardization, In: Joshua A. Fishman, ed., *Advances in Language Planning*. The Hague: Mouton, 457-77.

Barnes, Dayle. 1983. The implementation of language planning in China, In: Cobarrubias & Fishman, eds., 291-308.

Beijing. 1986. *Xiandai Hanyu Pinlü Cidian* [*Dictionary of Word Frequencies in Modern Chinese*], Beijing: Languages Institute Press.

Bolton, Kingsley and Helen Kwok. eds. 1992. *Sociolinguistics Today: International Perspectives*, London: Routledge.

Chao, Yuen Ren. 1968. Chinese language, *Encyclopedia Britannica* 5:630-34.

Chao, Yuen Ren. 1977. *Yuyan Wenti* [*Topics on Language*], 3rd ed. Taipei: Shangwu yinshuguan.

Chen, Chungyu. 1986. Xinjiapo Huayu yufa tezheng [Syntactic features of Singapore Mandarin], *Yuyan Yanjiu* [*Linguistic Studies*] 1: 138-52.

Chen, Enquan. ed. 1989. *Shuangyu Shuangfangyan* [*Bilingualism and Bi-dialectalism*], Guangzhou: Zhongshan University Press.

Chen, Jianmin. 1989. *Yuyan Wenhua Shehui Xintan* [*New Explorations into Language, Culture, and Society*], Shanghai: Shanghai Educational Press.

Chen, Ping. 1992. Diversity and uniformity in Chinese syntax, In: Bolton & Kwok, eds., 180-91.

Cheng, Chin-Chuan. 1979. Language reform in China in the seventies, *Word* 3:45-57.

Cheng, Robert L. 1990. Cong Taiwan dangdai xiaoshuo kan Huayu yufa yanbian [Change in Chinese grammar as viewed in contemporary novels in Taiwan], In Singapore 1990, 145-66.

Christian, Donna. 1988. Language planning: The view from linguistics, In: Frederick Newmeyer, ed., *Linguistics: The Cambridge Survey, IV: The Socio-cultural Context*, Cambridge & New York: Cambridge University Press, 193-209.

Cobarrubias, Juan and Joshua A. Fishman. eds. 1983. *Progress in Language Planning: International Perspectives*, Berlin: Mouton.

Cooper, Robert L. 1989. *Language Planning and Social Change*. Cambridge & New York: Cambridge University Press.

Coulmas, Florian. 1989. The function of loan translations for the modernization of Japanese during the Meiji period, *Transactions of the Asiatic Society of Japan*, 4th series, 4:49-65.

Davies, Peter. 1992. The non-Beijing dialect component in Modern Standard Chinese, In: Bolton & Kwok, eds., 192-206.

Ferguson, Charles A. 1959. Diglossia, *Word* 15:325-340, Reprinted in Dell Hymes, ed., *Language in Culture and Society: A Reader in Linguistics and Anthropology*, New York: Harper & Row, 1964, 429-439.

Ferguson, Charles A. 1968. Language development, In: Joshua A. Fishman et al., eds., *Language Problems of Developing Nations*, New York: Wiley, 27-35.

Hashimoto, Anne Yue. 1988. Hanyu fangyan yufa de bijiao yanjiu [A comparative study of Chinese dialectal syntax], *Bulletin of the Institute of History and Philology*, Academia Sinica 59:23-41.

Haugen, Einar. 1983. The implementation of corpus planning: Theory and practice,

In Cobar-rubias & Fishman, eds., 269-89.

Ho, Wai Kit. 1989. *Yixue Xinlun [Translating Revisited]*, Taipei: Shulin.

Hoosain, Rumjahn. 1991. *Psycholinguistic Implications for Linguistic Relativity: A Case Study of Chinese*, Hillsdale, NJ: Erlbaum.

Hsu, Raymond S. W. 1979. What is standard Chinese? In: Robert Lord, ed., *Hong Kong Language Papers*, Hong Kong: University Press, 115-141.

Huang, Guoying. 1988. Taiwan dangdai xiaoshuo de cihui yufa tedian [Lexical and grammatical features in contemporary novels in Taiwan], *Zhongguo Yuwen [Chinese Language and Writing]* 3:194-201.

Kubler, Cornelius C. 1985. *The Development of Mandarin in Taiwan: A Case Study of Language Contact*, Taiwan: Student Book Co.

Kuo, Eddie C. Y. 1985. *Xinjiapo de Yuyan yu Shehui [Language and Society in Singapore]*, Taipei: Cheng Chung Book Co.

Li, Charles N. and Sandra A. Thompson. 1981. *Mandarin Chinese: A Functional Reference Grammar*, Berkeley: University of California Press.

Li, Chen-ching. 1983. The sociolinguistic context of Mandarin in Taiwan: Trends and developments, In: Chauncey C. Chu et al., eds., *Papers from the 14th International Conference on Sino-Tibetan Languages and Linguistics*, Taipei: Student Book Co., 259-278.

Li, Jinxi. 1934. *Guoyu Yundong Shigang [Outline of History of National Language Movement]*, Shanghai: Shangwu Yinshuiguan.

Li, Xingjian. 1985. *Putonghua yu Fangyan [Putonghua and Dialects]*, Shanghai: Shanghai Educational Publishing House.

Liu, Yongquan. 1986. Terminological development and organization in China, *International Journal of the Sociology of Language* 59:33-46.

Lock, Graham. 1989. Aspects of variation and change in the Mandarin Chinese spoken in Singapore, *Australian Journal of Linguistics* 9:277-94.

Lu, Shaochang. 1990. Xinjiapo Huayu cihui de kaocha [Survey on Chinese vocabulary in Singapore], In: Singapore 1990, 336-41.

Lü, Shuxiang and Dexi Zhu. 1952. *Yufa Xiuci Jianghua [Lectures on Grammar and Rhetoric]*, Beijing: Kaiming Shudian.

Mao, Zedong. 1969. *Selected Works*, Beijing: Renmin Chuibanshe.

Newman, John. 1988. Singapore's Speaking Mandarin Campaign, *Journal of Multilingual and Multicultural Development* 9:437-48.

Norman, Jerry. 1988. *Chinese,* Cambridge & New York: Cambridge University Press.

Platt, John T. 1985. Bilingual policies in a multilingual society: Reflections of the Singapore Mandarin Campaign in the English language press, In: David Bradley, ed., *Papers in South-East Asian linguistics 9: Language Policy, Language Planning and Sociolinguistics in South-East Asia* (*Pacific Linguistics*, A-67), Canberra: Australian National University, 15-30.

Rubin, Joan. 1977. Language standardization in Indonesia, In: Joan Rubin et al., eds., *Language Planning Processes*, The Hague: Mouton, 111-129.

Singapore. 1990. *Shijie Huawen Jiaoxue Yantaohui Lunwenji* [*Proceedings of the International Symposium on Chinese Language Teaching*]. Singapore: Chinese Language Society of Singapore.

Tian, Xiaolin. 1992. Xianggang diqu de yuyan wenzi guifan wenti [The issue of standardization of language and writing system in Hong Kong], *Zhongguo Yuwen* 2:109-12.

Tse, Kwock-Ping J. 1986. Standardization of Chinese in Taiwan, *International Journal of the Sociology of Language* 59:25-32.

Wang, Huidi. 1990. Xinjiapo Huayu cihui de tedian [Features of the vocabulary of Singaporean Chinese], In Singapore 1990, 346-56.

Wang, Li. 1954. Lun Hanzu biaozhunyu [On standard language of Han people], *Zhongguo Yuwen* 1954, Reprinted in Yushu Hu, ed., *Xiandai Hanyu Cankao Ziliao* [*Reference Materials on Modern Chinese*], Vol. I, Shanghai: Shanghai Educational Publishing House, 1980, 23-40.

Wang, Li. 1980. *Hanyu Shigao* [*History of the Chinese Language*], Beijing: Zhonghua Shuju.

Wang, Peiguang. 1989. Xianggang Yueyu de diwei yu muyu jiaoyu, putonghua jiaoxue [The status of Cantonese, teaching of mother tongue, and teaching of putonghua in Hong Kong], In E. Chen, ed., 151-59.

Wu, Yingcheng. 1990. Cong Xinjiapo Huayu jufa shikuang diaocha taolun Huayu jufa guifanhua wenti [Discussion on standardization of Chinese syntax from the perspective of survey on the syntax of Singaporean Chinese], In Singapore 1990, 118-23.

Xu, Baohua and Bohui Zhan. 1988. Hanyu fangyan [Chinese dialects], In: Xianlin Ji, ed., *Zhongguo Da Baike Quanshu—Yuyan Wenti Juan* [*Encyclopaedia Sinica: Volume on Language and Writing System*], Beijing: Dabeike Quanshu Chubanshe, 137-149.

Zhou, Xiaobing. 1989. Xinjiapo Huayu xiaoshuo de yufa tedian [Grammatical features in novels in Singaporean Chinese], In E. Chen, ed., 212-22.

Zhu, Dexi. 1985. Hanyu fangyan li de liang zhong fanfu wenju [Two types of yes/no questions in Chinese dialects], *Zhongguo Yuwen* 1:10-20.

现代汉语书面语的发展

提　要　20 世纪之前很长一段历史时期里，汉语书面语呈现语言学文献中所谓的“双言”特征，即文言文和白话文两种文体并存，前者用于正式场合，后者用于非正式场合。19 世纪下半叶开始的语言现代化运动，一项重要内容便是在传统白话文的基础上建设现代汉语标准书面语，取代文言文，成为通用的、正式的汉语书面语文体。本文考察现代汉语书面语的确立和发展过程，研究语法和词汇方面的有关特点，以及汉语几个主要使用地区的地域特征，同时比较汉语和欧洲语言在确立和推行正式书面语问题方面的异同。

关键词　语言规划　汉语现代化　双语　双言　标准语与方言　现代汉语书面语　标准化

（This article was first published in *Language in Society* 22(4), 505-537, in 1993. Permission by Cambridge University Press to reprint the article in the present volume is gratefully acknowledged.）

Modern Written Chinese, dialects, and regional identity

Abstract This paper analyzes the major linguistic and sociopolitical factors responsible for the underdevelopment of written languages based on non-Mandarin dialects. It also explores the current language planning efforts in Taiwan to standardize a written language based upon the local dominant dialect. It will point out that the movement is mainly triggered by, and contributes to, the political cause built on the base of an increased assertion of regional identity. In spite of the enthusiasm and devotion on the part of some linguists and writers, such efforts have not yet won general acceptance. Drawing upon findings on the correlation between vernacular literacy and regional identity in Europe, it is argued here that the educational, social and political cost of the success of dialect writings may be too high for them ever to be generally accepted and extensively used in Chinese society.
Keywords Modern Written Chinese; Northern Mandarin; dialect writing; regional identity

1. Introduction

Aside from social, political and economic factors, the three major Chinese communities—mainland China, Taiwan, and Hong Kong—differ most prominently in respect to the native tongue of the majority of their respective populations. According to the latest statistics (Zhou 1992:23; Huang 1993:21), Mandarin is the predominant dialect on the mainland, with native speakers accounting for about 70 per cent of the Chinese-speaking population. On the other hand, it is Cantonese in Hong Kong, spoken by 96 per cent of the population, and Southern Min in Taiwan, spoken by 73 per cent.

Dialects, as remarked by Haugen (1966: 68), are potentially disruptive forces in a unified nation, as they appeal to local loyalties that could conceivably come into conflict with national loyalty. The regional identity based on dialectal diversities in Chinese society, however, has been blurred to a certain extent by the fact that the speakers of mutually unintelligible Chinese dialects have been using the same writing system and the same written language. Although the design and promotion of distinct writing systems for major dialects other than Mandarin have always been on the agenda of some language reformers, successive Chinese governments, regardless of whether such schemes use the traditional script or a phonetic one, have either discouraged, proscribed or prohibited such activity as potentially detrimental to the unity of Chinese society.

A most prominent indicator of an enhanced awareness of regional identity is the remarkable efforts that have been exerted in Taiwan since the mid-1980s to design and promote a written language based upon Southern Min. This paper attempts to offer an objective analysis of the linguistic and the sociopolitical significance of such endeavors within the context of language planning in China during the past century, with special reference to the features that characterize the current movement in Taiwan. I will begin with a brief explanation of the linguistic terms involved that are often a source of confusion in the literature on the Chinese language. I will then give an account of the major linguistic and sociopolitical factors that are responsible for the underdevelopment of written languages based on non-Mandarin dialects (henceforth called "dialect writing"). Following that will be an examination of the current movement in Taiwan to standardize a written language based upon Southern Min. I will discuss in detail the major motivating factors underlying the current movement, examining how it reflects and contributes to the rising awareness of local identity. I will also discuss how such efforts have been received by the wider community in Taiwan. Drawing upon findings on the correlation between vernacular literacy and sociopolitical development in Europe, I will conclude with a brief discussion of the possible consequences of such an undertaking of language planning on Taiwan and in the larger Chinese community.

2. Language, Dialect and Modern Written Chinese

Two of the most important criteria in terms of which ethnic groups are differentiated from each other are religion and language. In the case of Chinese, language plays a greater role than religion in establishing ethnic identity.

What is known as the Chinese language, however, comprises dozens of dialects which may be mutually unintelligible. In the literature of Chinese linguistics, these dialects fall into eight major groups, differentiated mainly on the basis of phonological features and, to a lesser extent, also in terms of vocabulary and grammar. The major dialect groups are Mandarin, Wu, Cantonese, Southern Min, Northern Min, Hakka, Xiang, and Gan, of which Mandarin is by far the largest group, its native speakers accounting for the majority of the Chinese population. The non-Mandarin groups are also called the Southern dialects. Each of the major dialect groups is in turn comprised of a large number of varieties that are related to each other in terms of a hierarchy with three main levels: sub-dialect, vernacular, and accent. For example, following the traditional classification, Mandarin is composed of four major sub-dialects, namely, Northern, Northwestern, Southwestern, and Jiang-Huai. What is called Southern Min comprises sub-dialects spoken in Xiamen, Zhangzhou, and Quanzhou, respectively.

The difference among the Chinese dialects is quite remarkable in comparison with the situation of dialects in languages like English or French. As assessed by Yuen Ren Chao (1943: 24), the sub-dialects of Mandarin differ from each other to the same extent as the varieties of the English language, whereas the other major dialect groups are about as far from Mandarin as Dutch or Low German from English.

Given such difference among the Chinese dialects, it is no wonder that they are more often than not referred to as separate languages by linguists and the general public alike (cf. Li and Thompson 1981; DeFrancis 1984, 1989). As a matter of fact, the terms language and dialect are sometimes used interchangeably with respect to the regional varieties of Chinese, in a way similar to what is reported for Western societies (cf. Fasold 1984, 1990; Wardhaugh 1986: 25).

Following the distinction between language and dialect conventionally drawn in linguistic literature in terms of whether they have a standardized written form or not, there is one important aspect in which the various geographical varieties of Chinese other than Mandarin are justifiably called dialects or underdeveloped languages: except for Mandarin, none of these dialect groups have an established writing tradition, in spite of their representing very large populations and being distributed over very large geographical areas—often much larger than was the case with most of the modern European languages. It is only a little more than 70 years since the present standard written language, known as Modern Written Chinese (MWC), established itself as the standard written code in Chinese society. As observed in Chen (1993), for millennia China was characterized by a situation in which the written language was divorced from vernacular speech. The standard written Chinese was *wenyanwen* "classical literary language" , which looks to the Classical Chinese of two thousand years ago for its vocabulary and grammatical norms and is the language of a substantial amount of literary texts in the pre-modern period. It is generally held that, due to the inconvenience of writing using knives or chisels in early times, and also because of the special economies possible in the written language, there were already considerable discrepancies between the written and the spoken language in the initial stage of the development of *wenyanwen*. The discrepancies grew more and more substantial throughout the following millennia, resulting in complete separation of the written language from vernacular speech. Since the Literary Revolution which started close to the end of 1910s, *wenyanwen* was replaced by the so-called *baihuawen* "the vernacular literary style" , which has developed since the late Tang dynasty (618-907) and is much closer to contemporary spoken Mandarin in terms of vocabulary and grammar. What is known as MWC today evolved from this *baihuawen*, being based for the the core of its lexical and grammatical norms upon Northern Mandarin, and also incorporating some features from Classical Chinese, other contemporary Chinese dialects, and foreign languages (cf. Chen 1993 for a detailed account). *wenyanwen*, on the other hand, is only used by very few people on highly restricted occasions.

As a result, when native speakers of the Southern dialects acquire literacy, it is in MWC, a written language whose lexical and grammatical norms are mainly based not on their indigenous vernaculars, but rather on Northern Mandarin. For the past 70 or so years, this superimposed norm has been the sole written form of Chinese in almost all situations and for speakers of all dialects. As long as speakers of Southern dialects look to Northern Mandarin instead of to their own vernacular for the standard in the written medium of communication, the Southern dialects will remain underdeveloped dialects unless and until standardized writing systems for each dialect have been developed that are extensively used by the community for all functions expected of a bona-fide written language.

Aside from the question of whether to call them languages or dialects, the situation has more important educational, and sociopolitical implications. To the extent that native speakers of all Chinese dialects have been using one or both varieties of the written language, *wenyanwen* before the Literary Revolution and MWC afterwards, the standard written code has provided a strong unifying force for speakers of dialects that may differ greatly in pronunciation. Linguistic distinctions are always important definitive features of national or regional identity. In the case of China, the remarkable divergence in speech between different regions is countered by an even stronger force of uniformity in the oneness of the written medium. In conventional wisdom, it is often argued that the Chinese character script has played an essential rule in unifying the Chinese people, and has prevented the possible disintegration of the vast land into autonomous regions formed along the linguistic lines of dialects. Although it is hard to validate or falsify such a claim, as contended by Defrancis (1950, 1984, 1989), it is a safe assumption that the writing system contributes to rather than detracts from the unifying forces in China. To be precise, however, it is not the Chinese characters per se, but the specific type of written Chinese encoded in the script that plays such a role (cf. Chen 1993, 1994, forthcoming). Characters can also be used to write non-Mandarin dialects, but only to produce texts that are largely unintelligible to outsiders, much in the same way as the spoken correspondents.

At the same time, it must be pointed out that the uniformity of a written code in MWC for all Chinese is achieved at the expense of non-native speakers of Mandarin. It is more difficult for Southern dialect speakers to acquire MWC than it is for native speakers of the base dialect of MWC. Actually, this difficulty was raised as an important objection to the replacement of *wenyanwen* by *baihuawen* as the standard written language (cf. Li 1934). It was argued that as *wenyanwen* was disassociated from all of the contemporary dialects, the dialectal background of learners did not make any difference in its acquisition; with *baihuawen*, on the other hand, southerners were at a linguistic disadvantage in comparison with native speakers of Mandarin. This concern, as it turned out, was overridden by the urgent need for a written language closer to the vernacular of the majority of population and thus more suitable for a society in the process of modernization. The fact that a large amount of vernacular literature written in *baihuawen* had already been extensively distributed all over China for several centuries also contributed significantly to the general ready acceptance of *baihuawen* as the base for a standard written language after the late 1910s. One of the major goals of language reform in China has been to achieve the unification of speech and writing, and the replacement of *wenyanwen* by *baihuawen* as the base of a standard written code is considered to be the decisive achievement in that direction. However, as MWC differs remarkably from Southern dialects in its lexical and grammatical norms, the positive import of its establishment does not hold for speakers of Southern dialects as much as for native speakers of Mandarin, unless they have become bilingual, speaking Mandarin in addition to their native dialect.

3. Dialect Writing

3.1 Dialect Writing in Traditional Chinese Script

Some of the Southern dialects also have a literary tradition—particularly Cantonese, Wu, and Southern Min—but this is mostly confined to writings of popular cultural functions, such as records of folk drama scripts, folk songs, stories and other literary genres that approach vernacular speech. Aside from literature that has been handed down from earlier times, there are also contemporary publications in dialect writing. In comparison with the other Southern dialects, Cantonese has a written form that is more conventionalized, and, theoretically at least, is competent for all functions expected of a written medium. As we will discuss shortly, however, Cantonese writing, as other dialect writing, is generally held to be low in prestige, often appealing to dubious taste rather than being appropriate for more formal purposes.

Several factors are responsible for the underdevelopment of Southern dialects with respect to writing. The most important linguistic factor is that the traditional Chinese writing system, namely the character script, is less suitable for Southern dialects than for Mandarin. When the script is used to render the Southern dialects in writing, there are many words and expressions that do not have adequate representation in characters. As observed by Cheng (1989), Xu (1992), and Huang (1993), about 25 per cent of the most commonly used words in Southern Min do not have conventional representation in the traditional Chinese script. When they choose to write in these dialects, writers usually resort to the following devices to solve the problem of inadequate representation (cf. Cheng 1978; Bauer 1988; Fan and Wu 1992).

1) *Benzi "original characters"*. Some words in dialects did once have representation in characters, but these characters, called *benzi* "original characters", have long since fallen into disuse and are preserved only in dictionaries handed down from ancient times. Not all the words in dialects can be traced to their original representations without much controversy. In most cases, there is a lack of consensus among scholars as to which character correctly represents a particular word.

2) *Phonetic borrowing*. This method consists of borrowing characters of similar pronunciation to write the words in dialects, and is preferred by people whose educational level is not very high. The shortcoming of this device is that the dialect words in question may have no characters with the same pronunciation. Furthermore, as each character is associated with an intrinsic semantic meaning, it is not always easy for readers to tell when the characters are used for their original meanings and when they are borrowed for their phonetic values only.

3) *Semantic borrowing*. Characters representing the corresponding words in MWC may be borrowed to write words of the same meaning but with different pronunciation in Southern dialects. This is called "diglossic paraphrasing" by Bauer (1988: 247) and is resorted to mostly by persons with a high level of education.

4) *New characters*. Occasionally, new characters are designed to represent dialect words. Very few have gained acceptance by people other than the inventors. Disagreement among writers on which devices to choose in particular cases is an important reason for the present pre-standardized status of dialect writings.

3.2 Dialect Writing in Phonetic Script

Western missionaries in China in the nineteenth century were the first to opt for a totally different approach to dialect writing. Primarily in avoidance of the difficulty of learning the traditional script, but also in view of the mismatch between characters and Southern dialects, they chose to design a phonetic script that is used exclusively to write the major Chinese dialects, especially the Southern coastal area dialects. As discussed in the literature (Ni 1948a, 1948b; Zhou 1979), distinct writing systems were designed for each of the major Southern dialects. Literature in such phonetic script included the translation of the Bible, catechisms, and other religious tracts. People acquainted with the writing systems also used them for secular purposes.

The Western missionaries demonstrated, for the first time and on a large scale, that it is possible and feasible to write Chinese for regular purposes with a script other than the traditional characters, and to write on the basis of one's own dialect instead of Mandarin. This provided much inspiration to later, native Chinese proponents of phonetic script, most notably the proponents of phonetic script around the turn of the century, beginning with Lu Zhuangzhang (1892) and followed by Wang Zhao (1900) and Lao Naixuan (1905), among others. Between 1892 and 1911 thirty or so schemes of phonetization were proposed, mostly based upon Southern dialects. Among the dialects represented are Southern Min, Northern Min, Cantonese and Wu, plus varieties of Mandarin (cf. Ni 1948a, 1948b; Zhou 1979). In addition to being extensively used in the publication of books and journals, some of the schemes were also taught in schools and won popular support from various strata of society.

Latinxua Sin Wenz (LSW) "Latinized New Script" represents the third peak of interest in writing in phonetic script based upon the major dialects. Designed by left-wing intellectuals in exile in the Soviet Union in collaboration with Soviet linguists, LSW was published in 1929 in the Soviet Union. First employed among the 100,000 Chinese living in the Soviet Union, and later introduced into China, it was the first romanized scheme that was put to large-scale use as a fully independent writing system intended to supersede the character script. The proponents of LSW differ remarkably from the proponents of previous and contemporary schemes in that they were opposed, in theory and in practice, to making Northern Mandarin the base of a standard national spoken and written language for speakers of all the Chinese dialects. They contended that there was as yet no dialect in China that was qualified to form the base of a national language. Furthermore, they argued, if the romanized writing system were to be based upon the Beijing dialect, it would be as difficult to learn as a completely foreign language for native speakers of Southern dialects like Southern Min, Cantonese or Wu. They maintained that instead of basing the romanized writing system on the pronunciation of one particular dialect, a separate scheme should be designed for each of the important dialects, thus ensuring easy access to literacy by its native speakers. In line with that theory, there were at least thirteen schemes of LSW designed for the major Chinese dialects, which were used in more than 300 publications totaling half a million copies (Ni 1948a: 142-143).①

---

① Although full-scale LSW schemes were proposed for the major dialects, the most influential one, the one that was actually promoted and widely learned and used, was based upon Northern Mandarin (cf. Ni 1948a, 1948b).

4. Causes of the Underdevelopment of Dialect Writing

4.1 Underdevelopment of Dialect Writing

In comparison to literature in Mandarin, texts in other dialect writings account for a negligible fraction of the traditional Chinese literature, much less influential in terms of the number of publications and range of functions. While in Europe Dante opted to write his masterpiece in the Tuscan vernacular rather than the standard literary language, Latin, and Chaucer chose to write in Southeast Midland English, rather than Latin (the language of the church and courts) or French (the language of polite literature), there was no Chinese writer of any prominence in Southern dialect areas who deviated from the established literary tradition and produced great vernacular literature to rival that of the North. Partly because of its scarcity, and partly because of reasons to be discussed below, literature in dialects other than Mandarin has almost been ignored by history. In the volume on literature in the *Encyclopedia Sinica* (cf. Zhou 1986), which represents the most up-to-date and comprehensive scholarship on the study of literature in China, non-Mandarin literature does not even receive a passing mention.

Apart from the inadequacy of the traditional Chinese writing system in representing Southern dialects, as discussed above, the underdevelopment of dialect writing and its failure to gain wider usage are mainly attributable to prestige and policy.

4.2 Popular Attitudes and Official Policy towards Dialect Writing

Dialect writing has always been held in low esteem by both the literati and the general public. On the one hand, it lacked the prestige that had been accorded to *wenyanwen* before the twentieth century. On the other hand, it did not enjoy the widespread usage of *baihuawen*, based on Northern Mandarin. When even the borrowing of vernacular expressions into *wenyanwen* or dialectalisms into *baihuawen* met with disapproval (cf. Chen 1993), it is only to be expected that general attitudes towards dialect writing over the past centuries have ranged from indifference to contempt and opposition. Even in present-day Hong Kong, where over 90 per cent of the population speak Cantonese, and read and write written Cantonese more than anywhere else in the world, dialect writing is to a certain extent looked upon with contempt by most educated Chinese, and is sometimes referred to as "low-class" Chinese, as reported in Bauer (1988: 285-287).

Actually, as a linguistic issue, dialect writing received little attention until the second half of the nineteenth century. Almost right from the beginning there have been two opposing attitudes towards dialect writing. The group in favor of it has demanded that more effort should go into the design and promotion of writing systems for each of the major dialects, which may be used by native speakers of the dialect in question either as the sole written code, or as one that is supplementary to the standard written language if they can afford the money and time to learn the latter. The group opposing it has maintained that there should only be one standard written language, and that dialect writing should be discouraged or prohibited in the interests of the uniformity of written Chinese within Chinese society. The opposition from the latter group appears to be the major non-linguistic factor responsible for the current underdevelopment of dialect writing.

The language reform in progress in China during the past century has two major goals: unification of speech and writing, and unification of the national language. The former demands easy access to literacy via a written language that approximates actual speech as much as is practically possible, and the latter aims at the establishment of a standard language, in the spoken and written modes, that is to be used across dialectal barriers for all formal purposes. The controversy over dialect writing to a great extent hinges upon whether to assign primacy to the unification of speech and writing, or to the unification of the national language.

Opponents of dialect writing are mainly motivated by the concern for the uniformity of written Chinese, which they believe has served a most important role in Chinese history—that of a unifying bond between speakers of mutually unintelligible dialects. To develop distinct writing systems based on various dialects, whether in the traditional script or a phonetic script, would serve to weaken the bond and to strengthen regional identity in a way that could have negative impact upon the unity of the Chinese nation-state. The first to point out the potential negative impact of separate writing systems for dialects (in phonetic script) is S. Wells Williams, an American missionary who was in China for more than forty years following 1833. He wrote (1883: 608):

> Local, unwritten phrases, and unauthorized characters, are so common, however, owing to the partial communication between distant parts of so great a country and mass of people, that it is evident, if this bond of union were removed by the substitution of an alphabetical language, the Chinese would soon be split into

> many small nations. However desirable, therefore, might be the introduction of a written language less difficult of acquisition, and more flexible, there are some reasons for wishing it to be delayed until more intelligence is diffused and juster principles of government obtain.

While scholars may argue as to what extent the written language has served as the bond of union for distinct dialectal regions in Chinese history, it seems that the point made by Williams was not lost on language planning institutions of successive Chinese governments, as will be discussed in detail shortly.

Furthermore, it is maintained that one standard language for the whole country, both in spoken and written mode, would greatly facilitate communication among Chinese, contributing substantially to the cause of modernization of China. Granted that dialect writing systems are effective tools of communication among speakers of the same dialect, the learners of such writing systems would have only limited access to specific parts of the Chinese community. Rather than learn a written language that has only restricted use and is confined to a limited readership, native speakers of Southern dialects should learn what is taken as the standard language by the majority of the Chinese population, with the consequent benefits more than compensating for the extra effort demanded by its acquisition. In the words of a commentator from around the turn of the century, for the long-term benefits to learners and the state it is necessary to *qiang Nan jiu Bei* "to force the South to follow the North" (cf. Ni 1958: 59).

On the other hand, the proponents of separate writing systems for each of the major dialects give priority to ease of learning. Assuming that it is much easier for children or adults to gain literacy in a writing system that is close to their speech than in one that is far removed from it, those in favor of dialect writing maintain that distinct writing systems for Chinese dialects, especially those in a phonetic script, enable native speakers to acquire literacy with much less time and effort than is the case with *wenyanwen* or MWC. [①]This is particularly true for Southerners, as it would remove the disadvantage that is entailed by the dialectal base of MWC.

While scholars and language reformers may differ in their personal opinions on the issue, successive Chinese governments, be it that of the Qing dynasty, the Kuomintang (KMT) in the Republic of China, or the Chinese Communist Party in the People's Republic, have been conspicuously consistent in discouraging or proscribing any form of dialect writing, in either the traditional Chinese script or in a phonetic script. For want of space, I will discuss the issue in detail in a separate paper. Suffice it to observe here that consistent opposition to dialect writing on the part of official language planning institutions has been another determining factor in the underdevelopment of Chinese dialect writing.

5. Current Efforts in Taiwan as an Indicator of Rising Awareness of Regional Identity

5.1 Proposals of Dialect Writing

Since the mid-1980s efforts to develop dialect writing have continued

① The ideal situation in which speech and writing are unified is prescribed by the famous slogan raised in the second half of the nineteenth century, *wo shou xie wo kou* "my hand writes what my mouth says". Indeed, at a time when the promotion of Northern Mandarin as a lingua franca across Chinese dialects had achieved far from satisfactory success even among officials and educated people, separate phonetic writing systems for different dialects seemed to be the only means of attaining this goal.

in Taiwan, where there has been an upsurge of interest in the design and promotion of a standard writing system for Southern Min. The participants have the same objective in mind: to design and promote a standard writing system based upon the dominant local dialect rather than Mandarin. They differ, however, in regard to the type of script that should be used for the writing system. As reported in the literature (Cheng 1989; Hong 1992; Huang 1993), there are two major groups of schemes for Southern Min writing in Taiwan.

The first group is composed of schemes that use mainly Latin script. Most of these are modified versions of the writing that has been used by church for about a century and a half, with some opting for letters instead of superimposed diacritics to indicate tones. While some of this first group employ Latin script exclusively, others also make occasional use of traditional Chinese characters to enhance clarity. The other group includes schemes that use mainly the traditional script. Many also use phonetic script to write common grammatical morphemes or for words that have no conventional representation. Several articles in Cheng (1989), for instance, are written in this way.

There are also those, for example Hong (1992), who are not satisfied with either of the two major groups, mainly in regard to the adoption of the Latin script, which they see as incongruous with the traditional Chinese script in the same text. What they suggest for words without conventionalized representation in Chinese characters is a new script modeled on Korean that is phonetic and assumes the square shape of traditional Chinese script. So far, however, no details have been proposed for this new script. Dialect writers write mainly either in the Latin script or in the traditional Chinese script, in each case often using the other script as a supplementary device as well.

5.2 Motivating Factors

The current movement to develop a standard writing system for the major local dialect, Southern Min, represents the most intense interest yet shown towards such activities in non-Mandarin areas. It shares with the previous efforts the concern for easier access to literacy for the native speakers of dialects. On the other hand, it is unique in that it aims at objectives beyond mere native literacy. Correlated with an increased assertion of regional identity of which language is a significant defining feature, the current linguistic undertaking constitutes a very important part of the overall effort to elevate the status of the language and the culture, and to advance the political interest of the dialect's speakers, who constitute the majority of the island's population. In other words, it is mainly triggered by, and contributes to, a political cause.

Since being returned to China in 1945 after 50 years of cession to Japan, Taiwan has been under the rule of the KMT Government. Following the language policy it pursued on the mainland, the government continued the promotion of the national language on the island. If the language planning policy of the KMT government in Taiwan differed in any way from the policy it held on the mainland before 1949, or from that of the CCP on the mainland after 1949, it is that the official measures adopted to promote the standard language became harsher, sterner, and more effective. School children were penalized for using dialects other than Mandarin when in school, TV programs in local dialects were restricted to not more than one hour a day (in spite of their popularity among local residents), and Western missionaries were expelled for using dialect writing systems in phonetic script in church (cf. e.g. Cheng 1989; Hong 1992; Xu 1992; Huang 1993).

With the formation in 1987 of the largest opposition party in Taiwan—the Democratic Progressive Party (DPP), which appeals strongly to the rising awareness of regional identity—the language policy of the government came under attack. This may be seen partly as a backlash against the stern language planning measures, and best understood in the context of the heightened assertion by a large number of local residents of an identity based, not on Mandarin, but on their native dialects of Southern Min and Hakka. Language has become a highly politicized issue on which the DPP fights against the ruling KMT government. The long-standing policy of stipulating Mandarin as the standard language is denounced as an act of linguistic imperialism that is unfair to native speakers of non-Mandarin dialects. It is argued that the success in promoting Mandarin on the island has been achieved at the expense of local dialects, which are allegedly on the way to extinction. Among the objectives of the language policy in the program of the DPP are bilingual education and equal rights for all dialects in mass media and public life, although details of the policy issues, such as how to reconcile different opinions on dialect writing, how to achieve the goals, and how to deal with the negative consequences of the policy, etc., have yet to be furnished. It is also proposed that Mandarin should ultimately be replaced by Southern Min, the native tongue of the majority of the local population, as the island's lingua franca. Essential to achieving this goal is the standardization and promotion of a written language based upon the dialect.

With local dialects, Southern Min in particular, taken to be *the* defining feature of the regional identity, the linguistic issue of dialect writing has become the symbol of a wider political and cultural cause. Promoting the dialects to the status of languages (in every sense of the word) through the standardization of a written code is seen as an integral part of the cause to preserve and promote the local culture represented in the dialects, and to protect and advance the interests of the people who speak them. As explained in the relevant literature (Cheng 1989; Hong 1992; Xu 1992; Huang 1993), the special emphasis placed on dialect writing is motivated on the following grounds.

First, assuming that dialects are an important medium/carrier of the sentiments that bind the local people together, it is maintained that they play an essential role in fostering and strengthening the sense of regional identity. As it is, however, the linguistic situation in non-Mandarin areas is characterized in terms of what is called diglossia in linguistics. As defined in the literature (cf. Ferguson 1959; Fishman 1967; Fasold 1984), diglossia refers to the situation where two types of linguistic code are used and are functionally differentiated. One is used for high-level purposes such as for educational, scientific, and administrative functions; the other is for low-level purposes, used among native speakers for informal occasions such as communications within the family and among friends. The former, called High Language, is learned in schools, while the latter, called Low Language, is the native tongue acquired in childhood. At present in Taiwan, Mandarin is the High Language, used for almost all formal functions such as education and administration, and until recently as the sole language in mass media, while the native dialects are for use in everyday life. Unless the Southern dialects become as fully standardized in terms of a well-developed written code as Northern Mandarin, they will always be viewed as Low Languages. To some people, the status quo of the local dialects and the inequality between their native tongues and Mandarin are unacceptable. As they see it, to develop and standardize a written language based upon the local dialect constitutes the first step towards changing the situation in a fundamental way, which is also generally attested in the studies of similar situations elsewhere in the world (cf. e.g. Haugen 1966, 1983; Ferguson 1968; Fishman 1968; Cooper 1989; Coulmas 1989; Clyne 1992).

Furthermore, as dialects are regarded as a component part of the cultural heritage of native speakers, a written language is seen as essential for the preservation of the dialect-unique culture and of regional identity. As estimated in Huang (1993), if the current language policy in Taiwan continues for a certain number of years, Northern Mandarin will emerge as the dominant language of the island, not only in terms of the major functions but also in terms of the number of native speakers. Needless to say, many find it unacceptable that the local dialects, as the most important means by which much of the local culture has been preserved and as a defining feature of the regional identity, should be replaced by a non-indigenous language.

5.3 Responses to Writing in Southern Min

The movement to develop a standard writing system for Southern Min has met with mixed responses from the academic and educational community, and from the general public on the island.

Linguists in Taiwan and abroad who are native speakers of Southern Min are the most enthusiastic participants and supporters. While they may disagree on issues such as the intended functions of dialect writing, or argue over technicalities of the proposed schemes, they have been devoted, often with a missionary zeal, to the study of the major aspects of Southern Min as the foundation for the design and standardization of an optimized scheme for the writing of the dialect, and to the promotion of dialect writing in the wider community. Southern Min dictionaries, textbooks and readers in the dialect writing have been compiled with the aim of providing orthographic norms for the language as it continues to standardize.

The entertainment sector and the literary circle echo the enthusiasm for dialect writing. Concurrent with the increasingly widespread use of Southern Min in all sectors of society, there are a large number of movies, songs, and television programs in Southern Min which have proved to be very popular among the general audience. Script writers for these productions find it much more effective and convenient to write directly in dialect, adopting one of the schemes most familiar to co-workers in the field. Meanwhile, the number of dialect writers of other literary genres is increasing. More and more stories, poems, essays, etc. written in dialect or containing a large amount of dialectalisms are published regularly in print media alongside writings in MWC. Publications exclusively in dialect writing have also increased remarkably with years. Many literary works originally written in MWC are being translated into the local dialects.

Responses from schools and other sectors of the community towards dialect writing have been much more cautious. So far, the teaching of Southern Min writing in various schemes has been conducted mainly in an ad hoc way, depending upon the efforts of enthusiastic individuals. It is mostly confined to nonaccredited institutions or programs and has not been included in the regular curriculum of the formal educational system in Taiwan or abroad. Writings of a formal nature, whether by individuals, the government, or non-government institutions, most often use MWC instead of the local writing. In contrast to the enthusiasm for dialect writing within some circles, the general public in Taiwan does not seem to be particularly interested in the whole issue, at least for the time being. While the gradual replacement of Mandarin by Southern Min as the common speech has been a topic of heated debate that attracts widespread attention, dialect writing has failed to draw much interest from the general community other than in relatively small linguistic and literary circles.

Lack of a standardized or widely recognized writing system is just one reason that dialect writing has not been as successful as the promoters have wished. Given the present momentum, however, it may only be a matter of time before the completion of the standardization of Southern Min in terms of a written code that represents the consensus of linguistic opinion of the community and is regularly used by those opting to write in the dialect instead of MWC. If the current endeavour in Taiwan is emulated in other major non-Mandarin speaking areas such as the Cantonese or Wu dialect areas, it may also be only a matter of time before a situation emerges in which there are standardized distinct written languages in Chinese communities, representing the dominant dialects used in the area concerned.

A more important factor underlying the underachievement of dialect writing in Taiwan, in my view, is that the wider community is not prepared yet to accept these efforts to standardize and promote a separate orthography for Southern Min. Whether these efforts will ever be accepted hinges upon how the pros and cons surrounding dialect writing are perceived and judged by the general public in the present circumstances.

6. Negative Consequences of the Success of the Efforts

The full standardization of the non-Mandarin dialects in the form of generally accepted and extensively used written codes would have considerable implications for the educational, cultural, social, and political aspects of the non-Mandarin speaking regions, and for Chinese society as a whole. We don't expect that the current movement in Taiwan will win extensive support in the wider community before it is convincingly demonstrated that the efforts in the direction of a standardized separate orthography for Southern Min will benefit the general public in a way that outweighs the cost and what many see as undesirable consequences.

As discussed above, what the proponents of dialect writing are aiming at, according to their own accounts, is a society characterized by multilingualism in the full sense of the word—the coexistence of several languages, each with its own standardized written literature. It remains then to be seen what type of interrelationship these languages would form. In my view, two possible scenarios could emerge in the three major Chinese-speaking communities, if the process of the standardization of the regionally dominant, non-Mandarin dialects is fully completed in the form of well-developed and widely used written code based upon the dominant dialect in each of the major dialectal areas. In either of the scenarios, in my view, there will be so many foreseeable problems that the majority of the population may decide that they prefer the present linguistic situation rather than the brave new world painted by the language reformers.

The first scenario is that the multilingual community will be characterized by diglossia, not only in speech, but also in writing (cf. Ferguson 1959; Fishman 1968; Fasold 1984; Chen 1993, 1994, 1996). Given the fact that the written language based upon Northern Mandarin has been used as the sole written code for a long period of time and over all geographical areas, it is most likely to remain as the High Language in all bilingual Chinese communities. Actually, this is what was envisaged by the early promoters of dialect writing. As Lu Zhuangzhang (1892) and Qu (1931) indicate, the writing systems of the local dialects are intended to be used for bookkeeping in everyday life. People who are literate in the local dialect writing system can then go on to learn the written language of wider acceptance, presumably the one based upon Northern Mandarin, as the tool for acquisition of science and arts and for participation in political and social activities at the national level, if they have the time and economic means to do so. In this case, as with the learning of standard Modern Spoken Chinese (MSC), students mostly have to learn two separate written languages. That extra effort must be added in to the educational cost of the diglossic community, which may turn out to be higher than that of the present situation.

It is also possible that the languages concerned will differ not in regard to the High or Low sociocultural functions, but in regard to the targeting of the intended readership. As proposed in Cheng (1989: 86), whether materials be in the fields of politics, administration, literature or news reporting, those that are important will be published in all three languages, namely Mandarin, Southern Min, and Hakka (in the case of Taiwan), and those that are unimportant will be published in a language that is learned by the majority of the people in the particular community. The measure would in effect dampen the motivation to acquire literacy in another language. While it may save persons the trouble of learning to speak or write in a language other than their own, there are obviously substantial disadvantages. Their communicative competence will be severely restricted if their native language happens to be a relatively small one. In the meantime, written communication across the major linguistic groups in the community could be a serious problem, if each learns writing only in its own dialect. This may further lead to undesirable social segregation along linguistic lines, as reported in the literature (cf. Fishman et al. 1968).

The second, and I think much less likely (though not totally impossible) scenario is the outcome of what might be called Quebecanization. By that term I refer to a situation in which the regionally dominant language in a multilingual community that is itself part of a larger community is promoted to the status of sole official language through the process of legislation, against a background of increasing assertion of a regional identity of which language is the most important definitive feature. In the case of Taiwan, the language that is most likely to assume such a status is Southern Min. By a political act, the native tongue of the majority of the population of the region could become the standard language in every sense of the word. Children may feel motivated to learn Mandarin, the language of wider usage, but only in the same way that a Dutch student is motivated to learn English.

This inevitably reminds one of S. Well Williams' prediction that the Chinese language could follow the fate of Latin if writing systems for its substantially differing dialects are developed, generally accepted, extensively used, and officially endorsed (cf. Williams 1883). To what extent is the comparison sustainable?

There appears to be a similarity between Williams' scenario and that which occurred in Europe during the past two centuries. According to the statistics in Deutsch (1968: 599), in the hundred years between 1800 and 1900 the number of full-fledged national languages in Europe increased from 16 to 30, at a faster rate than in any of the preceding ten centuries. Again, in the 37 years between 1900 and 1937 Europe's standard languages further multiplied to 53, adding almost as many to their number as in the entire thousand years that went before. It is observed that the native speakers of half of these newly developed languages have attained various degrees of political autonomy since 1800. Deutsch (1968: 601) highlights the correlation between the written language and enhanced sense of regional identity when he remarks that "most of these nationalistic movements, new states, and new autonomous districts have grown up from existing language groups, among people who were already speaking some old vernacular in their families and in their simple, mostly rural life. These now, on becoming commercialized, industrialized, and literate, are elevating their idiom to the status of a written standard language with its own grammar, literature, and claims for social recognition."

Admittedly, it is not the language factor alone, but a combination of the whole range of historical, political, economic and sociocultural factors that contribute to determining whether a people who have a distinct standard language will attain the status of nationhood or statehood with that language as a/the defining feature. As maintained by Deutsch (1968: 603), it is not, in the first instance, these languages that made history; it was history that made these languages. On the other hand, from the correlation between standardized language and statehood that was witnessed in Europe, it appears sensible to contend that the language factor does play an important role in the assertion of regional identity. As said previously, for thousands of years of Chinese history there was a standard written language for speakers of all dialects, and dialect writing as an issue did not arise until comparatively recently. The least we can say about this is that, in spite of the remarkable difference between dialects, the fact that there has been a single written standard makes the Chinese language less of a disintegrating factor than would otherwise be the case. Those who cherish the time-honored literary tradition in the Chinese community, and who cherish the role of the standard written Chinese as a most important medium that connects distinct dialectal regions, will most likely if only for that reason alone be ill disposed to any efforts to promote dialect writing at the expense of MWC. Judging from the lack of enthusiasm for dialect writing from the general public, it seems that, at least for the time being and possibly also for the foreseeable future, these people constitute the majority of the population even in Taiwan.

7. Conclusion

The shift from conventionalized literary Chinese *wenyanwen* to speech-based colloquial Chinese *baihuawen* as the standard written language since the late 1910s raised the question of which speech form to take as standard. The Mandarin-based MWC became the standard written language for speakers of all dialects, leaving a different language learning burden for southerners and northerners. The outcome is attributable to the traditional prestige enjoyed by the precursor of MWC, and to language policy. The concern for a nationally unified written language has prevailed over a better fit between writing and speech for speakers of various Chinese dialects. In spite of the enthusiasm for dialect writing on the part of many indigenous linguists and writers in Taiwan in the context of growing assertion of regional identity since the 1980s, there are so far no signs that the status quo of MWC will be seriously affected. Careful thinking and intensive debate are needed on how the negative consequences will be dealt with if a standardized written language based upon the local non-Mandarin dialect is generally adopted, either as a supplementary system to MWC or as a system that supersedes the latter. Unless the general public is convinced that the advantages will clearly outweigh the disadvantages, they are unlikely to follow the writing reformers.

References

Bauer, Robert S. 1988. Written Cantonese of Hong Kong, *Cahiers de inguistique Asie Oriental* 17: 245-293.

Chao, Yuen Ren. 1943. Language and dialects in China, In Anwar S. Dil, ed., *Aspects of Chinese Sociolinguistics: Essays by Yuen Ren Chao*, Stanford: Stanford University Press, 21-25.

Chen, Ping. 1993. Modern Written Chinese in development, *Language in Society* 22/4: 505-537.

Chen, Ping. 1994. Four projected functions of new writing systems of Chinese, *Anthropological Linguistics* 36/3: 1-16.

Chen, Ping. 1996. Towards a phonographic writing system of Chinese: A case study in writing reform, *International Journal of the Sociology of Language* 122:1-46.

Clyne, Michael. 1992. Language planning, In: William Bright, ed., *International Encyclopedia of Linguistics*. New York: Oxford University Press, 84-87.

Cooper, Robert L. 1989. *Language Planning and Social Change*, Cambridge University Press.

Coulmas, Florian. 1989. *The Writing Systems of the World*, London: Basil Blackwell.

DeFrancis, John. 1950. *Nationalism and Language Reform in China*, Princeton University Press.

DeFrancis, John. 1984. *The Chinese Language: Fact and Fantasy*, Honolulu: University of Hawaii Press.

DeFrancis, John. 1989. *Visible Speech: The Diverse Oneness of Writing Systems*, Honolulu: University of Hawaii Press.

Deutsch, Karl W. 1968. The trend of European nationalism—The language aspect, In: Joshua A. Fishman, ed., *Readings in the Sociology of Language*. The Hague: Mouton, 598-606.

Fan, Guo and Xinjie Wu. 1992. Xianggang dianhuabu Guangzhou Hua paijian xitong pingshu [Review of the Cantonese indexing system of the yellow pages of Hong Kong] (ms.), Hong Kong: Hong Kong Baptist College.

Fasold, Ralph. 1984. *The Sociolinguistics of Society*, London: Basil Blackwell.

Fasold, Ralph. 1990. *The Sociolinguistics of Language*, London: Basil Blackwell.

Ferguson, Charles A. 1959. Diglossia, *Word* 15: 325-40.

Ferguson, Charles A. 1968. Language development, In: Joshua A. Fishman et al., eds., 1968: 27-35.

Fishman, Joshua A. 1967. Bilingualism with and without diglossia; diglossia with and without bilingualism, *Journal of Social Issues* 13/2: 29-38.

Fishman, Joshua A. 1968. Nationality/nationalism and nation/nationism, In: Joshua A. Fishman et al., eds., 1968:39-52.

Fishman, Joshua A., Charles Ferguson and Jyotirindra Das Gupta. eds. 1968. *Language Problems of Developing Nations*. New York: John Wiley & Sons.

Haugen, Einar. 1966. Dialect, language, nation, *American Anthropologist* 68: 922-935.

Haugen, Einar. 1983. The implementation of corpus planning: Theory and practice, In: Juan Cobarrubias and Joshua A. Fishman, eds., *Progress of Language Planning: International Perspectives*. Berlin: Mouton, 269-289.

Hong, Weiren. 1992. *Taiwan Yuyan Weiji* [*Language Crisis in Taiwan*], Taiwan: Qianwei Chubanshe.

Huang, Shuanfan. 1993. *Yuyan, Shehui yu Zuqun Yishi* [Language, Society and Group Consciousness], Taipei: Wenhe Chubanshe.

Lao, Naixuan. 1905. Chongding Hesheng Jianzi Pu Xu [Introduction to Revised Phonetic Letters], In: Haishu Ni, ed., 1958: 52.

Li, Charles N. and Sandra A. Thompson. 1981. *Mandarin Chinese: A Functional Reference Grammar*. Berkeley/Los Angeles: University of California Press.

Li, Jinxi. 1934. *Guoyu Yundong Shigang* [*Outline of History of National Language Movement*], Shanghai: Shangwu Yinshuguan.

Lu, Zhuangzhang. 1892. *Yimuliaoran Chujie: Zhongguo Qieyin Xin Zi Xia Qiang* [*First Steps in Complete Understanding at a Glance: A New Chinese Script for the Xiamen Dialect*], Reprinted 1956, Beijing: Wenzi Gaige Chubanshe.

Ni, Haishu. 1948a. *Zhongguo Pinyin Wenzi Gailun* [*Introduction to Phonetic Writing in China*], Shanghai: Shidai Shubao Chubanshe.

Ni, Haishu. 1948b. *Zhongguo Pinyin Wenzi Yundong Shi* [*History of the Movement of Phonetic Writing in China*], Shanghai: Shidai Shubao Chubanshe.

Ni, Haishu. ed. 1949. *Zhongguo Yuwen de Xinsheng* [*Rebirth of the Chinese Language*]. Shanghai: Shidai Shubao Chubanshe.

Ni, Haishu. ed. 1958. *Qingmo Wenzi Gaige Wenji* [*Writings on Language Reform during the Final Years of Qing Dynasty*], Beijing: Wenzi Gaige Chubanshe.

Qu, Qiubai. 1931. Luomazi de xin zhongguowen hai shi rouma zi de xin Zhongguowen [New Chinese writing in Latin Script or in the sickening script], In: Haishu Ni, ed., 1949: 29-47.

Wang, Zhao. 1900. Guanhua Hesheng Zimu Xu [Introduction to Phonetic Letters of Mandarin], In: Haishu Ni, ed., 1958: 19-23.

Wardhaugh, Ronald. 1986. *An Introduction to Sociolinguistics*, London: Basil Blackwell.

Williams, Wells S. 1883. *The Middle Kingdom*. London: W.H. Allen & Co.

Zhou, Yang. ed. 1986. *Zhongguo Da Baike Quanshu: Zhongguo Wenxue* [*Encyclopedia Sinica Volume on Chinese Literature*], Beijing: Zhongguo Da Baike Quanshu Chubanshe.

Zhou, Youguang. 1979. *Hanzi Gaige Gailun* [*Introduction to Chinese Character Reform*], 3rd ed. Beijing: Wenzi Gaige Chubanshe.

Zhou, Youguang. 1992. *Zhongguo Yuwen Zonghengtan* [*Aspects of the Chinese Language*], Beijing: Renmin Jiaoyu Chubanshe.

现代汉语书面语、方言与地域认同

提　要　现代汉语书面语的基础语言是北方官话，其他方言没有标准化的书面语。对于造成这种现象的主要原因，本文做了详细分析。从 1980 年代起，台湾主要方言闽南话的文字化工作受到一些本土人士的关注，但迄今为止尚未被社会各界普遍接受。根据欧洲的经验推论，汉语方言文字化在凝聚和增强地域意识的同时，在教育、社会文化及政治方面得付出高昂的代价，未必会得到当地社会的广泛支持。

关键词　现代汉语书面语　北方官话　方言书写　地域认同

(This article was first published in *Language Problems and Language Planning* 20(3), 223-243, in 1996. Permission by John Benjamins Publishing Company to reprint the article in the present volume is gratefully acknowledged.)

Toward a phonographic writing system of Chinese: A case study in writing reform*

Abstract This article is devoted to a systematic study of the efforts to design and promote a phonographic writing system of Chinese. The undertaking is mainly motivated by the claim that the traditional logographic writing system is difficult to learn and inconvenient to use. Phonetic schemes that have been proposed differ with regard to the intended functions, the form of script, the dialectal base, and the phonological representation of the syllabic structure. Various linguistic and sociopolitical factors have interacted in a complicated way in the determination of the success or failure of the schemes.
Keywords writing system; phonographic; logographic; script reform; phonetic scheme

1. Introduction

The Chinese character script is one of the oldest writing system in the world and is the only one that has been in continuous use for at least four millennia (cf. Li 1985: 156). As generally reported in the literature, while the great majority of modern languages have adopted phonographic writing systems, Chinese is conspicuous as the most

* I would like to acknowledge my indebtedness to Professor Florian Coulmas for bis comments and suggestions on this paper. I am also grateful to One-Soon Her, Thomas Lee, Malcom Skewis, Xu Liejiong, and Eric Zee for their help. All responsibility for errors resides with the author.

important language to retain a logographic writing system (cf. Coulmas 1989, 1992; DeFrancis 1989; Gelb 1963; Sampson 1985). Tremendous efforts have been made during the past 350 years, especially the past 100 years, to design and promote a phonetic writing system for Chinese. In fact, nowhere in the world has there been a writing reform comparable in magnitude to the Chinese endeavors to shift from a logographic to a phonographic writing system. This article is devoted to an in-depth analysis of the undertaking, which I hope will lead to a better understanding of the interrelationships between a writing system and the spoken and written forms of the language it represents, specifically in the case of Chinese script reform, but also of writing reform in general.

The article is organized in the following way. I will begin with some basic facts about the writing system of Chinese as a background for the later discussion. After a brief analysis of the pros and cons of script reform in Chinese, I will explicate the motivations and principles underlying the more than 1,000 schemes of phonetic writing that have been proposed during the past century, with special reference to the intended functions of the schemes, the form of script, the dialectal base, and the representation of the syllabic structure. By way of Illustration, I will also present a brief account of five representative schemes of phonetic writing that have been proposed in different periods of the script reform movement that constitutes an important part of the intellectual life in Chinese communities.

2. Basic facts of the writing System of Chinese

2.1 Typological characterization

Writing systems in the world can be differentiated along two dimensions.

First is the size of the speech segments that are represented by the basic graphic units, and second is whether the graphic units encode speech sound only, or both speech sound and meaning.

Following DeFrancis (1989: 54), I use the term *grapheme* to refer to the basic graphic unit in a script that corresponds to the smallest segment of speech represented in the writing. English graphemes are letters, whereas Chinese graphemes are characters. Writing systems differ with regard to whether it is phoneme or syllable that is represented by the grapheme. Graphemes in languages like English and Finnish represent phonemes, which may assume the form of a letter or group of letters. Graphemes in languages like Chinese and Japanese, on the other band, represent a syllable, encoded by a character in the case of Chinese and a *kana* symbol in the case of Japanese. Thus, the writing systems of languages like English and Finnish are said to be phonemic, whereas those of Chinese and Japanese, in the form of characters or *kana* respectively, are syllabic.

Furthermore, graphemes differ with regard to whether they encode pure phonetic values, or phonetic values together with meaning. As is generally recognized in the literature (cf. Coulmas 1989, 1992; Haas 1983; Hill 1967; Pulgram 1976; Sampson 1985; Trager 1974; inter alia), those used as pure phonetic symbols devoid of any meaning are called phonographic or cenemic, whereas those encoding phonetic value together with meaning are called logographic, pleremic, or morphemic. The former are exemplified by letters in languages like Finnish, and *kana* symbols in Japanese, and the latter by characters in Chinese. Writing system are characterized as phonographic or logographic, depending upon whether they are mainly composed of phonographic or logographic graphemes. As observed in Bolinger (1946) and Sampson (1985), however, the distinction between phonography and logography drawn here is a relative one, in the sense that many writing system, including those of Chinese and English, while mainly phonographic or logographic, also display features of logography or phonography to varying degrees. The writing system of English, for example, is more logographic than that of Finnish, although both are generally recognized as phonographic.

On the basis of the above definition, the writing system of Chinese is characterized as logographic, and its graphemes, that is, characters, as morphosyllabic. Typically, a Chinese character represents one syllable. In addition to the phonetic value, it in most cases has its own meaning, thus representing a morpheme. It is not uncommon that the same syllable can be represented by dozens of distinct characters, which have at least as many different meanings. For example, in *Xiandai Hanyu Cidian* (*Modern Chinese Dictionary*) under the syllable *ji* are listed a total of 137 distinct characters (excluding variant forms of the same character), which encode different morphemes, as shown in Table 1.

Table 1. Number of characters pronounced as *ji*

Tone	Number of characters
1	47
2	33
3	12
4	45

2.2 Brief history of the Chinese script

Chinese writing as a well-developed system dates back to the fourteenth century BC, although individual characters may have an even longer history (Jiang 1987; Li 1985: 156; Qiu 1988: 22). The script at the earliest stage of development is represented by what is generally known as *jiaguwen* ‘oracle bone script’, with characters inscribed or painted on ox bones and tortoise shells and mostly recording divinatory outcomes. As is the case with the other two ancient writing systems, Sumerian cuneiform and Egyptian hieroglyphs, most Chinese characters during the initial phase are logographic signs, indicating both the sound and meaning of the morphemes they represent. In the literature of traditional Chinese philology, these characters fall into three major groups according to the principles underlying their graphic structure, *xiangxing* ‘pictographic’, *zhishi* ‘ideographic’, and *huiyi* ‘compound indicative’. *Xiangxing* characters bear a physical resemblance to the objects they indicate. Examples are familiar characters like 日 *ri* ‘sun’, 月 *yue* ‘moon’, 山 *shan* ‘hill’, 水 *shui* ‘water’. Supplementary to the principle of pictographic resemblance is *zhishi*, which refers to a more diagrammatic method used to create characters that represent more abstract concepts. Examples are 上 *shang* ‘up’, and 下 *xia* ‘down’. On the basis of *xiangxing* and *zhishi* characters evolved the third method, *huiyi*, which combines graphs of the first two categories on the basis of their semantics to create new characters that imply a combination of the meanings of the component parts. A good example is 明 *ming* ‘bright’, which is made of two graphs, 日 ‘sun’ and 月 'moon'.

All three groups share the feature that the characters were shaped in a way that attempted to capture the semantic content of the morphemes they represent in a more or less iconic fashion. Characters formed on the iconic principle constitute the bulk of the early stage of the Chinese writing system as represented by *jiaguwen* (cf. Guan 1988; Qiu 1988: 32).

It is obvious that the iconic principle has severe limitations. There are words indicating complicated concepts that are difficult to map onto graphic shapes. Furthermore, the most fertile imagination would find it difficult to use iconic means to represent words that serve purely grammatical functions. To meet the growing demands for graphemes in the writing system to record increasingly complicated texts, Chinese did what the Sumerians and Egyptians did by turning to the method of phonetic borrowing, whereby the originally logographic characters are used as pure phonetic signs, representing homophonic or near-homophonic morphemes that have no or little semantic relation to the original characters. It is reported that even among the characters in *jiaguwen*, many were found to have been used as cenemic syllabograms only, although the percentage of these phonetic loans is quite small in comparison with characters used as pleremic logograms (cf. Guan 1988; Qiu 1988).

As discussed in Coulmas (1989, 1992: 225), with more and more pleremic logograms simultaneously serving as cenemic syllabograms, it became more and more necessary to introduce some sort of differentiation into the writing system, usually in the form of some markers that are attached to the grapheme to indicate or hint at the phonetic or semantic value of the sign for the particular occasion. The same process is attested in all of the four major ancient writing systems, namely Egyptian, Sumerian, Maya, and Chinese (Gelb 1963; Haas 1976b: 177, Qiu 1988: 151; inter alia). In Chinese, some graphs are attached to cenemic syllabograms as semantic determinatives, and some are attached to pleremic logograms as phonetic determinatives. The addition of the semantic or phonetic determinatives serves to enhance the clarity of the writing system by reducing the possibility of ambiguity, either through the reduction of the number of homophonous graphemes by the addition of semantic determinatives to cenemic syllabograms, or through the differentiation of graphically similar characters by the addition of phonetic determinatives. When it comes to the positioning of the determatives in relation to the root characters, however, it seems that the aesthetic consideration that characters be of equidimensional shape led Chinese to pursue an approach different from that adopted in Egyptian and Sumerian. Instead of preceding or following the grapheme in question as a separate sign, the determinative in Chinese was incorporated into the root grapheme as an integral part of a new character, constituting what is called *xingsheng* 'semantic-phonetic' characters. As discussed in the literature (cf.Coulmas 1989, 1992; Qiu 1988), Chinese would most probably have evolved into a phonographic writing System, in the same way as the other writing systems in the world, if the characters initially created on the iconic principle were more and more used as cenemic syllabograms, instead of becoming a component part of *xingsheng* characters.

Xingsheng characters are typically composed of two parts, a phonetic component and a semantic component. Although they are more complex in graphic shape, the *xingsheng* characters hold an advantage over the pleremic logograms in that they carry more information in terms of phonetic or semantic value, and over the purely phonetic borrowings in that they carry more semantic information. From the way in which their writing system developed, it appears that the Chinese opted for clarity over economy. *Xingsheng* provided an efficient method to create a large number of characters on the basis of the current stock, and consequently after the *jiaguwen* period it became the major principle by which new characters were made, bringing about a sharp increase in characters in the following two millennia. Table 2 demonstrates the number of characters contained in the major dictionaries in different periods (cf. Norman 1988; Zhou 1988:198).

Table 2. Number of characters in Chinese history

Number of characters	Dictionary	Period	Date
3,300	*Cangjiepian, Yuanlipian, and Boxuepian*	Qin	221-206 BC
9,535	*Suowen Jiezi*	Eastern Han	100 AD

续表

Number of characters	Dictionary	Period	Date
16,917	*Yupian*	Liang	543
26,149	*Guangyun*	Northern Song	1011
32,200	*Hongwu Zhengyun*	Ming	1375
47,043	*Kangxi Zidian*	Qing	1716
48,000	*Zhonghua Da Zidian*	Minguo	1916
56,000	*Xiandai Hanyu Da Zidian*	PRC	1986-1990

According to several statistics, *xingsheng* characters constitute only about 37 percent in *jiaguwen*, but more than 80 percent in *Shuowen Jiezi*, and around 90 percent in dictionaries after *Guangyun* (cf. Guan 1988:109; Qiu 1988:32; Wu and Ma 1988:20). As observed in Qiu (1988:32), however, the percentage is lower with commonly used characters, with *xingsheng* characters constituting 74 percent of the list of 2,000 common characters published in 1952.

2.3 Characters, syllables, morphemes, and words in Modern Chinese: Interrelationships

Much discussion on the phonetization of Chinese was based upon an impressionistic assessment of the complicated interrelations among characters, syllables, morphemes, and words in Chinese, which is partly responsible for some of the gross misunderstanding and shaky argumentation once prevalent in the field. Since the 1980s, a number of quantitative studies have been made to establish the basic facts regarding the major phonological and morphological features of characters in Modern Chinese. The findings that have been reported provide the basis for a proper understanding of the important issues involved in Chinese script reform.

2.3.1 Number and structure of common characters

Although around 56,000 characters have been accumulated in Chinese, only a couple of thousand are needed to write Modern Chinese. Two important lists have recently been published in China that contain characters in common use in Modern Chinese.

One is a List of Common Characters in Modern Chinese, published by the State Language Commission and the State Education Commission in January, 1988, which is composed of two parts. Part 1 contains 2,500 common characters, and part 2 contains 1,000 less common characters. The other is a List of Regular Characters in Modern Chinese, published by the State Language Commission and the State Press and Publication Administration in March, 1988, which contains 7,000 entries (cf. Fu 1989). The coverage rate of the commonly used characters in modern publications is given in Table 3 (cf. Chang 1989; Su 1992:7; Yin 1991:19).

Table 3. Coverage rate of characters in publications in Modern Chinese

Number of characters	Coverage rate (%)
500	80
1,000	91
2,400	99
3,800	99.9
5,200	99.99
6,600	99.999

Literacy in Chinese is measured by how many characters, instead of words as in Western languages, have been acquired by learners. The threshold is generally set at around 2,000 characters. Graduates from primary schools are expected to have learned around 2,500 characters, and the number increases to 3,500 for college graduates.

The primary part in the graphic structure of characters is called the stroke, of which the average number per character for the 7,000 or so most common characters is 11 (Wu and Ma 1988:50). Strokes in turn combine to form one of the three types of component parts of characters, which are called phonetic determinatives, semantic determinatives, and what is generally known as mnemonic symbols, which, due to graphic attrition, do not indicate any semantic or phonetic value and are used merely as differentiating symbols.

2.3.2 Characters, syllables, and morphemes

Standard Chinese, as represented in *Xiandai Hanyu Cidian*, has 1,332 basic syllables if tones are counted, and 419 if tones are not counted. Given the monosyllabic nature of characters, and the tremendous discrepancy between the number of characters and the number of syllables, it is only to be expected that there are a large number of characters that are homophonous. By way of Illustration, let's consider the 3,500 characters in the List of Common Characters in Modern Chinese, published by the State Language Commission and the State Education Commission in 1988. In the list only 31.5 percent of the tonal syllables are represented by only one character; 68.5 percent are represented by at least two homophonous characters, with 15.8 percent by six or more (cf. Qian 1990:550). Needless to say, homophony increases when a larger number of characters is counted. Obviously, the distinctive graphic shapes of characters play a most important disambiguating role in writing.

The correspondence between characters and morphemes is much closer than is the case between characters and syllables. As ascertained in Yin (1988:255; 1991:17), there are about 4,800 morphemes in common use in Modern Chinese. Table 4 displays how they are represented by characters in Modern Chinese. As Table 4 shows, the great majority of characters encode one morpheme, and little more than 10 percent represent two or more.

Table 4. Correspondence between characters and morphemes

Character: morpheme correspondence	Number of characters	Percentage
1:1	3686	87.5
1:2	429	10.2
1:3	73	1.7
1:4	18	0.4
1:5	6	0.1

On the other band, it is also reported in the literature that about 95 percent of morphemes in Chinese are monosyllabic and represented by single characters (cf. Qian 1990:546; Yin 1988, 1991). The close match between characters and morphemes in Chinese accounts for many of the other features of the character script, which will be discussed later.

2.3.3 Morphemes and words

In Classical Chinese, the majority of the monosyllabic morphemes are simultaneously words. A remarkable distinction between Classical Chinese and Modern Chinese is that many of the free morphemes in Classical Chinese have become bound in Modern Chinese, used only in combination with other morphemes as component parts of words and other types of expressions. Statistics reveal that while words in Classical Chinese are overwhelmingly monosyllabic, there occurred an increase in the number of bi- or polysyllabic words as Classical Chinese evolved into Modern Chinese. In the literature of Chinese historical linguistics, this is generally known as the drift toward bi- or multisyllabification (cf. Wang 1980). Table 5 presents the percentage of monosyllabic words in prose of different periods.

Table 5. Percentage of monosyllabic words in Chinese history

Date	Period	Monosyllabic words(%)
before 221 BC	pre-Qin	96
618-1279 AD	Tang-Song	93
1368-1911	Ming-Qing	90
1910s-1930s	Mingguo	62
1950s-1980s	PRC	46

The percentage of bi- or multisyllabic words in the whole vocabulary of Modern Chinese is even higher. Of the 50,000 or so entries contained in *Xiandai Hanyu Cidian*, about 2,500 are monosyllabic, accounting for only 5 percent of the total, and about 40,000 are bisyllabic (cf. Chen 1981). It is generally believed that the drift toward bi- and multisyllabic words was largely an outcome of functional compensation for attrition in differentiation of syllables due to drastic reduction of the syllabary through these periods.

Far from falling into obsolescence, a large number of bound morphemes that were free words in Classical Chinese are still very active in Modern Chinese, constituting the important stock of components in word formation. Many of them are quite versatile in their capacity to combine with other morphemes to form words or nonce words. For a detailed account, cf. Cao (1988).

3. Pros and cons of script reform

Although the character script has functioned as the sole writing system of the Chinese language since ancient times, its shortcomings were actually recognized early in history, and this awareness came notably as a result of comparison with the phonographic writing systems of other languages. What is more significant is that the difference in writing systems was judged in terms of the benefits or disadvantages that they brought to the countries that employed them. It is reported that as early as more than 1,000 years ago, there was a Deng Su who remarked that, "The advantage of foreign countries lies in the simplicity of their writings, which accounts for their swiftness; whereas the problems of China lie in the complexity of the writing, which is responsible for her slowness" (cf. Zhou 1979: 25).

3.1 Shortcomings of the character script

Most experts in the field of Chinese linguistics would agree that the greatest shortcoming of the Chinese script, in comparison with romanized writing system, is that it is very difficult to learn and use.

Difficult to learn

First, it is generally maintained that characters are difficult to learn both to read and to write.

As mentioned above, over 90 percent of characters in Modern Chinese belong to the *xingsheng* category. It must be pointed out that the phonetic determinatives of *xingsheng* characters are not to be treated on a par with the sound-indicating symbols like *kana* in Japanese or letters in Finnish or English. While the number of basic phonetic symbols in a phonographic system is usually no more than a few dozen, an analysis of the *xingsheng* characters in Modern Chinese shows that there are around 1,300 distinct symbols that are used as phonetic determinatives, and 250 as semantic determinatives. Not counting the characters in the other categories, the number of the basic phonetic symbols in *xingsheng* characters alone is already much higher than that in English or Japanese, demanding strenuous effort on the part of learners.

Furthermore, contrary to what is generally assumed, a large portion of these phonetic and semantic determinatives provide only a vague hint as to the phonetic value and semantic category of the characters that contain them. Due to historical sound change, more often than not there is considerable discrepancy between the Modern Chinese pronunciation of the phonetic determinatives and their pronunciation at the time when they were first incorporated into the *xingsheng* characters in question. The syllable represented by a Chinese character is traditionally analysed into three parts: initial, final, and tone. The latest investigation reveals that, out of the 5,990 common *xingsheng* characters in Modern Chinese, only 1,578 are pronounced exactly the same as the phonetic determinative with regard to the initial, final, and tone, accounting for 26.3 percent of the total (Su 1992: 8). The percentage is even lower with the *xingsheng* characters that are most commonly used. The indicative ability is higher with semantic determinatives. Out of the most commonly used 2,522 *xingsheng* characters, 2,082 have semantic determinatives that indicate the thesaurus-like category of the containing characters in a way that ranges from precise to remotely suggestive (Su 1992: 8).

With characters other than the *xingsheng* type, there is no cue whatsoever in the graphic structure as to the phonetic value. As a result of attrition in the graphic structure, a large number of the graphemes of the *xiangxing*, *zhishi*, and *huiyi* categories discussed earlier have lost all traces of the iconicity of the original shape and become mere mnemonic symbols, which are known in the literature as *jihao* ‘sign’ characters. The same happened to a large number of graphs that were incorporated into *xingsheng* characters as phonetic or semantic determinatives. According to the latest statistics, characters that compose such *jihao* constitute at least 20 percent of the characters in common use in Modern Chinese (Qiu 1988:36). Needless to say, students can do little with these characters beyond rote memorization.

As mentioned above, in Modern Chinese there is an average of 11 strokes per character. In order to differentiate between characters, the configurations of these strokes are necessarily complex. As the graphic shape of the characters provides little or no indication of their pronunciation, learning to read and write thousands of graphically complex characters becomes a massive mnemonic task. The success of this task demands a large amount of time and energy on the part of Chinese schoolchildren, which could be used in learning other subjects. It is estimated that 30 percent of the total class hours in Chinese primary and secondary schools are devoted to learning the Chinese language, and much of that time is spent on learning characters. A comparative study shows that the reading materials in language class up to year 4 in Chinese schools are only about one-sixth of the length of those at the comparable level in countries that use phonographic writing system (cf. Zhou 1979). It also shows that while it takes only 3 to 4 months of intensive learning for people in countries like the former Soviet Union and North Korea to achieve literacy, the process takes much longer in China. It is estimated that in order to learn this difficult writing system, the Chinese, on average, spend two years more than people who use phonographic writing (Wu and Ma 1988:74-75). This is one of the reasons for the comparatively high illiteracy rate in China, especially in rural areas where peasants can hardly afford the time and money for such an enormous task. Before the 1950s, illiteracy in China reportedly reached 90 percent, and it is recorded at 30 percent around 1980 (cf. Chen 1988; DeFrancis 1950). The latest statistics report that in 1990 there are still 46 million illiterates in the age group of 15-39 (cf. Li 1993). Admittedly there are many factors that contribute to a nation's literacy rate. However, given the extra time needed to learn the Chinese script, it seems sensible to guess that China would enjoy a much higher literacy rate if it used a phonographic writing system.

Difficult to use

The use of such a large number of characters as basic symbols makes the Chinese writing System a very clumsy tool for many purposes. Due to the complicated nature of the graphic structures, the Chinese script is much less convenient than a phonographic system when it comes to indexing and retrieving, such as in cataloging, dictionary compilation, etc., where the ordering of the writing symbols is involved. Indexing system often differ with regard to the number and kinds of so-called radicals, a term used to refer to the distinguishing component parts of characters on the basis of which characters are arranged. There are scarcely two Chinese dictionaries that have exactly the same indexing of entries on the basis of the graphic structure. In many similar applications, the lack of uniformity in the ordering of characters stands in sharp contrast to the neatness of a phonographic system that uses far fewer basic symbols.

The deficiencies of the Chinese script become even more apparent in the present-day information age with its widespread use of computers. The input and output facilities of the computer as we know it today best suit phonographic writing that makes use of a relatively small number of basic units combined in a systematic way to represent the language. Near the end of 1980s there were more than 700 input schemes for the Chinese script, which testifies to the tremendous amount of effort that has gone toward solving the problem. In spite of all the time and money invested in the endeavor, we have yet to see a scheme that is truly satisfactory and widely adopted.

Furthermore, it is generally believed that the logography of the script is a contributing factor to the dialectal diversity of the Chinese language, which is notoriously complicated. There are seven major dialect groups in Chinese, namely Mandarin, Wu, Xiang, Hakka, Gan, Min, and Cantonese, all of which can be further divided when required by a higher level of analytical refinement. The non-Mandarin groups are called the Southern dialects. The seven dialect groups are mutually unintelligible (cf. Chen 1993; DeFrancis 1984b; Li and Thompson 1981). As characters can have different phonetic values in different dialects, they constitute a uniform writing system for all Chinese dialects that does not require the promotion of a spoken lingua franca among the speakers of dialects in the same way as a phonographic system does (cf. Wu and Ma 1988: 78).

3.2 Merits of the character script

There is no denying that, as a writing system that has been serving the Chinese language for thousands of years, the character script does have its own strengths, in terms of suitability for the language, which have enabled it to survive as the sole major logographic system in the world. From a purely linguistic perspective, the Chinese writing system has two major advantages in comparison to the various phonographic writings that have been proposed for the language. First is its capacity to differentiate homophonous morphemes, and second is its versatility in bridging time and dialects, although it has to be pointed out that these are both claims that have to be qualified to some extent, as will be discussed in detail later in this article.

Differentiation of homophonous morphemes

As Table 4 demonstrates, the great majority of Chinese morphemes are monosyllabic, and, due to the limited number of syllables in Chinese, there are many homophonous morphemes. When morphemes are represented by characters, there is little danger of ambiguity, as distinct characters serve the important function of differentiating the homophonous morphemes. This function is essential for writing Classical Chinese, where most monosyllabic morphemes are independent words that would hardly be differentiable if encoded in a typical phonographic system. Homophony, on the other band, is much less of a problem with a written language based upon the vernacular of Modern Chinese, largely because of the presence of a much higher percentage of bi- or multisyllabic words, as shown in Table 5, which are less likely to be homophonous than monosyllabic ones. It is no coincidence that the advocacy of phonographic writing to either replace or exist side by side with the traditional characters rose in concomitance with the rising call to bring written Chinese closer to the present day vernacular, instead of relying on the classics of 2,000 years ago for its lexical and grammatical norms. For a detailed account of the process, see Chen (1993). As observed in Chen (1993), however, Modern Written Chinese still retains many features from Classical Chinese in spite of attempts to get rid of them. To the extent that features of Classical Chinese persist in Modern Chinese writing, homophony would remain a serious problem for any attempt to devise phonographic writing for Chinese. However, the problem would be less serious if Modern Written Chinese were closer to colloquial speech in Modern Chinese, which, being subject to the constraints of oral communication, is unlikely to contain a large number of homophonous words.

Use across times and dialects

One of the most lauded merits of the Chinese script is its ability to span time and dialects. As characters can have different phonetic values in different times and at different places, they can be used to represent the Chinese language spoken in different periods and in different geographic areas. It is largely by virtue of this feature that it is much easier for present-day Chinese to read the writings of more than 2,000 years ago than it is for the users of a phonographic system, such as English, to read texts from very early times. To a certain extent, it is also by virtue of this feature that the Chinese people can sometimes communicate in writing even if they speak mutually unintelligible dialects.

Some caveats are in order here with regard to the use of characters across dialects. Strictly speaking, the characters fit Mandarin, especially Northern Mandarin, much better than the Southern dialects like Cantonese, Wu, and Min. For native speakers of non-Mandarin dialects to be literate, and thus able to communicate in writing with others across dialectal barriers, customarily means that they have acquired a written language that is in the main based upon Northern Mandarin and removed from their native tongue in many respects. Obviously, it takes more effort on their part to achieve literacy than on the part of native speakers of Northern Mandarin. Attempts have been underway to write the non-Mandarin dialects in the Chinese script. There are many native words in the Southern dialects that do not have appropriate or conventional representation in characters, which often causes a lot of inconvenience and confusion on the part of the native speakers who attempt to write on the basis of their vernacular. Among the non-Mandarin dialects, Cantonese is the one with the best developed written code. As observed in Bauer (1988), however, there is still high inconsistency in the use of written symbols in its representation. For Southern Min, it is estimated in the literature (cf. Cheng 1989; Hong 1992; Xu 1992) that about 5 percent of the words in the dialect do not have appropriate or fixed characters to represent them. As most of them are high-frequency grammatical words, they make up about 15 percent of all the words occurring in the common written texts in the dialect. The situation is worse with the Wu and

Hakka dialects, which have an even higher percentage of morphemes or words that have no conventional representation. The fact that the great majority of vernacular-style literature that has been handed down is based upon Northern Mandarin is attributable in large part to the poor fit between characters and non-Mandarin dialects. Recently, there have been redoubled efforts on the part of linguists and educationalists in Taiwan to design a written language for the local Min dialect (cf. Cheng 1989; Hong 1992; Huang 1993; Xu 1992). The problems they have encountered with the representation of the local dialect in characters demonstrate that the alleged versatility of the Chinese script across dialects has to be accepted with some reservation.

4. Approaches to script reform

Script reform as an issue did not attract serious attention until it was embraced by the language reform movement that started after the Opium War (1840-1843) and gained momentum at the turn of the century, when China suffered a series of military defeats and humiliations at the hands of Western powers and Japan. The cruel reality that faced China as a nation forced people to look hard for the underlying reasons for the country's backwardness, and they found them in areas ranging from technology and sociopolitical institutions right up to the traditional Chinese set of values and ideology. It was the prevailing feeling that China must undergo a reform in all these areas if she was to avoid the fate of being annihilated by foreign forces. The Chinese written language was picked up by a group of intellectuals as one of the major targets for reform. It was, and has been, argued that the written language encoded in the traditional Chinese script is to a large measure responsible for the country's high illiteracy and poor performance in comparison with the Western countries, standing as an impediment to the process of modernization, because it is difficult to learn and inconvenient to use. At this time, the abolition of characters was seriously proposed as an objective of language reform and won some support among contemporary intellectuals.

The language reform movement had three major tasks, namely, (1) promotion of a spoken standard in a country that has many dialects that are mutually unintelligible; (2) promotion of a new modern written language based on the vernacular, as a replacement for the traditional written language whose grammar and basic vocabulary is based upon the classics of more than 2,000 years ago; (3) reform of the script to facilitate its learning and use. Of the three tasks, script reform has always been considered the most important and most urgent, and an end the other two tasks were meant to subserve. Script reform was taken to be the key issue in the reform of the Chinese language.

Two main approaches have been pursued in order to address the problems of the character script. One is to simplify the script by reducing the number of characters and the number of strokes in characters. The other is to adopt a phonographic writing system as an auxiliary, or supplementary, or alternative, or superseding system for the character script. As the simplification approach is not our concern in this article, we will continue with the second.

5. Phonetization of Chinese

5.1 Efforts by Western missionaries

The first schemes for the phonetization or, more specifically, romanization of Chinese were all developed by Western missionaries in China. Matteo Ricci (1552-1610), the Jesuit who went to China from Italy in 1583, is generally believed to be the first person who designed a systematic romanized writing system for Chinese. His scheme was later modified by another Jesuit missionary in China, Nicolas Trigault (1577-1628). Basically, their schemes served two purposes, to transcribe Chinese proper names, and to help foreigners learn Chinese, especially the Chinese characters. As recorded in the literature (DeFrancis 1950; Li 1934; Ni 1948a, 1948b; Zhou 1979: 19; inter alia), quite a few dictionaries were compiled on the basis of the schemes for the convenience of missionaries.

Because of the conflict between the Jesuits and the Imperial Court of the Qing Dynasty, the influence of the Jesuits in China was reduced to a minimum in the next century. As a consequence, the romanization of Chinese that they had initiated was dormant for nearly a century and was not revived until the early 1800s. The British Protestant missionary Robert Morrison (1782-1834) published a dictionary during 1815-1823, in which he introduced a romanization system that he had designed for Mandarin Chinese. Since 1940, similar schemes were designed for almost all of the important dialects of Chinese, mainly for the purpose of replacing characters as a bona fide writing system in the translation of the Bible, and for other communicative purposes. Known as *jiaohui romazi* 'romanization by the missionary', these schemes were quite influential both at the time and in the years to come. At least 17 dialects had their own romanized writing system, and about 137,000 copies of the Bible printed in romanization were sold between 1891 and 1904 (Ni 1948a: 18). Although, by the founding of the Republic of China in 1912, the use of these schemes as a regular writing system had declined in all but some isolated parts of China (cf. Hong 1992; Huang 1993), their contribution to the movement toward a phonographic system for Chinese should not be underestimated. They demonstrated, for the first time and on a large scale, that it is possible, and feasible, to write Chinese for regular purposes with a script other than characters, and to write on the basis of one's own dialect instead of Northern Mandarin. This provided much inspiration for endeavors to reform the Chinese script in the following century, though these later attempts were mainly initiated by native Chinese and were on a much larger scale, with farther-reaching consequences. As Ni (1948a: 21) put it, "the achievements of missionary romanization have been cited by almost every worker for the romanization of Chinese as strong evidence in favor of the use of phonetic system in the promotion of education."

5.2 Schemes proposed by native Chinese

1892 marks the beginning of the era in which script reform became an integral part of the endeavor to rejuvenate and modernize China. In this year, Lu Zhuangzhang published a phonographic system that he specifically designed for his native tongue, the dialect of Xiamen (Amoy), which is a Southern Min dialect. His goal was clearly stated in the preface to his book:

> Chinese characters are probably the most difficult script in the world... I believe that the strength and prosperity of the country depends upon the physical sciences, which can grow and flourish only if all people—men and women, old and young—are eager to learn and sensible. For them to be eager to learn and sensible depends upon the phonetization of the script in such a way that, after they have acquired the alphabet and the spelling, they will know how to read without further instruction. It also

> depends upon speech and writing being the same so that what is said by the mouth will be understood by the mind. Furthermore it depends upon having a simple script that is easy to learn and write. As a result, this will save more than ten years' time. If all that time is applied to the study of mathematics, physical sciences, chemistry and other practical studies, how can there be any fear that our country will not be rich and strong?(Lu 1956 [1892]: 3)

In terms of the motivation and theoretical assumptions underlying the proposals, what was said in the preface summarizes nicely the features characteristic of Lu's scheme and the dozens of similar schemes proposed by his contemporaries and followers. First, most of the proponents maintained that, from the point of view of learners and users, the Chinese script is inferior to the phonographic writings of Western languages and Japanese and should be replaced by a phonetic system, or at least supplemented by one. Second, it is obvious that all the proposals were motivated by a strong desire to contribute to the cause of modernizing the country, rather than being a purely intellectual pursuit. As noted above, it was widely believed, but never proved, that the difficulty of the writing system was largely responsible for the high rate of illiteracy in China, which in turn accounted for the country's weakness and ineptitude in the face of foreign powers. Since Lu Zhuangzhang, these assumptions have been part of the foundation underlying the whole process of script reform. We will return to this point later in this article.

This approach to script reform has been an important part of intellectual life in China ever since, engaging the keenest attention of linguists, educationalists, and politicians. Roughly speaking, this one century of script reform is divisible into four periods. During the first period, from 1892, when Lu published his scheme, to 1911, 30 or so schemes of phonetization were proposed. The second period is represented by *Zhuyin Zimu* (ZZ) 'Sound-annotating Alphabet', designed in 1913 and published in 1918, which was the first phonetic writing of Chinese that won official acceptance. Eight years later, *Gwoyeu Romatzyh* (GR) 'National Language Romanization' was published, which was, though arguably overcomplicated, the most sophisticated scheme of romanization of the time. 1929 saw the publication of *Latinxua Sin Wenz* (LSW) 'Latinized New Script', which was designed by several Communist scholars in exile in the Soviet Union in collaboration with Soviet linguists. These two important schemes of romanization mark the third period of script reform. The fourth period starts with the beginning of the 1950s, when there was a tremendous upsurge of enthusiasm for the romanization of Chinese. In less than a decade, more than 1,000 schemes were submitted to the *Wenzi Gaige Weiyuanhui* 'Committee for Writing System Reform' in Beijing (Zhou 1979:50). This enthusiasm showed no sign of abating even after the *Pinyin Zimu* 'Phonetic Alphabet' scheme was endorsed by the National People's Congress in 1958, and new schemes kept pouring into the language planning institutions. Largely stimulated by the practical need to design computer input/output system for the Chinese script, the number of new schemes has been growing fast during the past decade or so (cf. Conference 1987).

5.3 Groupings of schemes

The more than 1,000 schemes of phonetic writing for Chinese that have been proposed during the past century differ mainly along four dimensions: (1) intended role in relation to the traditional characters;

(2) graphic form of the script; (3) dialect upon which the system is based; (4) way to represent the phonological structure of the syllable.

5.3.1 Intended roles in relation to the traditional characters

All schemes of phonetic writing were conceived with the aim of tackling the problems that confront the learners and users of characters. The solutions differ with regard to the roles that are stipulated for the schemes in relation to the traditional script. In this regard, four distinct though closely related roles can be identified, namely auxiliary, supplementary, alternative, and superseding.

5.3.1.1 Auxiliary

A phonetic writing that is intended only to play an auxiliary role is not meant to be a writing system in the strict sense of the word. It does not affect the status of the character script as a writing system. It is merely used to facilitate the learning and use of characters, serving such functions as annotating the pronunciation of characters, transcription, indexing, etc.

The usefulness of an auxiliary phonetic writing system, if well designed and promoted, is indisputable. Since such a writing system does not threaten the status quo of the established one, there is usually little resistance to the design and promotion of the system other than on the technical grounds of script form, dialectal base, and the representation of the syllabic structures of characters, etc. As will be discussed in detail, most schemes proposed in the first period, as well as ZZ, GR and *Pinyin*, actually play such a role, although some of these schemes were designed for more radical roles in the first place.

5.3.1.2 Supplementary

A supplementary phonetic writing system is intended to be used together with characters in all situations that characters are used.

Either the phonetic symbols are used in juxtaposition with characters, creating a new type of symbols that are composed of two parts, that is, the character and phonetic symbols that annotate its sound; or they are used to replace characters in some parts of the text, resulting in a mixed writing system, as we have witnessed for Japanese, where *kanji*, *kana* (*hiragana* and *katakana*), and *romaji* can be found together in the same text. The phonetic writing system assigned a supplementary role is bound to have a considerable effect upon the character script, either substituting a new type of composite symbols for the traditional characters, or reducing the number of characters normally used in writings by customarily encoding some of the words or morphemes with the phonetic symbols. A well-known example of such a supplementary phonetic writing system is the Japanese *kana*. Some of the proponents of ZZ hoped that ZZ would play a supplementary role in much the same way as the *kana*, although it turned out to be confined to an auxiliary role.

5.3.1.3 Alternative

An alternative phonetic writing system is one that can properly fulfill the basic functions that are performed by the character script as a writing system. Rather than initiate any change into the logographic writing per se, it takes over some of its functions. More often than not, there is a division of labor between the two kinds of autonomous writing system. One is used for low-level practical purposes in everyday life, the other for more formal occasions, such as for literary, legal, and academic purposes. If put in place, the two writing system would constitute what is known in the linguistic literature as digraphia (cf. Dale 1980; DeFrancis 1984a).

Such a role was intended for most of the schemes of phonetic writing proposed during the past century, although few actually succeeded in attaining that goal, as we will discuss in detail later.

5.3.1.4 Superseding

A phonetic writing system of this type is designed to supersede the logographic system, forcing it into disuse and oblivion, as Quoc Ngu and Hangul did to Chinese characters in Vietnamese and Korean respectively (partially in South Korea and completely in North Korea).

Proponents of a superseding phonetic writing system hold the most radical view toward Chinese characters. It is argued that characters are irremediable, and the best way to solve the problems associated with learning and using them is to replace them by a phonographic system that would better meet the needs of a modernizing society. As we will see later, some of the proposed schemes, notably LSW in the 1930s, were intended to play exactly such a role.

In spite of frequent reiteration of the need to abolish characters during the past century of language reform, it now seems more and more unlikely that any phonetic writing system would ever succeed in superseding Chinese characters. In the literature, we are reminded that characters were not indigenous to the languages in which they have been superseded, but rather had been borrowed because those languages had no writing system of their own. As Coulmas (1989, 1992) reports, it has never happened that a logographic system native to a language has been superseded by a phonographic system for that language. It is doubtful whether this would succeed with Chinese in the future.

5.3.2 Form of script

The graphic forms of the proposed schemes fall into three major categories:

5.3.2.1 Shorthand-style scripts

Schemes adopting scripts modelled after shorthand symbols were mainly proposed during the first period from 1892 to 1912. As reported in Wu and Ma (1988: 89) and Zhou (1979), of the 30 or so popular schemes of this period, five adopted such scripts, although this type fell out of favor with later designers.

5.3.2.2 *Kana*-style scripts or characters

The fact that Japanese *kana* symbols are adapted forms of Chinese characters used purely as phonetic symbols has lent much inspiration to designers of phonetic writing for Chinese, especially during the first and second periods. Most of the schemes proposed during this time were designed after the pattern of *kana*. Sets of phonetic symbols were proposed that either were based upon existing Chinese characters or their components, or were completely new creations. As reported in Ni (1948a) and Zhou (1979), 24 of the 30 schemes in the first period adopted this form of script, constituting the mainstream of this period. It culminated in ZZ, the first phonetic script promulgated by the central government. We will discuss this scheme in more detail later.

In addition, there were some schemes that retained Chinese characters as the basic symbols of the script but used them largely as phonetic symbols that represent the syllables in the language. Examples are *yinbiaozi* 'phonetic characters', proposed by Zhai Jiaxiong in the mid-1930s, which contained 454 characters that were meant to represent all the Chinese syllables without tonal differentiation; and the scheme proposed by Zhang Gonghui in 1947, which comprised two syllabaries, one with more than 1,000 characters representing all the tonal syllables, and the other with more than 400 characters for non-tonal syllables (cf. Wu and Ma 1988: 134). The most influential representative of this category is the system of General Chinese Characters (GCC) or *tongzi,* proposed by the eminent Chinese linguist Yuen Ren Chao in Chao (1976). The GCC is based upon a phonological system of Chinese that is a kind of lowest common denominator between the major dialects. Roughly speaking, the phonemic syllables in the GCC comprise the main features of the initial consonants of the Wu dialects, the vowels of Mandarin, and the endings of Cantonese, totalling 2,082 in number. Each syllable is represented by a unique character, which in about 80 percent of the cases may represent a group of regular characters that are etymologically related, hence the name *tongzi* 'General Chinese character'. Only in about 20 percent of the cases do characters represent homophonous morphemes that are not etymologically related. The GCC is designed to write Chinese in general, both classical Chinese and modern dialects, and without limitation in style or vocabulary.

5.3.2.3 Roman alphabet

In comparison, the schemes using the roman alphabet came as a late development. The first full-scale scheme in this category is represented by Zhu Wenxiong's *Jiangsu Xin Zimu* 'New Alphabet of Jiangsu', which appeared in 1906. With the mainstream of schemes during the first and second periods in favor of a *kana*-style script, romanization did not become a serious contender until near the beginning of the 1920s, but it has been the most popular form since then. The most influential entries in this category are GR, which was proposed In 1926, LSW, in 1931, and *Pinyin*, in 1958. These schemes will be discussed in detail later.

5.3.2.4 Comparison of the forms of script

As I see it, there have been two major factors at work in the choice of script form. One is the technical advantages of the script in terms of ease of learning and efficiency of use. The other is how it appeals to the nationalistic sentiment that has traditionally attached itself to the Chinese characters, not necessarily among Western-minded Chinese scholars, but certainly among the general public in China. These two factors may stand in conflict when it comes to the selection of a particular form of script.

Shorthand-style scripts score low on both criteria. It was soon realized among the designers that the shorthand-style forms are easy to write, but not easy to read, because they are typically comprised of symbols that are not sufficiently differentiated to ensure speedy and unambiguous recognition. For similar views with reference to English, cf. Sampson (1985). Furthermore, bearing little resemblance to characters, they do not enjoy the reverence that is accorded to the traditional script. Phonetic writings of this category may serve an auxiliary role of subservience to the character script, but they fall well short of the qualifications of a bona fide writing system. Very few of the proposals that were raised after the first period advocated this type of script.

The real competition is between the character-based type, especially those formed after the pattern of *kana*, and the romanized type.

During the early period, it was the nationalistic sentiment toward the traditional script that prevailed over technical considerations in choice of script form. As characters were regarded by some as an inextricable part of the Chinese language, and of Chinese culture for that matter, it was believed, and is still believed by many people, that, if the Chinese language is to adopt a phonographic writing system to replace or supplement the logographic one, at least the basic symbols of the new writing should be created from the traditional stock of characters.

As discussed above, some schemes simply adopt regular characters as the basic symbols of the phonetic writing system, each representing a single syllable. The major difference between such schemes and traditional writing is that there are many more phonetic loans in the former than in the latter. To reduce homophony, some schemes introduce distinctions from non-Beijing dialects into the syllabary, resulting in a richer ratio of characters to syllables. The GCC is such a scheme. As the characters that are retained in such schemes are all traditional ones so far as the graphic shape is concerned, they enjoy whatever reverence has been accorded to the traditional script. Also, because students only have to grapple with around 400-2,000 characters, depending upon which scheme is adopted, instead of the more than 3,000 required for full proficiency in the regular writing system, the burden on learners and users is alleviated.

Schemes of this category, however, have serious shortcomings that prevent them from being accepted beyond a small circle. Obviously, they only alleviate to some extent the difficulties encountered by learners and users of characters, rather than providing a thorough solution to the fundamental problems. Furthermore, potential ambiguity poses a serious problem for schemes of this type. While in most cases the characters can be used as pure phonetic symbols without incurring the danger of ambiguity, there are also quite a few cases where the original meanings of the characters used for their phonetic values may persist, engendering meanings that are not intended. Given the logographic nature that has been characteristic of the Chinese script for thousands of years, it is hard for Chinese readers not to "read into characters". Also, given the heavy functional load of syllables in Chinese as discussed earlier, it may not always be easy for readers to identify the writer's intended meaning from the whole range of homophonous morphemes that a single character, now employed as a pure phonetic symbol, represents. This probably explains why only a very tiny portion of the proposed schemes advocate this type of all-character script.

To the extent that the *kana*-type script resembles the graphic shape of the traditional Chinese characters, it is superior to the romanized script in terms of its nationalistic appeal. As the *kana*-type symbols are not conventional characters either, they serve better as phonetic symbols, being free from the semantic meaning that has been associated with logographic characters.

In comparison with *kana*-type symbols, on the other band, the roman alphabet scores higher in terms of technical convenience and efficiency. It is economical in terms of the number of basic symbols, and it is easy to memorize as the letters are already in common use in everyday life. As the most widely used script at the international level, it serves Chinese better in relating to the world. The romanized script normally represents the language in a phonemic manner, which is more precise and flexible than the semi-phonemic and semi-syllabic representation that is typically adopted by a *kana*-type script. Furthermore, the roman letters are easier to write, as the ending strokes easily lead to the beginning strokes of the following letters, and are easy to recognize. In comparison, *kana*-type letters, like those in ZZ, are less differentiated than roman letters in terms of graphic shape and are more prone to confusion in handwriting. Also, based upon characters, typical *kana*-type symbols still preserve the visually solitary shape, making it less easy to mark word boundaries in text. What is more, only a language with a very simple syllable structure, such as Japanese, is suitable for such a script.

It took several decades for technical advantage to become the more important factor in the choice of script form. Since the 1930s, the roman alphabet has become the mainstream type of script, having been adopted in all the important schemes like GR, LSW, and *Pinyin*. However, this does not mean that there is no resistance to this script. The roman alphabet is a foreign script in both origin and graphic form. It does not appeal to those who insist that a phonetic Chinese script should draw upon indigenous resources rather than borrowing from the outside. Views like this have often struck a sympathetic chord with nationalistic-minded Chinese of the twentieth century. A good example is Mao Zedong, who, while endorsing the phonetization of the Chinese writing system with enthusiasm, insisted in the early 1950s that it should be national in form and should be elaborated on the basis of the existing Chinese characters (cf. DeFrancis 1979: 140). In the explanatory note that accompanied the introduction of the romanized *Pinyin* in 1956, there was a whole section devoted to the justification of adopting this non-Chinese script for the new phonetic writing. While there is no denying that technical efficiency has prevailed over nationalistic sentiment in the mainstream of script reform, the view in favor of a native script for the phonetic writing of Chinese is far from being abandoned in Chinese communities. The *kana*-type ZZ is still the normal phonetic script used in Taiwan, rather than the roman-based GR that was promulgated by the same government. It appears that the tension between technical efficiency and nationalistic sentiment will remain an issue in the field for many years to come.

5.3.3 Dialectal basis

As discussed earlier, in relation to dialects, Chinese characters function somewhat like algebraic symbols, which can be realized by different though systematically related phonetic values by speakers of different dialects. In designing a phonetic writing system for Chinese, the issue naturally arises as to what particular phonological system of Chinese is to be represented.

As regards the dialectal basis, schemes of phonetic writing of Chinese that have been proposed so far fall into two major groups, those that are non-dialect-specific, or interdialectal, and those that are dialect-specific.

5.3.3.1 Non-dialect-specific

Some romanized schemes are designed to serve as the writing system of all Chinese dialects, playing basically the same role as the traditional Chinese script but, in theory at least, without the problems associated with characters. Such a writing system is possible in principle, by virtue of the fact that all the modern dialects of Chinese can be traced to the phonological system of Middle Chinese as represented in the rhyme book *Qieyun* that was compiled in the year 601. It can be demonstrated that the modern dialects were derived from the *Qieyun* system by means of systematic phonological rules that relate particular phonemes and tonemes in the former to the corresponding segments in the latter. The differences between dialects are manifested in terms of the different phonological rules that were operative in the course of derivation. Instead of being based on any particular modern dialect, an interdialectal phonetic writing system typically represents an approximation of the phonological system of *Qieyun*. Speakers of modern dialects arrive at the specific pronunciation in the particular dialect by applying to the word a set of phonological rules equivalent to those operative in the historical derivation of the word from the *Qieyun* system. In other words, the same set of phonological rules that operated diachronically is meant to work synchronically to derive the specific pronunciation of the word forms in the modern dialect.

The first scheme in this category is called *La Romanization Interdialectique* 'The Interdialectic Romanization', proposed by the Catholic priests Henri Lamasse and Ernest Jasmin in 1931-1932 (cf. Wang 1990 [1940]: 363; Zhou 1979: 24). Based upon the pronunciation of Chinese as represented in *Qieyun*, it is meant to be realized differently in different dialects. The eminent Chinese linguists Wang Li (1990 [1940]) and Yuen Ren Chao (1976) each designed system based on roughly the same principle. Wang's was called *wenyan luomazi* 'classical literary Chinese romanization' and was intended mainly to encode Classical Chinese rather than Modern Chinese. Chao's system was called General Chinese Romanization (GCR) and, as a romanized form of the GCC, was intended to be a full-scale writing system suitable for all dialects and for all literary styles (cf. Chao 1976).

5.3.3.2 Dialect-specific

The great majority of the proposed schemes are dialect-specific, either representing the phonology of a single dialect, or mainly based upon one dialect while incorporating a few features from other dialects.

As mentioned earlier, the romanization schemes created by Western missionaries in China represent the first attempts at designing separate phonetic writing system for different dialects. Most of the schemes proposed by native Chinese during the first period were based upon non-Mandarin dialects. Among the dialects represented in this way are Southern Min, Cantonese, and Wu (cf. Ni 1948a, 1948b; Zhou 1979). Concomitant with the advocacy of a nationwide lingua franca based upon Northern Mandarin, the trend moved toward taking Northern Mandarin, especially the Beijing dialect, as the basis of romanization. Starting from 1913, serious attempts were made to decide, on a character-by-character basis, upon a standard pronunciation for the lingua franca. It was this standard, called *guoyin* 'national pronunciation', that the new phonetic writing was intended to represent. Two types of *guoyin* were proposed, known respectively as the "old *guoyin*" and the "new *guoyin*" Though based upon the pronunciation of the Beijing dialect for more than 90 per cent of the vocabulary, the old *guoyin* also incorporates some features that are prominent in the other dialects, notably with regard to the pronunciation of entering-tone syllables, which end with one of the stop consonants [p], [t], [k], and [ʔ] in the overwhelming majority of Southern dialects. Later in 1924, it was decided to base the *guoyin* exclusively upon the Beijing dialect without those features from other dialects, hence the "new *guoyin*", which served as the standard of pronunciation for several prominent romanization schemes proposed thereafter (cf. Li 1934).

The issue of a phonological standard was raised again later in the 1930s in the LSW movement that was initiated by left-wing intellectuals, first among Chinese communities in the Soviet Union, then among many cities and regions in China. The idea of basing the phonetic writing of Chinese on a single dialect or on *guoyin* was explicitly rejected in favour of separate romanizations for each of the major dialects in China, along the same line as pursued by the missionaries in the nineteenth century. Full-scale LSW schemes were proposed for the major dialects, although the most influential one, the one that was actually promoted and widely learned and used, was based upon Northern Mandarin (cf. Ni 1948a, 1948b).

So far as the issue of dialectal base is concerned, the proponents of *Pinyin* in the 1950s discarded the LSW's characteristic approach of designing separate writings for different dialects, in spite of the fact that the design and promotion of *Pinyin* was mainly conducted under the leadership of the proponents of LSW. Instead, they took the approach of creating a single system for a single standard language, basing the phonetic writing upon the Beijing dialect in much the same way as ZZ and GR. As little provision was made for the system to represent the other dialects, it is an inadequate tool even for the auxiliary purpose of indicating the pronunciation of characters in those dialects. The language planning institutions of the central government put little, if any, effort into designing romanized schemes for dialects other than the Beijing dialect. However, recent years have witnessed a noticeable resurgence of enthusiasm for romanization of non-Mandarin dialects in Taiwan and Hong Kong. It is reported that a group of linguists have been working hard at new schemes for Southern Min (cf. Cheng 1989; Hong 1992; Huang 1993; Xu 1992). There was a workshop in Hong Kong in December, 1992, that focused on the design and standardization of a romanized writing for Cantonese. Although a great variety of schemes has been proposed for these purposes, we have yet to see a definitive scheme that has been widely accepted for either Southern Min or Cantonese (cf. Bauer 1988; Cheng 1978; Fan and Wu 1992; Hong 1992).

The design of an interdialectic romanization for Chinese is a very demanding task. The proponents have to be expert in Chinese historical phonology, as well as in Chinese modern dialectology. As noted above, although the major dialects of Modern Chinese are mutually unintelligible, due to their derivation from a common source they do have regular phonological correspondences, which are exploited by the designers of such schemes. The symbols in the phonographic writing are to be realized in dialects through the application of phonological rules in a way that parallels the evolution of the dialects in question from the common source. In such a way, it was hoped, the phonographic system would work equally well for all dialects.

In spite of their theoretical soundness, however, all schemes of interdialectical romanization have had very little impact beyond a small group of linguistic experts. They are learned by hardly anyone and are little known outside a narrow academic circle. Most academics consider the creation of such schemes to be more of an intellectual exercise in historical phonology than an activity that has any practical application. The reason for the lack of success, in my view, lies in the fact that while such systems have lost most of the disambiguating power of the logographic script, the way in which they encode phonological information does not represent any significant compensatory gain. As the basic symbols in such a system are supposed to represent pure phonetic value, the ease of recognition afforded by the logographic system with its distinct graphic forms for homophonous morphemes is lost. On the other band, as the "phonographic" symbols are quite removed from the actual pronunciations in any of the Chinese dialects, it demands a lot of effort on the part of users before they can establish the correspondences between the graphemes and their speech (cf. Haas 1983).

In more serious contention are two mutually opposing approaches: those advocating a single phonographic system for the standard dialect and those arguing for separate system for different dialects. The former are represented by proponents of ZZ, GR, and *Pinyin*, and the latter by the missionaries, the proponents of a large portion of the phonetic scripts before ZZ, and, most notably, the proponents of LSW. The controversy between the two groups is essentially a matter of whether to assign primacy to the standardization of the Chinese language for the whole Chinese community, or to assign primacy to easy access to literacy, especially on the part of native speakers of dialects other than Northern Mandarin.

At the initial stage of script reform, when attention was mainly devoted to a drastic reduction of the illiteracy that rated at least as high as 90 percent in China, the approach of designing separate phonetic writings for different dialects was the most popular. It seemed to those engaged in script reform that the best way for the mass of people to attain literacy was to have a phonetic writing based on the vernacular, which would be much easier to learn than the character script. The approach of designing a single writing system for a standard dialect gained ascendancy only after the call to promote a lingua franca, called *guoyu* ‘national language’, as a bridge across dialectal barriers won widespread support in China around the turn of the century. Since then, it has been the major approach to script reform.

As the proponents of the latter approach see it, a single phonetic writing system that is based upon a standard dialect facilitates the modernization of China by providing a uniform writing system for all Chinese and by promoting a lingua franca across the country. It is widely believed that the Chinese characters have served a most important role in Chinese history—that of a unifying bond between speakers of mutually unintelligible dialects. In this respect, the standard phonographic writing system is intended to play the same role as the traditional characters for Chinese as a nation. Furthermore, such a phonetic writing system would greatly facilitate the acquisition of the lingua franca by speakers of the other dialects, by virtue of the close match between writing and speech.

Aside from the potential linguistic problems for a phonetic writing system for Chinese that were discussed earlier, a single standard phonographic system, based upon Northern Mandarin, should serve the intended functions well, albeit to the disadvantage of native speakers of other than the standard dialect. So far as the acquisition of the characters is concerned, non-Mandarin speakers are by and large on an equal footing with Mandarin speakers. The former are at a greater disadvantage, however, if what they have to learn is a phonetic writing system that is only remotely related to pronunciation in their native dialects.

So far as literacy in Standard Modern Written Chinese is concerned, non-native speakers of Northern Mandarin are at another disadvantage, which is not alleviated by switching from a character script to a phonetic writing system. As discussed in detail in Chen (1993), Modern

Written Chinese is based upon Northern Mandarin for its lexical and grammatical norms, which differ to varying extents from those of other dialects. As a result, even if they have learned the standard phonographic system, speakers of the other dialects still have to adapt to the lexical and grammatical norms of Northern Mandarin before they can achieve full literacy. What this means is that, even if a phonetic writing system is adopted, it would not be as easy for them as it is for native speakers of Northern Mandarin to read and write Modern Written Chinese. The approach of creating separate phonetic writing system for different dialects, on the other band, promises an adequate solution to the above problems. It would certainly be much easier for people to learn a phonetic writing system based upon their own pronunciation, and to achieve literacy in a written language that also looks to their speech for its lexical and grammatical norms. During the first period of script reform, when ease of learning and use was the primary concern, there was a famous slogan, *wo shou xie wo kou* ‘my hands write what my mouth says’ , which prescribes the ideal situation that should eventuate as the result of the language reform. Indeed, at a time when the promotion of Northern Mandarin as a lingua franca across Chinese dialects had achieved far from satisfactory success even among officials and educated people, separate phonographic writing system for different dialects seemed to be the only means of attaining this goal.

It must be pointed out that the advocates of separate phonetic writing system for dialects differ in their attitudes toward the concept of a standard writing system, and a standard written language. The concept is rejected by some as linguistic-imperialistic, as is the case with the LSW camp, and some present-day proponents of separate writing system for Southern Min and Cantonese. Most people, however, accept the concept and recognize the importance of the promotion of a standard language that may coexist with the dialects. Lu (1956 [1892]: 5-6) represented such a point of view when he maintained that, first, the traditional script should be accompanied by a phonetic writing system based upon various dialects so that people could learn both the dialect-based phonetic system and the traditional characters more easily. Following that, he argued, one phonographic system should be taken as a standard across the country, as the basis for which he proposed the Nanjing dialect (Lu 1956 [1892]: 5-6). A similar view was raised by the eminent phonologist Lao Naixuan in 1906 when he proposed his schemes for non-Mandarin dialects, as the means by which to attain what he called *yin Nan gui Bei* 'guiding the South to merge into the North', in contrast to *qiang Nan jiu Bei* 'forcing the South to follow the North', which is how he saw the approach of stipulating a single phonographic writing system based upon Northern Mandarin. According to such people, literacy in the dialects is just a first step, after which most people should learn another writing system and written language, presumably the standard that is based upon a dialect of wider usage. Otherwise they would have only limited access to people outside their own dialect area. In any case, it is assumed that it would be easier to learn the standard language after the learners are literate in their own dialect.

It seems then that whatever approach is adopted with regard to the dialectal base of romanization, it will be weighted against the speakers of Southern dialects. Either they have to work harder to learn a phonographic writing system that is removed from their own speech, or they will achieve literacy in a system that is little used beyond their own dialectal areas. The difficulty in learning the standard phonographic writing system based upon Northern Mandarin is relieved only if the speakers of Southern dialects become truly bidialectal, speaking Northern Mandarin in addition to their own dialect.

6. Representation of syllabic structure

In traditional Chinese phonology, aside from the tone, the syllabic structure of a character is taken to be composed of two parts, initial and final. The initial indicates the consonant that begins the syllable, although some syllables may not begin with any consonant, in which case they are said to have "zero-initial" . The final represents the remaining part of the syllable, with a vowel as the core. Finals may begin with one of the three gliding sounds, [i], [u], and [y], called *jieyin* "medial sound" , which is followed by the main vowel. Also, the main vowel may be followed by what is called *yunwei* "terminal sound" , which can be one of the two terminal vowels, [i] and [u], or one of the two terminal nasals, [n] and [ŋ]. Thus, the syllabic structure of characters in Modern Chinese can be represented as in Table 6.

Table 6. Syllabic structure of characters in Chinese

Initial	Final		
	medial	main vowel	terminal
(C)	([i]) ([u]) ([y])	V	([i]) ([u]) ([n]) ([ŋ])

Phonographic schemes differ with regard to the manner in which the segmental structure of syllables is represented. They fall into three major groups, namely, syllabic, semisyllabic and semiphonemic, and phonemic:

6.1 Syllabic

One symbol is used to represent a whole syllable, as do characters in the traditional script. All schemes comprising characters used as purely phonetic symbols belong to this category, such as those proposed by Zhai, Zhang, and Chao (1976) that were discussed earlier.

6.2 Semisyllabic and semiphonemic

Two or three phonetic symbols are used to represent the syllabic structure of the character, some encoding phonemes and some encoding syllables. Schemes using two symbols are known as *shuangpin* "double spelling", and those using three as *sanpin* "triple spelling". Schemes of double spelling may use one symbol for the initial, representing a phoneme, and the other for the final, representing a syllable. Alternatively, they may use one symbol for the initial and the medial, when there is one, and the other for the remaining part of the final. With schemes of triple spelling, the medial is always represented by a separate symbol, with the initial and the remaining part of the final represented by the other two respectively. Almost all the schemes adopting a *kana*-type script represent the syllabic structure in this semisyllabic and semiphonemic fashion.

6.3 Phonemic

Each segment is represented by one symbol. The majority of the romanized schemes adopt this method of representation. The syllabic representation found little favor in script reform, mainly for the reason that more than 400 distinct phonetic symbols are needed in such a writing system, making it clumsy in comparison to the other types. The main choice has been between semisyllabic and semiphonemic, and phonemic.

The semisyllabic and semiphonemic method of representation relates closely to an age-long linguistic tradition in which the phonetic value of a character is indicated by two other characters according to the so-called *fanqie* method: one character having the same initial as the character in question, and the second having the same final and tone. It is as if one were to indicate the pronunciation of the word *pie* by (p)ea and m(y). However, in the case of this type of phonetic writing, pure phonetic symbols are used instead of characters. A feature of the semisyllabic and semiphonemic method of representation is that, although it needs more distinct letters than the phonemic system, the average length of the written word is shorter in the former than in the latter.

The phonemic representation reflects a more sophisticated analysis of the syllabic structure. In comparison with the semisyllabic and semiphonemic system, it is characterized by two features that decidedly make it preferable to most phonetic writings. First, it employs a smaller inventory of phonetic letters. Second, it is capable of representing a greater variety of syllabic types and thus is better suited to many functions that the phonographic system is expected to serve, such as transcribing from other dialects or languages.

7. Brief account of five important schemes

To illustrate the above discussion on the major aspects of the schemes of phonetic writing of Chinese, let us briefly examine five schemes that played, or have been playing, important roles in the script reform movement during the past 100 years, with special attention to the functions they are intended to serve within the broad context of language reform.

7.1 Wang Zhao's *Guanhua Zimu* (GZ) "Mandarin Phonetic Alphabet"

Proposed in 1900, Wang Zhao's GZ was the most influential of the 30 schemes proposed during the first period of script reform. The alphabet contains 49 symbols for initials and 12 symbols for finals, representing the syllabic structure of characters by the method of double spelling. It differs from most of the contemporary and following schemes in that the medial sound is integrated with the initial rather than the final, as shown in Table 6. The symbols are all adapted from component parts of characters, assuming a graphic form that is very similar to that of *kana*. As discussed earlier, given that the traditional reverence toward Chinese characters was still prevalent among the masses of Chinese at that time, GZ's close resemblance to the character script contributed to its popularity during the first period of the movement.

Table 7. *Guanhua Zimu (GZ) "Mandarin Phonetic Alphabet"*

Initials				
匕 [pi]	攵 [pʰi]	† [mi]		
卜 [pu]	扌 [pʰu]	才 [mu]	扌 [fu]	
卄 [t]	犭 [tʰ]	亻 [n]	ι [l]	
乁 [ti]	ㄏ [tʰi]	ㄈ [ni]	厶 [li]	
ナ [tu]	士 [tʰu]	ㄡ [nu]	ㄊ [lu]	▭ [ly]
七 [k]	ㄐ [kʰ]	扌 [h]		
ㄋ [ku]	刂 [kʰu]	ㄅ [hu]		
丄 [tɕ]	卄 [tɕʰ]	× [ɕ]		
尸 [tɕy]	屮 [tɕʰy]	ン [ɕy]		
ξ [tʂ]	爪 [tʂʰ]	寸 [ʂ]	日 [ɻ]	
丁 [tʂu]	刀 [tʂʰu]	セ [ʂu]	入 [ɻu]	
マ [ts]	千 [tsʰ]	么 [s]		
二 [tsu]	厂 [tsʰu]	ク [su]		
< [i]	立 [u]	于 [y]		
Finals				
了 [a]	丶 [ɛ]	乀 [o]		
一 [ai]	フ [ei]	ɔ [au]	丨 [ou]	
⊣ [an]	ㄴ [ən]	乙 [aŋ]	ㄱ [əŋ]	
儿 [ɚ]				

GZ was later expanded, by Lao Naixuan, to write other dialects, mainly Wu, Cantonese, and Min. New symbols were designed and added to Wang's scheme to accommodate sounds not found in the Beijing dialect. The scheme, including its variants for other dialects, found favour among literati and bureaucrats in China and was promoted on a scale unmatched by any other contemporary schemes. A large number of books were compiled and published, on a wide range of subjects like ethics, history, geography, geology, botany, zoology, etc. It was reported that more than 60,000 copies of books in this script were sold in a decade after its publication, and there were many newspapers and magazines printed in this script. It was also used for posters and personal communications (cf. Ni 1948a, 1948b; Zhou 1979).

Wang Zhao was prominent among his contemporaries in that he was among the first to advocate a standard language in China. He argued that such a standard should be based upon the Beijing dialect, as it was the most widely understood. It was on the basis of this dialect that his own phonographic scheme was designed. Advancing the concept of a standard language both in theory and in practice, Wang Zhao heralded what later became known as the National Language Movement. It was due to his zealous advocacy that the necessity of the promotion of a lingua franca gained quick and wide acceptance in China (cf. Li 1934). Furthermore, his scheme exerted remarkable influence upon contemporary and succeeding schemes with regard to both the script form and the dialectal base, paving the way for the first alphabetic script for Chinese to be promulgated by the government 18 years later.

As was typical of the schemes proposed during the first period, GZ was intended to serve a dual function in much the same way as *kana* in Japanese. First, it played an auxiliary role in relation to characters, standing as an aid to indicate the pronunciation of the latter. Second, it served as a fully independent writing system that was an alternative to the character script, mainly for those who could not afford the time and energy needed for the mastery of characters. On one band, Wang Zhao maintained that it was impractical to abolish the characters, because of the existence of the myriad of Chinese classics; on the other band, he argued that there should be an alternative script like GZ, much easier to learn, but fully capable of serving the needs of everyday, non-literary functions. It is obvious that, in proposing the second role of GZ, Wang Zhao had in mind what is now called digraphia: the character script was to stand as a High writing System, learned by people of sufficient leisure, and GZ as a Low writing system merely for the mundane, practical purposes of everyday life.

7.2 *Zhuyin Zimu* (ZZ) "National Phonetic Alphabet"

Promulgated in 1918 by the Ministry of Education of the Republic of China, ZZ was the first phonographic writing system of Chinese that was sanctioned and promoted by the language planning institution of the government. In much the same way as Wang Zhao's GZ, the symbols of ZZ were adapted from simple characters in Classical Chinese, characterized by few strokes and simple forms, as shown in Table 7. It adopted the method of triple spelling in the representation of the syllabic structure. Concerning the dialectal base, it was intended at the beginning to represent a phonological system that was based upon the Beijing dialect but also included features from other dialects, notably the Nanjing dialect. Later on, it was decided that it was to be based exclusively on the Beijing dialect. As a result, some symbols were abolished that represented sounds not found in the Beijing dialect (cf. Li 1934; Zhou 1979).

Table 8. *Zhuyin Zimu (ZZ) "National Phonetic Alphabet"*

Initials					
ㄅ [p]	ㄆ [pʰ]	ㄇ [m]	ㄈ [f]	ㄪ [v]	
ㄉ [t]	ㄊ [tʰ]	ㄋ [n]		ㄌ [l]	
ㄍ [k]	ㄎ [kʰ]	ㄫ [ŋ]	ㄏ [x]		
ㄐ [tɕ]	ㄑ [tɕʰ]	ㄬ [ɳ]	ㄒ [ɕ]		
ㄓ [tʂ]	ㄔ [tʂʰ]		ㄕ [ʂ]	ㄖ [ɻ]	
ㄗ [ts]	ㄘ [tsʰ]		ㄙ [s]		
Medials					
ㄧ [i]	ㄨ [u]	ㄩ [y]			
Finals					
ㄚ [a]	ㄛ [o]	ㄝ [ɛ]	ㄞ [ai]	ㄟ [ei]	ㄠ [ao]
ㄡ [ou]	ㄢ [an]	ㄣ [ən]	ㄤ [aŋ]	ㄥ [əŋ]	ㄦ [ɚ]

ZZ is generally taken to be the culmination of the first stage of script reform that was initiated by Lu Zhuangzhang in 1892. With respect to the script form, dialectal base, and representation of the syllabic structure, it embodies the major features characteristic of the mainstream of schemes proposed during the first period. However, ZZ stands in remarkable contrast to the previous schemes with regard to the stated purpose of the phonetic writing system. As mentioned above, most of the earlier schemes were intended to serve at least one of the three major functions in relation to the character script, namely supplementary, alternative, or superseding, in addition to the auxiliary role. At the time of promulgation, it was stated explicitly in the official document that ZZ was to serve only an auxiliary role, viz. that of annotating the pronunciation of characters. In comparison with the aspirations of the proponents of the earlier schemes, this represents a more conservative stance toward the traditional character script. Some of its chief designers did conceive of a more active role for ZZ, intending it to serve a supplementary or alternative function. For instance, Li Jinxi advocated that characters in all publications should be accompanied by ZZ, which essentially means that the traditional characters should be replaced in publication by a new type of script comprising characters in juxtaposition with ZZ. It was hoped that, with the widespread use of ZZ under the auspices of the government, the phonetic script could in practice play a role beyond the auxiliary or the supplementary one and either serve as a bona fide alternative to the character script or supersede the latter in due course. The developments of the following years, however, put an end to such dreams. In 1930, the government passed a resolution reiterating that the function of ZZ was confined to annotating sound only, and that it should in no way be treated as an autonomous writing system. Furthermore, it was proclaimed that, as the name of ZZ was misleadingly suggestive of a conventional writing system, it was to be changed to *zhuyin fuhao* (ZF) "sound-annotating symbols". At the same time, it began to be used to annotate the sound of characters in other dialects as well.

So far as the auxiliary function is concerned, ZZ or ZF has been very successful in facilitating the learning of character pronunciation in Northern Mandarin, especially in the Beijing dialect. It was a valuable tool in the promotion of *guoyu* during the several decades after its promulgation. It was replaced by *Pinyin* in mainland China after 1958 but has been in continuous use in Taiwan.

7.3 *Gwoyeu Romatzyh* (GR) "National Language Romanization"

Designed by a group of eminent linguists and scholars of the time, GR was published in 1926 and promulgated by the government in 1928, representing the first romanized system that was officially recognized by the language planning institution in China. See Table 8. Adopting a phonemic representation, GR was in the main based upon the Beijing dialect, with some features from other Northern Mandarin dialects added in. It was intended to serve as the standard romanization of Chinese characters for all relevant purposes at that time, such as transcription of proper nouns, in a context where the widespread use of several other romanizations, such as the Wade-Giles system and the Postal system, had created considerable chaos.

Table 9. *Gwoyeu Romatzyh (GR) "National Language Romanization"*

Initials					
b [p]	p [p^h]	m [m]	f [f]	v [v]	
d [t]	t [t^h]	n [n]		l [l]	
g [k]	k [k^h]	ng [ŋ]	x [x]		
j [tɕ]	ch [$tɕ^h$]	gn [ɳ]	sh [ɕ]		(before [i] or [y])
j [tʂ]	ch [$tʂ^h$]		sh [ʂ]	r [ɻ]	(before other sound)
tz [ts]	ts [ts^h]		s [s]	z [z]	

Finals			
y [ɿ] or [ʅ]	i [i]	u [u]	iu [y]
a [a]	ia [ia]	ua [ua]	
o [o]	io [iɔ]	uo [uo]	
e [ɤ]			
e [ɛ]	ie [iɛ]		iue [yɛ]
ai [ai]	iai [iai]	uai [uai]	
ei [ei]		uei [uei]	
au [au]	iau [iau]		
ou [ou]	iou [iou]		
an [an]	ian [iɛn]	uan [uan]	iuan [yɛn]
en [ən]	in [in]	uen [un]	iun [yn]
ang [aŋ]	iang [iaŋ]	uang [uaŋ]	
eng [ən]	ing [iŋ]	ueng [uəŋ]	
ong [uŋ]	iong [yŋ]		
el [ɚ]			

GR is characterized by another feature with regard to the function it is meant to play in relation to the character script. Not satisfied with the conservative stance the government assumed on the role of ZZ, a group of liberal intellectuals launched a heated debate on the fate of the character script as an integral part of the New Culture Movement, which, among other things, advocated that radical changes to the cultural and literary aspects of Chinese society were necessary to a modernizing state. As amply illustrated in the literature, it was a period that was marked by a mood in intellectual circles that favored radical change. So far as language is concerned, the National Language Movement that started more than two decades earlier had achieved remarkable success. A written language based upon the vernacular in Northern Mandarin, called *baihua*, was rapidly replacing *wenyan*, the traditional literary language based upon Classical Chinese, as the standard written language. A lingua franca based mainly upon the Beijing dialect, that is, *guoyu*, was being promoted vigorously across the country. Advances on the two fronts of language reform both prompted and encouraged scholars to take on the issue of script reform with renewed vigor. In the debate on the fate of Chinese characters in the then influential journals such as *Xin Qingnian* [*La Jeunesse*], *Guoyu Yuekan* [*National Language Monthly*], and *Guoyu Zhoukan* [*National Language Weekly*] the majority of articles entertained a fairly radical view, advocating the replacement of the character script by one that is easier to learn and use (cf. Li 1934). As remarked in Zhou (1979:42), the call to abolish characters in favor of a romanized alphabet reached a peak around 1923. As almost all of the designers of GR were ardent supporters of this radical view, it is only natural that, aside from serving the immediate auxiliary role of sound annotation, etc., their scheme was designed in such a way that it would be capable of serving all the functions expected of a bona fide writing system and would supersede characters in due course.

In GR, tones are represented in terms of spellings, instead of by diacritical marks. This, it has been argued, makes the system unnecessarily complicated. Due to that and some other factors, it turned out that the system itself was not as popular as ZZ/ZF in following years. However, it was influential in that it ushered in a new period in the design of phonetic writing system for Chinese: one that is characterized by a switch from character-based symbols to the roman alphabet as the preferred script, and by the renewed interest, after the conservative stance of ZZ/ZF, in the more fundamental roles to be assigned to schemes over and above the function of annotating character pronunciations.

7.4 *Latinxua Sin Wenz* (LSW) "Latinized New Script"

Designed by several prominent Chinese communist scholars in exile in the Soviet Union, in collaboration with Soviet linguists, LSW was first published in 1929 in the Soviet Union. First employed among the 100,000 Chinese living in the Soviet Union and later introduced into China, it was the first romanized scheme that was put to large-scale use as a fully independent writing system, intended to supersede the character script.

LSW differs from the preceding schemes in two remarkable aspects. First, all of the three schemes discussed above were designed and promoted as part of the effort to promote a national language based on the Beijing dialect, making it easier to learn by providing a set of symbols that can be used to annotate the pronunciation of characters in that dialect. Both in theory and in practice, the proponents of LSW were opposed to making the Beijing dialect the base of a standard national language for speakers of all the Chinese dialects, labeling the National Language Movement as an elitist endeavor that placed the speakers of non-Mandarin dialects at a linguistic disadvantage. They argued that there was as yet no dialect in China that was qualified to form the base of a national language. Furthermore, it was argued that if the romanized writing was to be based upon the Beijing dialect, it would be as difficult for native speakers of Southern dialects like Wu, Southern Min, or Cantonese to learn as a foreign language (Ni 1948a: 139). Instead of basing the romanized writing system on the pronunciation of one particular dialect, they maintained, a separate scheme should be designed for each of the important dialects, thus ensuring easy access to literacy by its native speakers. As a result, there were at least 13 schemes of LSW published for the major Chinese dialects (Ni 1948a: 142-143). The most influential was the one based upon Northern Mandarin, this being due solely to the larger population of the native speakers of that dialect. See Table 9.

Table 10. *Latinxua Sin Wenz (LSW) "Latinized New Script"*

Initials				
b [p]	p [p^h]	m [m]	f [f]	
d [t]	t [t^h]	n [n]		l [l]
g [k]	k [k^h]	ng [ŋ]	x [x]	(except before [i] or [y])
g [tɕ]	k [tɕ^h]		x [ɕ]	(before [i] or [y])
zh [tʂ]	ch [tʂ^h]		sh [ʂ]	rh [ɻ]
z [ts]	c [ts^h]		s [s]	r [ɚ]

Finals			
	i [i]	u [u]	y [y]
a [a]	ia [ia]	ua [ua]	
o [o]		uo [uo]	yo [yo]
e [ɤ]			
	ie [iɛ]		ye [yɛ]
ai [ai]		uai [uai]	
ei [ei]		ui [uei]	
ao [au]	iao [iau]		
ou [ou]	iu [iou]		
an [an]	ian [iɛn]	uan [uan]	yan [yɛn]
en [ən]	in [in]	un [un]	yn [yn]
ang [aŋ]	iang [iaŋ]	uang [uaŋ]	
eng [ən]	ing [iŋ]	ung [uŋ]	yng [yŋ]

The other feature that sets LSW apart from other schemes is the radical attitude its proponents held in relation to characters. While the auxiliary role of annotating the sound of characters was intended to be an important function of the above three schemes, LSW was designed, first and foremost, to supersede the character script. It was asserted that the Chinese characters were a product of the old feudal society and had become a tool with which the ruling class oppressed the laboring masses. They were an insurmountable impediment to higher literacy, and so unsuitable for a modern society. Because of that, they reasoned, they should be abolished in favor of a purely phonetic writing system.

LSW is notable as the scheme that was designed with the most radical intentions in relation to the traditional characters. In spite of the indifference and hostility on the part of the Nationalist government toward the scheme, LSW was very popular as an autonomous writing system in some parts of the country, particularly in those regions in the northwestern part of China that were under the control of the Communist Party. This was largely due to the support of a large number of prominent left-wing and liberal scholars. According to Ni (1948b: 209), more than 300 publications totalling half a million copies appeared in LSW. What is more important, by its considerable success, it demonstrated to later proponents of script reform just what a phonetic writing system for Chinese could achieve, thus paving the way for an even more influential scheme, *Pinyin*, that was to be published in the 1950s.

It is also worth pointing out that the promotion of LSW and its widespread use were concomitant with the growing movement for a truly popular written language, known as *dazhongyu yundong* "movement for a popular language", which aimed at a written language that was rid of all those words, expressions, and sentence patterns that originated in Classical Chinese and do not normally appear in the vernacular speech of the masses. The most outstanding man of letters of the time, Lu Xun, made a perceptive point when he claimed that "to promote the vernacular language, we must use a romanized writing" (Zhou 1979: 46). Similar views were also propounded earlier by linguists like Li Jinxi (cf. Li 1934: 67).

Arguments in favor of a romanized writing system for the popular language are built upon the following grounds. First, there are quite a few words and expressions in the vernacular that do not have conventional representation in Chinese characters. This is especially the case in the Southern dialects, as mentioned earlier. Second, many classicisms that are deemed incompatible with a popular written language owe their continuous use in writing largely to the logographic characters. Because of the high homophony of morphemes as discussed at the beginning of this article, it would be difficult, if not impossible, to differentiate these overwhelmingly monosyllabic residues from Classical Chinese if a phonetic writing system were to be adopted. As argued in Chen (1993), however, these classicisms have become an integral part of Modern Written Chinese and provide the sole linguistic device for certain important stylistic effects. The adoption of a phonetic writing system for Chinese would certainly take a heavy toll on the expressive range of the written language, by reducing the wide variety of stylistic effects currently made available by the logographic system.

7.5 *Pinyin Zimu* "Phonetic Alphabet"

Designed during the mid-1950s and promulgated in 1958 by the government of the PRC, *Pinyin* adopts the roman alphabet and assumes a phonemic representation, basically along the same lines as GR and LSW, as shown in Table 10.

Table 11. *Pinyin*

Initials				
b [p]	p [pʰ]	m [m]	f [f]	
d [t]	t [tʰ]	n [n]		l [l]
g [k]	k [kʰ]		h [x]	
j [tɕ]	q [tɕʰ]		x [ɕ]	
zh [tʂ]	ch [tʂʰ]		sh [ʂ]	r [ɻ]
z [ts]	c [tsʰ]		s [s]	
Finals				
	i [i]	u [u]	ü [y]	
a [a]	ia [ia]	ua [ua]		
o [o]		uo [uo]		
e [ɤ]				
ê [ɛ]	ie [iɛ]		üe [yɛ]	
ai [ai]		uai [uai]		
ei [ei]		uei [uei]		
ao [au]	iao [iau]			
ou [ou]	iou [iou]			
an [an]	ian [iɛn]	uan [uan]	üan [yɛn]	
en [ən]	in [in]	uen [un]	ün [yn]	
ang [aŋ]	iang [iaŋ]	uang [uaŋ]		
eng [əŋ]	ing [iŋ]	ueng [uəŋ]		
ong [uŋ]	iong [yŋ]			
er [ɚ]				

Unlike the other schemes, however, *Pinyin* has received the full support of the government, in a way unseen in any earlier period of language reform in China. It is the official phonographic scheme of Chinese in China, being extensively employed in all relevant areas such as textbooks, reference works, communications, signs, etc. It is also the most popular phonographic system of Chinese outside China, widely taught in schools and used in publications (Wu 1980). It was adopted by the International Standardization Organization in 1982 as the standard form for the transcription of Chinese words.

There are two aspects of *Pinyin* that are worth discussing here, one with respect to the dialect base of the system, the other concerning the functions it is intended to serve.

Language reform was high on the agenda of the government of the PRC right after it was established in 1949, which is evident from the focus that language issues received from 1950 onward (cf. Chen 1993; Wu 1958; Wu and Li 1958; Zhou 1979; etc.). In the initial stage attention was concentrated on the reform of the Chinese script. The few directives from Mao Zedong published in newspapers were exclusively on script reform (cf. DeFrancis 1979). The official language planning body, set up in 1954 to deal with all language related issues, was called *Zhongguo Wenzi Gaige Weiyuanhui* 'Committee for Writing System Reform of China'. Chairman of the Committee was Wu Yuzhang, a veteran communist scholar who was one of the masterminds of the LSW. Given that, one would expect that the new scheme *Pinyin* would have realized the hopes previously held for LSW on a national scale. As it turned out, however, *Pinyin* deviated from LSW in the following important aspects.

Pinyin is based exclusively upon the pronunciation of the Beijing dialect. In contrast to the LSW approach of separate schemes for the major dialects, no attempt has been made on the part of the language planning institution to design similar *Pinyin* schemes for other dialects. As discussed above, the LSW approach of designing separate schemes for each of the major dialects is based on a rejection of the concept of a standard language based on a particular dialect. It is obvious that this concept of a standard national language, which had been the main theme of the National Language Movement since the turn of the century, was whole-heartedly embraced by the newly established government. The promotion of such a language, renamed *Putonghua* "Common Speech", has been an essential part of the language planning activities of the government and a continuation of what all the preceding governments in China had done in the field of language planning. Indeed, one of the major stated functions of *Pinyin* is to facilitate the acquisition of *Putonghua*, which is based upon the pronunciation of the Beijing dialect, by speakers of other dialects. Thus, rather than assign primacy to creating easy access to literacy, as the LSW camp had done, the PRC government has opted for establishing uniformity of language (Wu 1958; Wu and Li 1958).

With regard to the intended function of the phonetic writing system, *Pinyin* also retreated from the more radical position of LSW. While LSW was to function as an alternative and superseding writing system in relation to the character script, *Pinyin* is intended to serve a mere auxiliary role.

It must be pointed out, however, that a close examination of the relevant literature reveals that there has been considerable vacillation on the part of the government concerning the function of *Pinyin*. There is ample evidence that when the Committee first set about the task of designing a phonetic writing system in the 1950s, there was no doubt in the mind of the designers that the scheme would eventually supersede the character script. In the early 1950s Mao Zedong was quoted as saying, "The writings system must be reformed, and it should take the phonetic direction common to the languages of the world" (cf. DeFrancis 1979; Wu 1978: 101). As was widely believed at that time, it was just a matter of how long it would take for the phonographic system to completely supersede the characters.

When *Pinyin* was promulgated in 1958, however, there was an obvious retreat from the previous stance with regard to its role. *Pinyin* is intended to serve an auxiliary role, mainly as a sound-annotating tool to facilitate the learning and use of characters, in much the same way as ZZ/ZF and GR; Furthermore, as *Pinyin* is based on the Beijing dialect, which provides the standard pronunciation of *Putonghua*, it also functions as an aid in promoting the lingua franca among native speakers of other dialects. When the first draft of the *Pinyin* scheme was distributed to the participants of the National Conference on Script Reform convened in October 1955, it was called *Hanyu Pinyin Wenzi* (*Lading Zimu Shi*) *Cao'an Chugao* "First Draft of Phonographic Writing System of Chinese (in Latin Alphabet)" . When promulgated in 1958, it was changed to *Hanyu Pinyin Fang'an* "Phonographic Scheme of Chinese" with the term *wenzi* "writing system" deleted. Also, it was stated in explicit terms that *Pinyin* was not intended as a supplementary, or alternative, or superseding writing system in relation to Chinese characters. This change in attitude became even clearer at the National Conference on Language and Writing System convened in January 1986, when it was announced for the first time that it was open to debate whether the Chinese writing system should take the direction of phonetization—a significant retreat from what Mao Zedong, the proponents of LSW, and their predecessors envisaged for the Chinese language.

8. Conclusion

The above discussion demonstrates how various linguistic and sociopolitical factors have interacted in the endeavors to design and promote a phonetic writing system for Chinese during the past century. As we can conclude from the above, some positive results have been achieved, mainly in the general acceptance of auxiliary phonographic system, which, by virtue of their sound-annotating functions, greatly facilitate the learning and use of characters, and the promotion of a standard language across the country. On the other band, while it seems very improbable that what Turkey's Kemal Ataturk accomplished in script change in 1928 would ever happen in China, no one can know for certain, any more than a century ago, whether any phonetic writing system for Chinese will play a role beyond the auxiliary one in the future. From what we have learned about writing reform in China during the past 100 years, we are in a better position to appreciate what Coulmas (1989: 261) observes about writing reform in general: "Every writing reform is a social experiment on a large scale, and since there are always sociolinguistic factors which interfere with the ideal solution from a strictly systematic point of view, the results are to some degree unpredictable."

References

Bauer, Robert S. 1988. Written Cantonese of Hong Kong, *Cahiers de Linguistique Asie Orientale* 17, 245-293.

Bolinger, Dwight. 1946. Visual morphemes, *Language* 22, 333-340.

Cao, Xianzhou. 1988. Hanzi de biaoyixing he Hanzi jianhua [The logographicity of Chinese characters and their simplification], In: Seminar 1988, 17-27.

Chang, Baoru. 1989. Xiandai Hanyu pinglü cidian de yanzhi [Complication of the dictionary of frequency of Modern Chinese], In: Yuan Chen, ed., *Xiandai Hanyu Dingliang Fenxi*, Shanghai: Shanghai Educational Publishing House, 30-59.

Chao, Yuen Ren. 1976. A preliminary sketch of General Chinese, In: Anwar S. Dil, ed., *Aspects of Chinese Sociolinguistics: Essays by Yuan Ren Chao*, Stanford University Press, 106-143.

Chen, Mingyuan. 1981. Shuli tongji zai Hanyu yanjiu zhong de yingyong [Application of mathematical statistics in the studies of Chinese language], *Zhongguo Yuwen* [*Chinese Language and Writing System*] 6/1981, 466-474.

Chen, Ping. 1993. Modern Written Chinese in development, *Language in Society* 22(4), 505-537.

Chen, Weizhan. 1988. Wo dui Hanzi qiantu de yixie kanfa [My views on the future of Chinese characters], In: Institute of Applied Linguistics of the Chinese Academy of Social Sciences, ed., *Wenzi Wenti Xueshu Taolunhui Lunwenji*, Beijing: Yuwen Chubanshe, 39-49.

Chen, Yuan. ed. 1989. *Xiandai Hanyu Dingliang Fenxi* [*Quantative Analyses of Modern Chinese*], Shanghai: Shanghai Educational Publishing House.

Chou, En-lai [Zhou, Enlai]. 1958. Current tasks of reforming the written language, In: Secretariat of National Conference on Language and Writing System, ed., *Reform of the Chinese Written Language*, Beijing: Foreign Languages Press, 7-29.

Conference. 1987. *Xinshiqi de Yuyan Wenzi Gongzuo: Quanguo Yuyan Wenzi Gongzuo Huiyi Wenjian Huibian* [*Work on Language and Writing System in the New Period: Proceedings of National Conference on Language and Writing System*], Beijing: Yuwen Chubanshe.

Coulmas, Florian. 1983. Writing and literacy in China, In: Coulmas and Ehlich, eds., 239-253.

Coulmas, Florian. 1989. *The Writing Systems of the World*, London: Blackwell.

Coulmas, Florian. 1992. Writing system. In: William Bright, ed., *International Encyclopedia of Linguistics*, Vol. 4, Oxford University Press, 253-257.

Coulmas, Florian and Konrad Ehlich, eds. 1983. *Writing in Focus*, Berlin: Mouton.

Dale, Ian R.H. 1980. Digraphia, *International Journal of the Sociology of Language*, 26, 5-13.

DeFrancis, John. 1950. *Nationalism and Language Reform in China*, Princeton University Press.

DeFrancis, John. 1979. Mao Tse-tung and writing reform, In: Joshua A. Fogel and William T. Rowe, eds., *Perspectives on a Changing China*, Boulder, CO: Westview, 137-154.

DeFrancis, John. 1984a. Digraphia, *Word* 35(1), 59-66.

DeFrancis, John. 1984b. *The Chinese Language: Fact and Fantasy*, Honolulu: University of Hawaii Press.

DeFrancis, John. 1989. *Visible Speech: The Diverse Oneness of Writing Systems*, Honolulu: University of Hawaii Press.

Fan, Guo and Xinjie Wu. 1992. Xianggang dianhuabu Guangzhou Hua paijian xitong pingshu [Review of the Cantonese indexing system of the yellow pages of Hong Kong], unpublished manuscript, Hong Kong Baptist College.

Fu, Yonghe. 1989. Xiandai Hanyu changyong zibiao de yanzhi [Design of the list of common characters in Modern Chinese]. In: Yuan Chen, ed., *Xiandai Hanyu Dingliang Fenxi*, Shanghai: Shanghai Educational Press, 107-115.

Gelb, Ignace J. 1963. *A Study of Writing*, 2nd ed. University of Chicago Press.

Guan, Xiechu. 1988. Hanzi jianhua wenti [The simplification of Chinese characters], In: Institute of Applied Linguistics of the Chinese Academy of Social Sciences, ed., *Wenzi Wenti Xueshu Taolunhui Lunwenji*, Beijing: Yuwen Chubanshe, 108-109.

Haas, William. ed. 1976a. *Writing Without Letters*, Manchester: Manchester University Press.

Haas, William. 1976b. Writing: The basic options, In: William Haas, ed., 1976a, Manchester: Manchester University Press, 131-208.

Haas, William. 1983. Determining the level of a script. In: Florian Coulmas and Konrad Ehlich, eds., *Writing in Focus*, Berlin: Mouton, 15-29.

Haugen, Einar. 1966. Dialect, language, nation, *American Anthropologist* 68, 922-935.

Hill, Archibald A. 1967. The typology of writing systems, In: William M. Austin, ed., *Papers in Linguistics: In Honor of Leon Dosiert*, The Hague: Mouton, 92-99.

Hong, Weiren. 1992. *Taiwan Yuyan Weiji* [*Language Crisis*], Taiwan: Qianwei Chubanshe.

Huang, Shuanfan. 1993. *Yuyan, Shehui Yu Zuqun Yishi* [*Language, Society and Group Consciousness*], Taipei: Crane.

Jiang, Shanguo. 1987. *Hanzixue* [*Studies of Chinese Characters*], Shanghai: Shanghai Educational Publishing House.

Li, Charles N. and Sandra A. Thompson. 1981. *Mandarin Chinese: A Functional Reference Grammar*, Berkeley and Los Angeles: University of California Press.

Li, Jinxi. 1934. *Guoyu Yundong Shigang* [*Outline of History of National Language Movement*], Shanghai: Shangwu Yinshuguan.

Li, Shiyi. 1993. Zhongguo renran shi fazhanzhong guojia [China is still a developing country], *Liaowang* [*Outlook*] 26/1993, 4-9.

Li, Xueqin. 1985. Kaogu faxian yu Zhongguo wenzi qiyuan [Archaeological discoveries and the origin of the Chinese script]. In: Shouhe Ding et al., eds., *Zhongguo Wenhua Yanjiu Jikan II* [*Collected Studies in Chinese Culture, Vol. 2*], Shanghai: Fudan University Press, 146-157.

Lu, Zhuangzhang. 1956[1892]. *Yimuliaoran Chujie: Zhongguo Qieyin Xin Zi Xia Qiang* [*First Steps in Complete Understanding at a Glance: A New Chinese Script for the Xiamen Dialect*]. Beijing: Wenzi Gaige Chubanshe.

Ni, Haishu. 1948a. *Zhongguo Pinyin Wenzi Gailun* [*Introduction to Phonetic Writing in China*], Shanghai: Shidai Shubao Chubanshe.

Ni, Haishu. 1948b. *Zhongguo Pinyin Wenzi Yundong Shi* [*History of the Movement of Phonetic Writing in China*], Shanghai: Shidai Shubao Chubanshe.

Norman, Jerry. 1988. *Chinese*, Cambridge: Cambridge University Press.

Pulgram, Ernst. 1976. The typologies of writing systems. In: William Haas, ed., *Writing Without Letters*, Manchester: Manchester University Press, 1-28.

Qian, Nairong. 1990. *Xiandai Hanyu* [*Modern Chinese*], Beijing: Higher Education Press.

Qiu, Xigui. 1988. *Wenzixue Gaiyao* [*Introduction to the Study of Script*], Beijing: Shangwu Yinshuguan.

Reform. 1958. *Reform of the Chinese Written Language*, Beijing: Foreign Language Press.

Sampson, Geoffrey. 1985. *Writing Systems: A Linguistic Introduction*. London: Hutchinson.

Seminar. 1988. *Hanzi Wenti Xueshu Taolunhui Lunwenji* [*Proceedings of the Seminar on Chinese Characters*], Institute of Applied Linguistics of the Chinese Academy of Social Sciences, ed., Beijing: Yuwen Chubanshe.

Su, Peicheng. 1992. Xiandai hanzi yanjiu jianshu [Survey of research on modern Chinese characters], *Yuwen Jianshe* [*Language Planning*] 7/1992, 6-14.

Trager, George L. 1974. Writing and writing systems. In: Thomas Sebeok, ed., *Current Trends in Linguistics*, Vol. 12: *Linguistics and Adjacent Arts and Sciences*, The Hague: Mouton, 373-496.

Wang, Li. 1990[1940]. Hanzi gaige [Chinese character reform], In: *Wang Li Wenji* [*Collected Works of Wang Li*], Vol. 7. Jinan: Shandong Educational Press.

Wang, Li. 1980. *Hanyu Shi Gao* [*History of Chinese Language: A Draft*], Beijing: Zhonghua Shuju.

Wu, Wenchao. 1980. The adoption of the Chinese Phonetic Alphabet as the international standard for romanization of Chinese names of persons and places, *Journal of Chinese Linguistics* 8(2), 320-321.

Wu, Yuzhang. 1958. Report on the current tasks of reforming the written language and the draft scheme for a Chinese Phonetic Alphabet, In: *Reform of the Chinese Written Language*, Beijing: Foreign Languages Press, 30-54.

Wu, Yuzhang. 1978. *Wenzi Gaige Wenji* [*Essays on Writing Language Reform*], Beijing: Chinese People's University Press.

Wu, Yuzhang and Jinxi Li. 1958. A summary of the efforts of the Chinese people over the past sixty years for a phonetic alphabet, In: *Reform of the Chinese Written Language,* Beijing: Foreign Languages Press, 63-70.

Wu, Zhankun and Guofan Ma. 1988. *Hanzi and Hanzi Gaige Shi* [*Chinese Characters and the History of Chinese Character Reform*]. Changsha: Hunan Renmin Chubanshe.

Yin, Binyong. 1988. Guanyu Hanzi pingjia de ji ge jiben wenti [On some basic issues concerning the evaluation of Chinese characters]. In: Institute of Applied Linguistics of the Chinese Academy of Social Sciences, ed., *Wenzi Wenti Xueshu Taolunhui Lunwenji*, Beijing: Yuwen Chubanshe, 251-262.

Yin, Binyong. 1991. Xiandai Hanzi de dingliang yanjiu [Quantitative studies on modern Chinese characters], *Yuwen Jianshe* 11/1991, 19-21.

Zhou, Zumo. 1988. Hanzi [Chinese characters]. In: *Encyclopaedia Sinica* (Volume on *Language and Writing System*), Beijing: Encyclopaedia Sinica Press, 195-199.

Zhou, Youguang. 1979. *Hanzi Gaige Gailun* [*Introduction to Chinese Character Reform*], 3rd ed. Beijing: Wenzi Gaige Chubanshe.

论汉语拼音书写系统

提　要　自利玛窦开始至今，为汉语设计的拼音系统数以千计。本文研究汉语拼音系统设计过程中的理论和技术问题。我们首先分析同汉语字、词和语素有关的主要特点的历史和现状，以此为基础探讨汉语拼音系统的主要特点，研究对象包括拼音系统的基本符号形式、语音基础、音节结构、字调表现以及设计目的，等等。同时选取最重要的五个拼音系统，对它们的历史渊源和系统特点作详细分析。

关键词　文字系统　标音性　音意性　文字改革　拼音方案

(This article was first published in *International Journal of the Sociology of Language* 122, 1-46, in 1996. Permission by Walter de Gruyter GmbH to reprint the copyright material in the present volume is gratefully acknowledged.)

Four projected functions of new writing systems for Chinese*

Abstract New writing systems for Chinese are mainly designed to perform one or more of four functions, in relation to the traditional logographic script, namely, auxiliary, supplementary, alternative, and superseding. So far only those intended for the auxiliary role have achieved success. Since schemes to perform each of the other three functions would affect the traditional script in one way or another, they have yet to overcome the resistance stemming from linguistic, psychological, pedagogical, political, and socio-cultural factors discussed in this paper.

Keywords logographic script; phonographic writing system; script reform

1. Introduction

In contrast to the great majority of modern languages that have adopted phonographic writing systems, Chinese retains a logographic writing system that has been in continuous use for more than 4,000 years. At the same time, tremendous efforts have been made during the past century to design and promote a phonetic writing system for Chinese. The scale

* Acknowledgments—I wish to express my gratitude to One-soon Her. Thomas H-T Lee, Lü Shuxiang, Malcom Skewis, Sandra A. Thompson, Xu Liejiong, Eric Zee, and Zhou Youguang for their help in my research on the development of Modern Chinese since the nineteenth century. This paper presents part of the findings of the project. I alone am responsible for the views and interpretations of data given herein.

of this endeavor to shift from logographic to phonographic writing is unequaled in the world (cf. DeFrancis 1950, 1984a, 1989; Zhou 1979, 1992; Chen 1993, 1996). In the relatively short period between 1958 and 1980, as recorded in Zhou(1992:214), as many as 1,667 schemes of phonetic writing for Chinese were submitted to the language planning institution in Beijing. Given the scale of this sustained effort, it is worthwhile to examine the linguistic undertaking, in its various dimensions, as a case study of designing a new writing system for a language with a time-honored literary tradition, in contrast to efforts for previously unwritten languages as discussed in Sjoberg (1966), Smalley (1964),Venezky (1970), Mithun (1992), inter alia. Following detailed discussions on aspects of this complex and multifaceted subject in Chen (1993, 1996), the present paper offers an in-depth analysis of the major functions that various schemes are intended to perform in relation to the traditional script. It is established in this paper that new writing systems for Chinese are mainly designed to fulfill one or more of four functions—namely, auxiliary, supplementary, alternative, and superseding. With influential schemes for illustration, this paper discusses each of the four functions expected by these schemes, giving special reference to the problems of the traditional script addressed by each scheme and the linguistic and extralinguistic implications of their solutions.

2. Motivation for designing new writing systems for Chinese

The basic units of the traditional Chinese writing system, customarily called characters, are notoriously difficult to learn and use. As elaborated in the literature, Chinese characters are described as morpho-syllabic, each representing a distinct morpheme, and at the same time a single syllable (DeFrancis 1984a,1989; Sampson 1985 inter alia; Coulmas 1989, 1992; Chen 1996). As morphemes in Modern Chinese greatly outnumber syllables, the language has a large number of homophonous morphemes, which are differentiated in writing by graphically distinct characters. Literacy in Modern Written Chinese (MWC) is defined as a thorough knowledge of a minimum of 2,000 characters. Since characters contain few reliable cues to their pronunciation, there is not much a learner can do beyond rote memorization.① It has been established through comparative studies of Chinese and other languages using phonographic writing that the Chinese, on average, have to spend an extra two years to acquire the characters of their writing system (cf. Zhou 1979; Wu and Ma 1988). It has been argued that, because it is difficult to learn and inconvenient to use, the traditional writing system is to a large extent responsible for the country's high illiteracy and low efficiency, and hence an impediment to the process of modernization. It has also been widely maintained that the best solution to the problem lies in the adoption of a phonetic writing system for the language (Qu 1931; Ni 1949; DeFrancis 1950; 1984a; Zhou 1979).

The development of phonetic writing for Chinese started in the sixteenth century, when the Jesuit missionary Matteo Ricci (1552-1610) designed the first romanization schemes for Chinese. After Ricci, other romanization schemes were designed by Western missionaries stationed

① Over 90 percent of the characters in Modern Chinese belong to the so-called *xingsheng* 'semantic-phonetic' category. Each character in this category is composed of two parts, a semantic and a phonetic determinative. As observed in the literature (cf. Qiu 1988; Yin 1991; Su 1992; Chen 1996), these semantic and phonetic determinatives provide only a vague cue for the phonetic value and the semantic category of the character in which they are contained.

in China. Lu Zhuangzhang, who proposed *Zhongguo Qieyin Xin Zi* 'New Phonetic Writing of Chinese' in 1892, represented the first native Chinese to partake in this endeavor. There are no precise statistics on the number of schemes proposed since then, but a conservative estimate would place it in the order of 2,000. Among theses chemes, there are five that are worthy of particular attention here. The first is *Guanhua Zimu* (GZ) 'Mandarin Phonetic Alphabet', which was proposed by Wang Zhao in 1900 and represents the earliest attempt to develop a phonetic writing system based on what was considered the standard dialect for speakers of mutually unintelligible Chinese dialects (i.e., the Beijing dialect). The second is *Zhuyin Zimu* (ZZ) 'Sound-annotating Alphabet', which was published in 1918, and became the first phonetic writing system for Chinese to win official approval and to be promulgated by the central government. Eight years later, *Gwoyeu Romatzyh* (GR) 'National Language Romanization' was published and became the first officially recognized scheme to adopt a romanized script. It was generally regarded as the most sophisticated, though arguably over-complicated, scheme of romanization in its time. The year 1931 witnessed the publication of another influential romanization scheme—*Latinxua Sin Wenz* (LSW) 'Latinized New Script', which was designed by several Communist scholars in exile in the Soviet Union, in collaboration with Soviet linguists. With the founding of the People's Republic of China (PRC) in 1949, there was a new upsurge of enthusiasm for the romanization of Chinese, which resulted in the promulgation of *Pinyin Zimu* (*Pinyin*) 'Phonetic Alphabet' in 1958. Among all the schemes of phonetic writing for Chinese, *Pinyin* is by far the most important, since it is the only one used in China and is widely accepted in other parts of the world as the standard system of romanization for Chinese characters.

3. Four functions of the writing schemes

All of the above schemes of phonetic writing were conceived with the aim of tackling the problems that confront learners and users of Chinese characters. The solutions differ in the type of functions stipulated for each scheme in relation to the traditional script. In this regard, four distinct, though closely related functions can be identified—namely, auxiliary, supplementary, alternative, and superseding.

3.1 Auxiliary

An auxiliary scheme is one that is designed to facilitate the learning and use of Chinese characters mainly by providing a set of phonetic symbols that indicate the pronunciation of the characters in a clear and straightforward fashion.

As already mentioned, characters in themselves provide poor cues to their pronunciation, an important factor contributing to the difficulties involved in their acquisition and use. In traditional lexicography, the pronunciation of characters was indicated by another character that had either the same or similar pronunciation. Later, under the influence of Sanskrit scholarship, which accompanied the introduction of the Buddhist classics at the beginning of the Eastern Han Dynasty (25-220 A.D.), a new method of sound annotation called *fanqie* was invented. According to this method, the syllable represented by the character is broken into two component parts, initial and final. The former can be a consonant, or empty, in which case it is called zero initial; the latter is composed of the main vowel, which may be preceded by another medial glide and followed by one of the three nasal consonants [m], [n], or [ŋ], or one of the consonant stops, [p], [t], or [k]. *Fanqie* uses two characters for sound annotation, with the first carrying the same initial as the annotated character, and the second, the same final and tone. ①

The shortcomings of the two methods of sound annotation are self-evident: it is not always easy to find characters that both provide the intended phonetic value and are common enough to be familiar to most users. More importantly, since characters have different pronunciations in different dialects, the annotation that works for one dialect may not indicate the intended pronunciation in other dialects.

Of the five most important schemes mentioned above, ZZ and *Pinyin* provide the best illustrations of this function. It was declared at their respective publications that the primary objective was to provide a set of precise, dialect-neutral phonetic symbols that could be used for sound annotation (cf. Li 1934). The name of ZZ highlights the principal function that the system is intended to perform. When *Pinyin* was promulgated by the State Council of the PRC, it was announced that it was intended to serve two purposes: first, to provide a sound-annotating tool for characters; and second, through the character-annotating function, to expedite the promotion of standard speech based on the Beijing dialect (cf. Proceedings 1957; Wu 1958). Of all the intentions cherished in designing phonographic schemes for Chinese, sound annotation for characters is the one that has met with the greatest success. Since their publication, ZZ and *Pinyin* have become indispensable tools for native and non-native learners of Chinese characters. Shortly after its publication, ZZ began to be taught in year one of primary school as an introduction to learning Chinese characters, until it was replaced by

① To give an example of *fanqie* in English, the sound of *bite* is indicated by the word *b*(ay) and (l)*ight*.

Pinyin on the mainland. As reported in the literature (Fang 1969), ZZ has played an essential role in promoting *guoyu* 'national language' in Taiwan since 1945.[①] Similarly, *Pinyin* has become an indispensable aid in character learning, and *putonghua* 'common speech' teaching in mainland China, and in the majority of overseas institutions where Chinese is taught.

Another important role of an auxiliary system is to facilitate the use of characters by providing an orthography, usually a romanization system, that enables characters to be arranged in a way that allows their convenient and efficient storage and retrieval with traditional printing materials and computers. It also serves as a tool for the transcription of characters in situations that require a rendering of Chinese names and words, such as those used in relating to the international community. The familiar Wade-Giles system and the Postal system were specially designed for such functions. As the first romanization scheme designed by native Chinese scholars, GR was also meant to address the contemporary chaos in transcription that existed as a result of several co-existing systems. *Pinyin* became the standard scheme for the transcription of Chinese names in 1958. It was adopted by the ISO in 1982 as the standard scheme for the transcription of Chinese names, and, with the exception of a few well-known names, *Pinyin* has been the only scheme used for this function.

If an auxiliary phonetic writing system is well designed and effectively promoted, it can play an indisputably useful role in facilitating the learning and use of characters, as well as promotion of the standard speech. In comparison with the schemes primarily designed

① *Guoyu* and *Putonghua* are different names for Standard Spoken Chinese, The former mainly used in Taiwan, the latter in mainland China and Hong Kong. It is called *huayu* 'the Chinese speech' in Singapore.

for the other functions, those playing an auxiliary role constitute the only category that has fully realized the expectations placed on them.

Writing systems designed for an auxiliary function do not pose any threat to the status quo of the established character script. Indeed, to the extent that the auxiliary schemes alleviate the difficulties confronting learners and users of characters, and address other inconveniences and inefficiencies associated with the logographic system, they actually serve to attenuate the need for a more drastic change to the traditional script, lending a new lease on life to the latter by enabling the language to be better accommodated to the needs of modern times. Given this situation, there is usually little resistance on the part of language planning institutions to designing and promoting such a system, other than on the technical grounds of script form, dialectal base, syllabic or phonemic representation, etc. (for a detailed discussion of these factors, cf. Chen 1996).

It is evident from the above discussion that a phonetic scheme that serves an auxiliary function alone is not meant to be a writing system in the strict sense of the word. Since traditional Chinese characters stand unaffected as the basic units of writing, such new schemes provide only a partial solution to the problems associated with the above mentioned characters.

3.2 Supplementary

A supplementary scheme is one that is intended to be used together with the traditional script in texts, seeking to improve on the latter or performing functions for which the latter is ill-suited.

Schemes of this category mainly perform the function in two different ways. Phonetic symbols are used either in juxtaposition with characters, creating a new type of symbol that is composed of two parts (i.e., the character and the phonetic symbols that annotate its sound), or they are used in the partial replacement of characters, resulting in a mixed writing system in the same text. Schemes of this type are best exemplified by *kana* in Japanese (Miller 1967; Shibatani 1990). Japanese *hana* can be attached to *kanji*, Chinese characters, to annotate the pronunciation of the latter, mainly in texts targeted for beginners. It is also used to encode functional words and grammatical morphemes as well as other words that either do not have adequate character representation or do not engender ambiguity among homonyms.

Roles similar to those of *kana* were intended for a large number of schemes in phonetic writing of Chinese, most notably ZZ and GR. Consider ZZ, for example. Most of its chief designers had studied in Japan and presumably drew inspiration from the Japanese writing system (cf. Li 1934). The role originally envisaged for the scheme was more ambitious than the auxiliary one later sanctioned by the government. The newly designed ZZ was intended to supplement the character script in the same way that *kana* does *kanji* in Japanese. Li Jinxi, one of the active participants in this work, advocated that the characters should always be accompanied by ZZ as the annotating symbols in all publications. This view was equivalent to suggesting that the traditional matrices in print be replaced by a new type comprising characters in juxtaposition with ZZ symbols. Such a change would either result in a new type of writing system that is an alternative to the character script, with the former used in printing and the latter in handwriting, or, as Li once admitted, when, under government auspices, constant contact familiarized people with the new matrix, ZZ could itself acquire the status of a full-fledged writing system.

On the other hand, there is also strong support for a hybrid writing system composed of the traditional script and a supplementary one like GR or *Pinyin*, similar to that of Japanese, where *kanji* are used side by side with *kana* or *romanji* in the same text. The most obvious advantage of such an approach is the drastic reduction of the number of characters to be used in Chinese, considerably alleviating the burden of learners. It is also contended that, by using a mixture of two writing systems, Modern Written Chinese (MWC) would be better equipped to deal with the translation of an ever increasing number of proper names and scientific and technological terminology from other languages (cf. Wu and Ma 1988; Zhou 1979). In contrast to high transferability of such names and terms among languages with a phonographic writing, much burden and chaos is incurred in reducing them to Chinese characters, due both to the considerable size of the task and the inconsistency among translators with regard to which particular characters are used in the rendition.

Furthermore, this type of hybrid writing also stands in good stead when it comes to writing non-Mandarin dialects. As discussed in detail in Chen (1993,1996), the language known as Chinese is composed of seven major dialect groups that are mutually unintelligible: Mandarin, Wu, Hakka, Min, Gan, Xiang, and Cantonese, with the last six customarily called the Southern dialects.① Each of these dialect groups are composed of subgroups. The dialects differ most remarkably in phonology, and only somewhat in lexicon and grammar. The language known as MWC is based on the vocabulary and grammar of Northern Mandarin. When native speakers of non-Mandarin dialects learn MWC, they are actually learning a written language with a vocabulary and grammar that may be quite different from that of their native tongue. Unless they have learned to speak Mandarin in addition to

① Some scholars in Chinese linguistics disagree on the classification of the Chinese dialects (cf. Atlas 1987; Ji 1988).

their native dialect, the attainment of literacy requires more effort for them than it does for native speakers of Mandarin. There have been intermittent attempts at writing the non-Mandarin dialects, producing several novels in which the vernacular has been recorded in dialects like Wu, Cantonese, and Min. However, since the traditional script best suits the representation of Northern Mandarin, many words in the Southern dialects, especially the high frequency function words, have no conventional representation in characters. As established in an investigation in Xu (1992:129), this is the case with twenty-five percent of the 200 most basic words in a Min dialect spoken in Taiwan. The past decade has witnessed a resurgence of interest in writing the non-Mandarin dialects, most notably Southern Min in Taiwan, in the context of rapidly changing social, economic, and political circumstances (cf. Cheng 1989; Hong 1992; Huang 1993). A few phonetic systems have been proposed to serve the supplementary function of representing the words that have no appropriate characters, creating a text characterized by the mixture of traditional characters and symbols of a phonographic writing system. Such a mixture of writing systems in texts would eliminate many of the problems of writing in the Southern dialects and provide easier access to literacy for native speakers of those dialects.

There are different views on mixing the traditional script and a supplementary one in the same text. While many people believe that such writing integrates what is best in both the logographic and phonographic systems by striking a balance between the ease of writing from the writer's perspective and ease of recognition from the reader's perspective, there are also many people who maintain that such a writing system adds to the difficulty of writing and printing, and, moreover, destroys the aesthetic beauty of the traditional script by disrupting the equidimentional arrangement of characters. The benefit acquired from the reduction of characters, in their view, is not substantial enough to offset the disadvantages caused by a mixture of scripts (cf. Hong 1992).

It is clear that a supplementary system goes further toward solving the problems of the traditional script than an auxiliary one. Unlike the latter, the former tends to have a considerable impact upon the character script, either substituting a new type of composite symbols for the traditional characters, or reducing the number of characters normally used in writing by customarily encoding some of the words or morphemes in phonetic symbols. This is exactly what has happened in Japanese, where many words erstwhile written in *kanji* are now encoded in *kana*, and a restriction has been imposed on the number of *kanji* in use (cf. Miller 1967; Shibatani 1990). Given the implications of such a writing system for the traditional script, schemes proposed to play a supplementary role have been typically regarded more cautiously by government language planning institutions than have the auxiliary systems.① So far, no governmental language planning institutions in China, either under the Qing dynasty or the Kuomintang government in Taiwan, or the Communist government in the PRC, have endorsed any phonographic system with a supplementary role.

3.3 Alternative

A scheme of this category is designed to serve the full range of purposes expected of a regular writing system, thus enabling it to stand as an alternative to the traditional script.

---

① For example, the language planning institution of the Kuomintang government renamed ZZ and GR as *Zhuyin Fuhao* 'sound-annotating symbols' and *Yiyin Fuhao* 'transcription symbols', respectively, in 1930 and 1940 to make it clear that they were not meant to play anything other than auxiliary roles.

In contrast to the auxiliary or supplementary systems, an alternative one takes a more radical approach to the problems of the traditional script. It does not initiate any change into the logographic writing per se. Instead, being an autonomous writing system that is presumably easier to learn and use, it is intended to compete with the traditional script across the wide range of applications that, for millennia, have been monopolized by the latter.

Of the approximately 2,000 schemes of phonetic writing for Chinese, a considerable number were primarily designed to perform such an alternative role. Most romanization schemes designed by Protestant missionaries in the eighteenth and nineteenth centuries actually served as a regular writing system that was used to translate the Bible and other religious materials (cf. Ni 1948b; DeFrancis 1950). Distinct systems were designed for the major dialects, mainly Wu, Cantonese, Southern Min, in addition to Mandarin. The first phonetic writing system designed by a native Chinese, that of Lu Zhuangzhang in 1892, sought to provide a writing system that offered easier access to literacy. Of the five most influential schemes noted above, GZ, developed by Wang Zhao, was the first scheme in this category that won widespread support among the literati and the general public. Within ten years of its publication, more than 60,000 copies of books written in the new writing system were sold; they covered a wide range of disciplines that included ethics, history, geography, geology, botany, and zoology (Ni 1948a, 1948b). As explained by Wang Zhao, it was meant to be a writing system employed to record the vernacular speech for everyday use by those who had neither the time nor economic means to learn the traditional script. Wang Zhao expected that GZ and the traditional script would coexist for a long period of time, leaving users to choose between them on the basis of their particular circumstances (cf. Wang 1900).

Although its designers had in mind an even more ambitious role than the alternative one, as will be discussed shortly, LSW in the 1930s and 1940s served a role similar to that of GZ, but on a much larger scale. Altogether thirteen schemes of LSW were designed for the major dialects of Chinese, with the most popular one based on Northern Mandarin. It was first taught to about 100,000 Chinese expatriates working in the Far Eastern areas of the Soviet Union in the early 1930s, and was then extensively learned in mainland China. According to the estimate in Ni (1948b), more than 200,000 copies of textbooks, readers, and reference books printed in LSW were sold within a short period of time. In the mid-1930s there were more than thirty newspapers and magazines printed in LSW.

The alternative writing systems exemplified by GZ and LSW hold two main advantages over the traditional script, both of which derive from the contrast between the phonological nature of the former and the logographic nature of the latter. First, the new writing systems that employ the roman alphabet are much easier to learn and more convenient to use. As reported in Ni (1949:141), it takes only 300-400 hours for complete illiterates to learn to read and write in LSW, ten days for junior high school students, and three days for senior high school and college students. In contrast, it takes at least two years to gain literacy in the traditional Chinese script (cf. Wu and Ma 1988:75). Second, the new writing systems are more flexible than characters in that they allow more latitude in the dialectal base that is represented in writing. Whereas the traditional Chinese characters are best suited to encode Northern Mandarin, the newly designed schemes, with slight modifications, can be conveniently used to reduce all of the remarkably differing Chinese dialects to writing, if there is such a need.

The situation in which two or more writing systems are used to represent a single language (or varieties thereof) is generally known as digraphia in the recent linguistic literature (cf. Dale 1980; DeFrancis 1984b). As mentioned earlier, the alternative system is intended to coexist with the traditional one. A natural development of such a situation is the creation of a division of labor between the two types of writings, resulting in what can be called partial digraphia. Partial digraphia was actually envisaged by all the designers of the schemes in question. When Lu Zhuangzhang published his first scheme of phonetic writing in 1898, he maintained that the characters should continue to be used, but only for functions related to the classics. Wang Zhao also suggested that while both GZ and the traditional script can be used in translation from Western languages, the latter alone should be used in learning the classics (cf. Wang 1900). A similar view was proposed by the proponents of LSW in the 1930s (cf. Ni 1949).

It is contended that schemes of an alternative nature offer a solution to the dilemma that faces a modernizing China. On the one hand, as the traditional script has been the medium of the literature of one of the most time-honored and magnificent civilizations of the world, it is unimaginable that such a tradition should become largely inaccessible to the Chinese people because of a switch from characters to a new script. On the other hand, the fact remains that, compared with the acquisition of a phonographic system, the acquisition of the traditional script consumes too much time and energy for learners, which they could use for other more worthwhile purposes. Digraphia, it is proposed, is a viable solution.

While the proponents of all such alternative schemes advocated a digraphic situation in which the proposed phonographic system is used concurrently with the traditional characters, they differ with regard to the long-term prospects. Some see the partial digraphia as a transitional arrangement that will ultimately lead to the abolition of characters. As the proponents of LSW proclaimed, it was their intention that the new phonographic scheme would eventually become the sole official writing system for Chinese, and that characters, an alleged product of the Chinese elite that has disadvantaged working people, should be abolished. Some, however, assign a more permanent status to the characters. They believe that the historical role played by the traditional script makes it irreplaceable for certain functions. As a result, even though the phonographic system may succeed as a regular writing system that is learned by school children to gain literacy, they will need to go on to learn the character script if they wish to engage in research in academic fields.①

In spite of the ardent advocacy of partial digraphia and the sporadic large scale promotions of schemes for this category in the course of language reform during the past century, schemes that were intended

① As a matter of fact, all year one students in China learn *Pinyin* as an auxiliary system and are normally quite proficient in it. As they advance to higher grades and learn more characters, however, they generally lose their skills in *Pinyin*. The regression in *Pinyin* proficiency has elicited little surprise or regret from educators and linguists. In a sense, *Pinyin* is meant to serve approximately the same role in schools that the ITA system in the United States and England did. Rather than being treated as full-fledged writing systems, they are intended to function as auxiliary systems that facilitate transfer to the traditional writing system (cf. Venezky 1970). One of the major reasons that such an auxiliary system fails to become a regular one is that there are very few publications printed in it. Although some publications in China, including a monthly newspaper, are printed exclusively in *Pinyin*, they have had scarcely any impact upon the general public. Without sufficient opportunity to practice *Pinyin*, and without enough motivation, *Pinyin* drops out of use before students graduate from primary schools. An experiment has been in progress in Heilongjiang Province in northeastern China that attempts to develop *Pinyin* into a regular writing system that would enable school children to gain literacy in this phonographic writing several years earlier than in the character script. Students are encouraged to write in *Pinyin* from year one, and devote much less time than usual to learning characters. At the same time, they are provided with a large amount of reading material printed in *Pinyin*. Such measures are intended to develop their writing skills from an early age without being hindered by the difficulties involved in learning the characters and, at the same time, help to retain their proficiency in *Pinyin* as an alternative writing system after they have later acquired literacy in the traditional script (cf. Ding et al. 1983).

to serve an alternative function have seldom survived more than two decades. There appear to be two primary factors underlying the failure to attain their goal. The first is the inadequacy of the proposed schemes to perform functions beyond an auxiliary or supplementary one. It is argued that, given the present structure of MWC as elaborated in Chen (1993), the new schemes like GR, LSW, or *Pinyin* cannot perform as wide a range of functions as the character script, mainly because they are poorly equipped to deal with the large number of homophonous morphemes,mostly from Classical Chinese, which, due to the rich variety of stylistic effects they convey, constitute an integral part of MWC. Without the differentiating capabilities of the graphically distinct characters in the logographic script, it is difficult for the phonographic schemes to write in anything other than a coarse, wordy style, approximating the vernacular of the most uneducated people. Secondly, the language planning institutions of successive Chinese governments, as well as a number of individual scholars, have been concerned about the prospect of distinct writings for different dialects made possible by the new schemes, fearing that this could disrupt the uniformity of the written language, which they allege has served as an important bond of unity for the Chinese nation-state. As discussed in detail in Chen (1996), then negative attitude toward such schemes on their part is a very important factor contributing to their failure.

3.4 Superseding

A scheme of this category is designed to supersede the traditional script, reducing it to disuse and oblivion, as in the case of what the Vietnamese Quoc Ngu and the Korean Hangul (partially in South Korea and completely in North Korea) did to the Chinese characters in their respective languages (cf. DeFrancis 1984a, 1989; Coulmas 1989).

Proponents of such a writing scheme hold the most radical view toward Chinese characters. It is argued that characters are irremediably difficult to learn and use, and the best way to solve this problem is to replace them by a phonographic system that would better meet the needs of a modernizing society. As discussed above, LSW was intended to play exactly such a role, although the proponents were resigned to the fact that in the short term LSW could at best fulfill the role of an alternative system.

For a new writing system to successfully supersede an old one, it has to fulfil the minimum requirement of being able to serve the major functions of the superseded one. In the case of Chinese, it means that, in addition to being the medium for MWC, the writing system has to be capable of serving both the users of Classical Chinese and the speakers of various contemporary Chinese dialects.

As discussed in detail in Chen (1996), the great majority of words in Classical Chinese are monosyllabic. Given the limited inventory of syllables, the number of homophonic words is too high to allow for a phonetic writing. Although it has been suggested that the most important classics in Chinese can be translated into Modern Chinese and are thus amenable to representation by phonetic writing, it is doubtful whether the particular literary styles in which so many works are composed are truly translatable, not to mention the tremendous amount of work that would be involved in such a project.

A phonetic writing system, as discussed above, cannot serve the speakers of mutually unintelligible dialects in the same way as the traditional script. Two possible scenarios may emerge if the characters are abolished in favor of a phonographic scheme. One is that in which the government stipulates that, in the place of the characters, a single phonographic writing based on a prestige dialect, most likely the Beijing dialect, is to be used as the official writing system for speakers of all Chinese dialects. Because of the direct speech-writing connection, such a system would also function to promote the standard dialect across dialect areas. As revealed in Zhou (1992), this scenario is precisely the one envisaged in the initial stage of designing *Pinyin* in the early 1950s. The second scenario is one in which, with or without the endorsement of the government, distinct systems are developed for the major dialects; then, after undergoing a process of standardization, the latter systems would become full-fledged written languages in the geographical areas in which the respective dialects predominate (cf. Cheng 1989; Hong 1992; Huang 1993). As noted above, such a scenario may be unacceptable to language planners who are concerned with the uniformity of the writing system and the written language.

In spite of continuous calls since the Literary Revolution at the end of the first decade of this century to abolish the traditional Chinese characters in favor of a phonographic writing system, it seems more unlikely now than ever before that any form of phonetic writing would ever succeed in superseding the traditional script. Although those who argue for the abolition of Chinese characters support the possibility of such a move by citing what happened to Chinese characters in Vietnamese or Korean, it is observed in the literature that Chinese characters were replaced only in other languages, languages that did not have their own indigenous writing systems and borrowed the Chinese script to fill that void (cf. Coulmas 1989; 1992). In fact, no instance has ever been found of a native logographic system being superseded by a phonographic system for it. It is also doubtful whether it would succeed with Chinese in the future.

During recent years, the validity of the fundamental theory

underlying the movement for phoneticization of Chinese has been called into question. It has been argued that, although characters are difficult to learn for beginners, once mastered, the script is better than a phonetic writing from the point of view of reading, since it provides more direct and quicker access to meaning. In otherwords, logography is a desirable feature for readers, since it offers greater graphic differentiation and thus facilitates more efficient decoding (cf. Venezky1970; Sampson 1985; inter alia).

Furthermore, as Chinese has become a language that extends beyond the confines of one country, it is becoming more and more difficult, if not impossible, for any language planning institution to suggest a measure as drastic as the abolition of the characters. According to a recent survey, there are thirty million ethnic Chinese who live outside mainland China, Hong Kong, and Taiwan. To the extent that the Chinese language, both spoken and written, serves as an important link among ethnic Chinese, any such move in language reform would have great impact on and strong feedback from overseas Chinese communities. Any drastic change to the writing system would have social and political repercussions, not only in China, but outside China as well, that could prove too serious to ignore. As often discussed, the simplification of characters that has been effected since the 1950s has already caused some inconveniences to mainland China in its dealing with other Chinese communities. A measure as drastic as the abolition of characters is therefore impractical in the foreseeable future.

Finally, with the increasingly widespread use of personal computers equipped with Chinese word processing facilities, learning and writing characters may well be less daunting than it used to be. Since it is much easier to write Chinese characters on computers than on a piece of paper, people who were turned away by the complicated script now tend to use more characters than before. Put in simple terms, computers may save characters, as Gottlieb (1993) observes is happening in Japan right now.

4. Conclusion

While one may think that in designing a new writing system there are only technical issues, in fact there are a range of linguistic and extralinguistic factors. As complicated as this undertaking may be for a previously unwritten language (cf. Smalley 1964; Sjoberg 1966; Venezky 1970; Mithun 1992), it is even more daunting when it involves a language like Chinese that has an entrenched literary tradition. For the previously unwritten language, the primary goal is to provide a new writing system that establishes the first instance of literacy in that language; whereas for a language with a long written tradition, a new writing system will perform one or more of the four projected functions in relation to the traditional writing system. As remarked in Venezky (1970), while political and socio-cultural factors must be considered in the design of new writing systems for unwritten languages, they are subordinate to the linguistic, psychological, and pedagogical variables that determine an optimal system, or range of systems, for the language and speakers involved. On the other hand, as demonstrated in this paper, when the goal is to reform or replace an existing writing system, it seems that political and sociocultural factors carry at least as much weight as technical considerations in determining the fate of the proposed schemes. Although four functions have been conceived in the design of thousands of writing schemes for Chinese during the past century, only those intended for the auxiliary role have achieved success. As schemes to perform the other three projected functions would all affect the traditional script in one way or another, the resistance they have encountered testifies to the difficulty of any attempt to change the status quo of a well-established writing system.

References

Atlas. 1987. *Language Atlas of China*, Compiled by Australian Academy of Humanities and the Chinese Academy of Social Sciences. Hong Kong: Longman Group (Far East) Ltd.

Chen, Ping. 1993. Modern Written Chinese in development, *Language in Society* 22(4):505-37.

Chen, Ping. 1996. Towards a phonographic writing system of Chinese: A case study in writing reform, *International Journal of the Sociology of Language* 122:1-46.

Coulmas, Florian. 1989. *The Writing Systems of the World*, London: Basil Blackwell.

Coulmas, Florian. 1992. Writing systems, In: William Wright, ed., *International Encyclopedia of Linguistics*, New York: Oxford University Press, 253-257.

Dale, Ian R. H. 1980. Digraphia, *International Journal of the Sociology of Language* 26:5-13.

DeFrancis, John. 1950. *Nationalism and Language Reform in China*, Princeton: Princeton University Press.

DeFrancis, John. 1984a. *The Chinese Language: Fact and Fantasy*, Honolulu: University of Hawaii Press.

DeFrancis, John. 1984b. Digraphia, *Word* 35(1):59-66.

DeFrancis, John. 1989. *Visible Speech: The Diverse Oneness of Writing Systems*, Honolulu: University of Hawaii Press.

Ding, Yicheng, et al. 1983. "Zhuyin shizi, tiqian duxie" shiyan baogao [Report on the experiment of learning characters with sound annotation and reading and writing ahead of schedule], *Yuwen Xiandaihua* [*Language Modernization*] Vol. 8,1985, Shanghai: Zhishi Chubanshe, 134-148.

Fang, Shiduo. 1969. *Wushi Nian Lai Zhongguo Guoyu Yundong Shi* [*History of the National Language Movement in China During the Past Fifty Years*]. 2nd edition. Taipei:Guoyu Ribaoshe.

Gottlieb, Nanette. 1993. Written Japanese and the word processor, *Japan Forum* (April 1993):115-132.

Hong, Weiren. 1992. *Taiwan Yuyan Weiji* [*Language Crisis in Taiwan*], Taipei: Qianwei Chubanshe.

Huang, Shuanfan. 1993. *Yuyan, Shehui yu Zuqun Yishi* [*Language, Society and Group Consciousness*], Taipei: Wenhe Chuban Youxian Gongsi.

Ji, Xianling. ed. 1988. *Zhongguo Da Baike Quanshu, Yuyan Weizi Juan [Encyclopedia Sinica, Volume of Linguistics*], Beijing: Zhongguo Da Baike Quanshu Chubanshe.

Li, Jinxi. 1934. *Guoyu Yundong Shigang* [*Outline of the History of the National Language Movement*], Shanghai: Shangwu Yinshuguan.

Lu, Zhuangzhang. 1892. *Yimuliaoran Chujie: Zhongguo Qieyin Xin Zi Xia Qiang* [*First Steps in Complete Understanding at a Glance: A New Chinese Script for the Xiamen Dialect*], Reprinted in 1956. Beijing: Wenzi Gaige Chubanshe.

Miller, Roy Andrew. 1967. *The Japanese Language*, Chicago: University of Chicago Press.

Mithun, Marianne. 1992. Orthography planning, In: William Wright, ed., *International Encyclopedia of Linguistics*, New York: Oxford University Press, 141-144.

Ni, Haishu. 1948a. *Zhongguo Pinyin Wenzi Gailun* [*Introduction to Phonetic Writing in China*], Shanghai: Shidai Shubao Chubanshe.

Ni, Haishu. 1948b. *Zhongguo Pinyin Wenzi Yundong Shi* [*History of the Movement of Phonetic Writing in China*], Shanghai: Shidai Shubao Chubanshe.

Ni, Haishu. ed. 1949. *Zhongguo Yuwen de Xinsheng* [*Rebirth of the Chinese Language*], Shanghai:Shidai Shubao Chubanshe.

Proceedings. 1957. *Di Yi Ci Quanguo Wenzi Gaige Huiyi Wenjian Huibian* [*Proceedings of theFirst National Conference on Language Reform*], Beijing: Wenzi Gaige Chubanshe.

Qiu, Xigui. 1988. *Wenzixue Gaiyao* [*Introduction to the Study of Script*], Beijing: Shangwu Yinshuguan.

Qu, Qiubai. 1931. Luomazi de Xin Zhongguowen Haishi Rouma Zi de Xin Zhongguowen [New Chinese writing in latin script or in the sickening script], In: Haishu Ni, ed., *Zhongguo Yuwen de Xinsheng* [*Rebirth of Chinese Language*], 1949, Shanghai: Shidai Shuban Chubanshe, 29-47.

Sampson, Geoffrey. 1985. *Writing Systems: A Linguistic Introduction*, London:

Hutchinson.

Shibatani, Masayoshi. 1990. *The Languages of Japan*, Cambridge: Cambridge University Press.

Sjoberg, Andree F. 1966. Socio-cultural and linguistic factors in the development of writing systems for preliterate peoples, In: William Bright, ed., *Sociolinguistics*, The Hague: Mouton, 260-276.

Smalley, William A., et al. 1964. *Orthography Studies: Articles on New Writing Systems*. London: The United Bible Societies & Amsterdam: The North-Holland Publishing Company.

Su, Peicheng. 1992. Xiandai hanzi yanjiu jianshu [Survey of research on Modern Chinese characters], *Yuwen Jianshe* [*Language Planning*] 7/1992:6-14.

Venezky, Richard L. 1970. Principles for the design of practical writing systems, *Anthropological Linguistics* 12(7):256-70.

Wang, Zhao. 1900. "Guanhua Hesheng Zimu" Xu [Introduction to the Phonetic Alphabet of Mandarin], In: Haishu Ni, ed., 1958, *Qingmo Wenzi Gaige Wenji* [*Writings on Language Reform During Final Years of Qing Dynasty*], Beijing: Wenzi Gaige Chubanshe, 19-23

Wu, Yu-chang [Wu Yuzhang]. 1958. Report on the current tasks of reforming the written language and the draft scheme for a Chinese phonetic alphabet, In: *Reform of the Chinese Written Language*, Beijing: Foreign Languages Press, 30-54.

Wu, Zhankun and Guofan Ma. 1988. *Hanzi and Hanzi Gaige Shi* [*Chinese Characters and the History of Chinese Character Reform*], Changsha: Hunan Renmin Chubanshe.

Yin, Binyong. 1991. *Xiandai Hanzi de Dingliang Yanjiu* [*Quantitative Studies on Modern Chinese Characters*], Yuwen Jianshe 11/1991:19-21.

Zhou, Youguang. 1979. *Hanzi Gaige Gailun* [*Introduction to Chinese Character Reform*]. 3rd edition, Beijing: Wenzi Gaige Chubanshe.

Zhou, Youguang. 1992. *Zhongguo Yuwen Zonghengtan* [*Aspects of the Chinese Language*], Beijing:Renmin Jiaoyu Chubanshe.

汉语新创书写系统的四种功能规划

提　要　过去数百年间设计了数以千计的汉语新文字方案，从与传统汉字系统关系的角度来看，可以根据这些新文字方案的设计意图和所拟功能将它们分为四个主要类型–辅助，补充、并行和取代。这四种类型的新文字方案在实际推广和使用过程中面对的问题不尽相同，涉及语言、心理、教学、政治和社会文化等种种方面的因素，本文对这些因素逐一加以分析，并指出这些问题的根源所在。
关键词 音意文字 标音文字 文字改革

(This article was first published in *Anthropological Linguistics* 36(3), 366-381, in 1994. Permission by University of Nebraska Press to reprint the article in the present volume is gratefully acknowledged.)

Language policy in Hong Kong before July 1, 1997

Abstract Hong Kong is characterized by trilingualism (English, Cantonese and *Putonghua*) and diglossia (Written English and Written Chinese). Language policy in Hong Kong before July 1, 1997 is divided into two periods — before 1974, and between 1974 and 1997. English was stipulated as the official language of Hong Kong in the Treaty of Tianjin between China and Britain in 1856. From then onward until the 1980s, English stood as the de jure and de facto official language for all administrative, legislative and judicial functions. In 1974 the Hong Kong government promulgated the Official Language Ordinance, which declared the English and the Chinese language to be the official languages of Hong Kong for the purposes of communication between the government or any public officer and members of the public. Other than granting the Chinese language de jure status as an official language in addition to English in the 1974 Ordinance, the government had no plan to adopt concrete measures to ensure that the Chinese language would enjoy equality of use at high levels. It was only after the signing of the Joint Declaration between China and Britain in 1984 that bilingualism in English and Chinese for all high level functions began to receive serious attention from the government, marking the beginning of the Chinese language becoming a de factor official language in Hong Kong.
Keywords language policy; language planning; trilingualism; diglossia; Hong Kong

1. A sociolinguistic profile of Hong Kong

Hong Kong was a small Chinese town with a population of 7,450 in

1841 when it was occupied by the British troops during the Opium War (1840-1842). It was ceded to the British in the next year after China lost the war and was forced to sign the Treaty of Nanjing. It returned to the sovereignty of China on July 1, 1997, and has become a special administrative region of China. Hong Kong has undergone tremendous growth during the past one and a half centuries. According to the latest census in 1996, it has a population of 6,218,000, with ethnic Chinese comprising about 98 per cent (cf. Bacon-Shore and Bolton 1998 for a historical profile).

The 1996 census also found that Cantonese is the most common language/dialect spoken at home by 89 per cent of the population. Another 7 per cent claim that they can speak the dialect. About one quarter of the population can speak *putonghua* 'common speech', the standard form of Modern Chinese that is based upon Northern Mandarin, either as the usual language/dialect or as another language/dialect. English is spoken at home by 3 per cent of the population while another 35 per cent claim that they can speak the language. While Cantonese differs remarkably from *putonghua* in terms of pronunciation, vocabulary, and to a lesser extent, grammar, speakers of the two varieties of Chinese share the same written standard, Modern Written Chinese, which is based upon Northern Mandarin (Chen 1996, 1999). A written code that approaches vernacular Cantonese is also found in magazines and newspapers. Unlike the standard written Chinese, it is generally considered to be too casual and vulgar to be appropriate for serious writing (Bauer 1988, Chen 1996). When the term 'Chinese language' is used in Hong Kong, it usually refers to Cantonese in spoken form, but Modern Written Chinese in written form. I will follow this usage in this chapter unless otherwise specified.

Hong Kong is thus characterized by both trilingualism and

diglossia. English, spoken and written, has been the traditional High language since the beginning of the colonial era up to the end of the twentieth century, serving as the norm for almost all administrative, legislative, judiciary, and high-level trade and business purposes. Cantonese has been the Low language, used by local Chinese residents at home, among friends, and for daily transactions other than those that call for the use of English. It has gained considerable power and prestige since July 1, 1997, particularly in the political arena. *Putonghua* has enjoyed increasing popularity since the early 1980s, and is frequently used on public occasions where people from the mainland are among the audience. Among Chinese who are bilingual in English and Cantonese, code mixing is extremely frequent in speech, particularly with topics involving a heavy amount of professional terminology and in places like offices and universities (Gibbons 1979; T'sou 1986; Yu 1986b; T'sou et al 1992).

The current linguistic situation ensued partly as a result of the official language policy of the colonial government of Hong Kong before July 1, 1997, and partly as a result of the interaction of other social, political, economical, educational and cultural factors during the period.

2. Language policy before 1974

English was explicitly stipulated as the official language of Hong Kong in the Treaty of Tianjin between China and Britain in 1856. From then onward until the 1980s, English stood as the de jure and de facto sole official language for all administrative, legislative and judicial functions. Almost all government documents, reports and directives were published in English, as were all laws adopted by the legislature. Only very few of the official announcements that were targeted at local residents on the lower rung of society were bilingual in English and Chinese. Court proceedings were conducted in English. A sound command of the English language was a prerequisite for admission into the civil service, while proficiency in Chinese was not a requirement at all. The great majority of the senior posts in the government were held by British expatriates. As English was both the statutory and the working official language, they seldom bothered to learn the local Chinese language. For the few local Chinese who were admitted into the higher echelon of the civil service, their performance depended crucially upon their competence in spoken and written English.

The colonial policy of promoting English rather than Chinese in Hong Kong was also implemented in relation to the medium of instruction in secondary schools. Since the great majority of the local residents were migrants or children of migrants from adjacent Cantonese-speaking areas in mainland China, Cantonese was the mother tongue of almost all school children in Hong Kong. While the overwhelming majority of Hong Kong primary schools adopted Cantonese as the medium of instruction, secondary schools fell into two major categories, the Chinese-medium and the English-medium. The former are known as Chinese schools, and the latter as Anglo-Chinese schools. In the early days of colonial rule, the government paid little attention to the education of local residents. The first school financially supported by the government, the Central School, was founded in 1866. The official policy of promoting English in schools at the expense of Chinese was formulated at the Conference on the Teaching of English at Government Schools in 1878. English language education was taken to be of primary importance in government-funded schools, while

Chinese was made an optional subject. Years later, the Education Commission further recommended that school children in the lower grades should be taught Chinese and English, and those over Year 14 should be taught English only. In 1902, another education commission report concluded that, in the best interests of the British Empire, the Hong Kong Government should encourage and support the development of the Anglo-Chinese schools rather than Chinese schools. In 1911, the University of Hong Kong was founded, with English stipulated as the medium of instruction. In comparison to the outdated curriculum in the great majority of the Chinese schools, the English-medium schools offered a modern education after the Western model, which was more attractive to most of the local residents. According to records, enrollment in English schools increased 60-fold between 1901 and 1911 whereas that for Chinese schools increased by ten times only (cf. W. So 1986; Yu 1986a:6).

Concurrent with the general surge of nationalism in all parts of China after the founding of the Republic of China in 1912, there was renewed enthusiasm for Chinese education which was sustained well after World War Two. A large number of Chinese schools were set up, many of which followed basically the same pattern as those in the adjacent Guangdong province in mainland China. The situation changed drastically after the end of the 1940s. On the one hand, there was much less communication between Hong Kong and mainland China when Britain joined with other Western countries in adopting a policy of containment after the founding of the People's Republic of China in 1949. Since traditionally Chinese schools in Hong Kong looked to the mainland for resources in terms of curriculum development, teaching materials, and staff support, the sudden termination of close contact had left the Chinese schools in an impoverished position. On the other hand, as Hong Kong grew into a cosmopolitan city that boasted a strong manufacturing industry and bustling international trade and finance, English and a westernized training became increasingly important for social mobility. Pragmatic local residents wanted their children to receive a sound training in the English language in schools so that they would have an edge in an extremely competitive society.

Over this period, several proposals were made by educators to adopt the native tongue as the medium of instruction in schools. All were rejected by the government on the grounds that parents of school children in Hong Kong preferred the English medium to the Chinese medium, as well as that of the assumed importance of English in the international and local community. The Chinese University of Hong Kong was founded in 1963, primarily to provide continued education in the Chinese medium for graduates of the Chinese schools. Although the policy of bilingualism was adopted by the University from its early days, with some subjects taught in English and some in Chinese, the higher proficiency in English of graduates from English-medium schools made them more competitive in matriculation examinations and after admission (Yu 1986a:15). As is evident from the statistics provided later in this paper, the enrollment in Chinese schools has continued to decline since the founding of the Chinese University of Hong Kong.

Starting from the late 1960s, there was another surge of nationalism among local residents of Hong Kong. The Chinese language served as an important symbol around which enhanced awareness of ethnic identity built up. In what was known as the Chinese Language Movement, there was a strong and growing demand for higher status and more widespread use of Chinese. The movement gained momentum into the 1970s. Following the assumption of the seat at the UN by the PRC, and the visit to China by the U.S. president Richard Nixon in 1972, China returned to the main stage of the world. Encouraged by the series of developments that enhanced the international status of mainland China, and with the general support of local residents, participants of the Chinese Language Movement proposed that the Chinese language should be granted the status of official language in Hong Kong. Responding to the rising sentiment over the language issue, the Official Language Ordinance was promulgated by the Hong Kong government in 1974 to provide for the official languages of Hong Kong and for their status and use. Clause 3 of the Ordinance reads as follows:

> (1) The English and Chinese languages are declared to be the official languages of Hong Kong for the purpose of communication between the Government or any public officer and members of the public;
>
> (2) The official languages possess equal status and, subject to the provisions of this Ordinance, enjoy equality of use for the purpose set out in subsection (1).

From the early 1970s, meanwhile, Chinese was used increasingly in the administrative activities of the Hong Kong government, motivated both by the rising demand from the local community and by considerations of improved efficiency in communication between the government and local residents. In addition to the enactment of the Ordinance in 1974, according to James So (1986:3), the Hong Kong government's Chinese language policy from the early 1970s was to promote the widest possible use of Chinese in official business. Two years before the 1974 Ordinance was enacted, a Commissioner for Chinese Language was appointed to head the Chinese Language Branch (later renamed Chinese Language Division) within the government. The major function of the office was to translate government documents and correspondence, and to provide interpretation services to meetings of all councils, boards and committees attended by monolingual members or a public audience. From the 1970s, simultaneous interpretation was also provided for meetings of the Legislative Council, the Urban Council, the Regional Council, the District Boards and other statutory bodies which were conducted bilingually in English and Chinese (Liu 1986:1; J. So 1986:6).

The Ordinance, however, did not grant the Chinese language the same range of official use as English. It is stipulated in the Ordinance that every ordinance shall be enacted and published in the English language. Proceedings in the following courts may be conducted in either the Chinese language or the English language:

(1) Magistrates' Courts

(2) Any inquiry by a coroner

(3) Any Juvenile Court

(4) Any Labor Tribunal

(5) Any Tenancy Tribunal

(6) Any Small Claims Tribunal

(7) Any Immigration Tribunal

whereas proceedings in the Count of Appeal, the High Court, the District Court and any other court not specified in the Ordinance shall be conducted in the English language.

It is clear that bilingualism was not on the agenda of the Hong Kong government in the 1970s. Other than granting the Chinese language de jure status as an official language in addition to English in the 1974 Ordinance, the government had no plan to adopt concrete measures to ensure that the Chinese language would enjoy equality of use for executive, legislative, judicial and educational purposes at high levels. No modification to the language requirement was made in the recruitment of civil servants. The plea for a Chinese version of the legislation was largely ignored. In 1974, furthermore, the government declined the recommendation submitted by the Education Commission that Chinese, not English, should be the medium of instruction in the lower years of secondary school across the board to better accommodate Hong Kong students, most of whom found it difficult to learn all subjects in English after receiving training in all subjects in their native tongue when in primary schools. Aside from the alleged benefits that the current language policy brought to the local community, it was first and foremost the interests of the colonial government and the UK that underlay the policy which ensured that English enjoyed the monopoly of being the sole working language in Hong Kong.

3. Language policy 1974-1997

Substantial changes to the language policy occurred only after the signing of the Sino-British Joint Declaration in 1984, according to which Hong Kong would return to the sovereignty of China, and become a special administrative region in 1997. It is stated in the Joint Declaration that

> 'In addition to Chinese, English may also be used in organs of government and in the courts in the Hong Kong Special Administrative Region'.

It is further stipulated in Article 9 of the Basic Law of the Hong Kong Special Administrative Region of the People's Republic of China adopted on April 4, 1990 that 'In addition to the Chinese language, English may also be used as an official language by the executive authorities, legislature and judiciary of the Hong Kong Special Administrative Region.'

As evident from the above wording, the political will dictated that the Chinese language was to be the primary official language in Hong Kong after 1997, while promising to reserve official status for the English language.

After the signing of the Joint Declaration, a series of concrete measures was initiated by the Hong Kong government to prepare for the inevitable events of 1997. Among other social, political, administrative and educational reforms, bilingualism in English and Chinese for all high level administrative, legislative and judicial functions began to receive serious attention from the government, marking the beginning of the Chinese language becoming a de facto official language in Hong Kong.

3.1 Administration

From October 1985, all papers in the Office of the Executive and Legislative Councils were prepared and published in both English and Chinese. In 1987, the Official Language (Amendment) Ordinance 1987 was promulgated which was to replace the Official Language Ordinance 1974. It was stipulated in the 1987 Ordinance that all ordinances should be enacted and published in both official languages, thus conferring upon Chinese the status of a working official language as well as a statutory one. The use of Chinese in administration and legislature increased significantly after that. All government documents for public consumption were thereafter issued bilingually. English, however, was still the primary working language for communications within the government, with the Chinese version provided on some occasions for the benefit of junior staff with low English proficiency. It was also the primary working language in government advisory boards and committees. While the government began to stress bilingual proficiency in the recruitment of civil servants, with written Chinese added on as an optional subject in the recruitment examination of administrative officers from the mid-1980s, competence in English was still of paramount importance, particularly for positions above the intermediate level.

Promotion of the use of Chinese within the government began in the 1990s. It was reported that, as a result of the long-standing oversight of Chinese language proficiency, the competence of Chinese civil servants in written Chinese was far from being satisfactory. Generally speaking, they spoke Cantonese as their first language, but did not feel comfortable with reading and writing in Standard Modern Chinese. In the 1990s, up to the time of the handover to China, the colonial government's goal was that all people in public service should be fluent in Cantonese and English, and competent in written Chinese and English. It was further suggested that senior public servants should acquire proficiency in *putonghua*. Starting from 1995, proficiency in Chinese was stipulated as a requirement in the recruitment of civil servants.

From the early 1990s to 1997, local members of the legislative Council regularly spoke in their native language, Cantonese, at meetings of the Council, very much different from the situation before the 1980s when English was the norm on such occasions.

3.2 Legislature and Judiciary

Bilingualism started later and more hesitantly in the legal domain than in government administration. In the early 1970s, while recognizing the need to expand the use of the Chinese language in government functions in order to improve communication with local residents, the government rejected the recommendation by the Chinese Language Committee to translate the laws of Hong Kong into Chinese on the grounds that "it cannot be regarded as essential" and "is not a practical proposition" (Chan 1986:4). In the changed sociopolitical circumstances after 1984, legal bilingualism returned to the forefront of the political arena.

It was declared in the Sino-British Joint Declaration that, after Hong Kong returned to China in 1997, the judicial system previously practiced in Hong Kong would be maintained except for those changes consequent upon the establishment of the Court of Final Appeal of the Hong Kong Special Administrative Region. It was further stipulated in the Basic Law of Hong Kong that the laws previously in force in Hong Kong, that is, the common law, rules of equity, ordinances, subordinate legislation and customary law would be maintained, except for any that contravened the Basic Law, and would be subject to any amendment by the legislature of the Hong Kong Special Administrative Region.

Law never exists independently of language. If the judicial system of Hong Kong was to be by and large preserved after 1997, given the projected importance of Chinese language in post-colonial Hong Kong, it had to be ensured that the law was workable in Chinese (cf. T'sou et al 1992; Sin et al 1992). The Executive Council decided in July 1985 that an authentic Chinese version of the statute law of Hong Kong should be produced, which, according to Chan (1986:2), represented the first official pronouncement of a move into legal bilingualism. The adoption of the Official Languages Ordinance (Amendment) in 1987 marked the end of the dominance of English as the sole legal language for almost a century (Chan 1986:2).

Steps were taken to implement the decision of the Executive Council. Top priority was given to the drafting and enacting of new legislation in Hong Kong in the English and the Chinese language at the same time. Second priority went to the bilingual drafting of new subsidiary legislation in the case of ordinances that already had a Chinese version. Next in order of priorities was the translation of the existing ordinances into Chinese on a selective basis. The work of bilingual drafting and translation proceeded after that, although not in a very satisfactory way in terms of quantity and quality. Before April 1989, of the laws promulgated in the Gazette of Hong Kong, only the English version was legally binding. Between 1989 and 1992, 34 bilingual laws were enacted, which are stipulated as being equally authentic. Up to 1992, only about a quarter of the more than 500 laws of Hong Kong had been translated into Chinese, and the Chinese translation had yet to be accepted by the Legislative Council as being of binding legal value.

Cantonese had been the language used in the lower courts and the Labor Tribunal. Although it was stipulated in the 1974 Ordinance that legal proceedings in Magistrates' Courts could be conducted in Chinese, this seldom happened before 1989, partly due to the lack of Chinese judicial personnel, and partly due to the conscious or subconscious notion of legal colonialism—English was the "proper" language to be used in court, and Chinese was not "formal" enough, as observed by Chan (1986:47). After 1989, Chinese was increasingly used in the Magistrates' Courts and other courts. For the first time in the history of Hong Kong, a civil case was conducted in Chinese in the Hong Kong High Court in December 1995. In March 1996, the District Court for the first time in the colonial era heard a criminal case in Chinese. In 1996-1997, about 60 per cent of cases were conducted in Chinese at the Magistrates' Courts.

The transition to legal bilingualism was by no means smooth. The Chinese version of the legal system as we knew it in the colonial period would be constrained by the essential role played by the Common Law of Hong Kong, which was in English, and could not be translated in totality into Chinese. In spite of the tremendous practical difficulty in the translation of the laws in Hong Kong from English to Chinese, the task was essential for a sound legal system in Hong Kong after 1997. The proposal that the law of Hong Kong after 1997 might as well be in the English language instead of Chinese, which sounded reasonable from a pragmatic and technical perspective, went against all sociopolitical considerations and sentiments based on ethnic and nationalistic factors. Johannes Chan, a Hong Kong lawyer, represented the sentiment of the local residents when he argued that "legal bilingualism can and should be justified in terms of social needs and local circumstances, and it is simply unreasonable that the legal system of a predominantly Chinese society should be built upon one single language which is alien to a large majority of the population" (Chan 1986:5). How to incorporate the English-based common law into a Chinese legal system would stand as a task that would challenge the wisdom of legal professionals in post-colonial Hong Kong after 1997.

3.3 Education

In spite of all the practical difficulties involved, there was little opposition to bilingualism in administrative, legislative and judicial domains. More controversial was language policy on the medium of instruction in secondary schools. This was open to much debate and controversy in the education sector and in the wider Hong Kong society. As noted above, in spite of the rising nationalistic sentiment among the general public in Hong Kong, there was an increasing demand for English on the part of students and their parents. The number of students who opted for English-medium schools had been increasing steadily after the 1960s, with a corresponding decrease in the number of students in Chinese-medium schools, as evident from the following statistics of the ratio between enrollments in Chinese-medium vs. English-medium middle schools (data from Cheung 1985, and Hou 1996).

Table 1: Ratio between enrollments in Chinese-medium vs. English-medium secondary schools

Year	Chinese:English
1967	1:2.6
1970	1:3.2
1975	1:4.3
1980	1:7.2
1990s	1:10

The majority of educators in Hong Kong maintained that the choice of English as the medium of education in secondary schools might not serve the best interests of students. It was true that, generally speaking, students in the English-medium schools attained a higher proficiency in English than those in Chinese-medium schools. At the same time, this had serious undesirable consequences. The following are some of the major arguments against the use of English as the medium of instruction in secondary schools:

(1) it had an adverse effect on content teaching;

(2) it had an adverse effect on the teaching of the Chinese language and traditional Chinese values;

(3) it was a cause of social division.

Since almost all of the students in secondary schools received education in the native language of Cantonese in kindergarten and primary school, it was doubtful that English was as effective as the native language of students in content teaching. In spite of the fact that most students learned English as a subject in primary schools, it was estimated that only about 30 per cent of students in secondary schools reached a level that was high enough to enable them to fully benefit from the use of English in subject teaching. For the majority of students, it would have been more effective if content subjects had been taught in their native language rather in English.

Chinese was taught as a subject in the English-medium secondary schools. Given the limited number of class hours devoted to the subject, and low motivation on the part of many students toward the subject, there was much to be desired in the Chinese language standard of students in Hong Kong. Although comparative studies on the linguistic attainment of students from the major Chinese communities were lacking, it was generally felt that, as a cost of their better proficiency in English, the Chinese proficiency of students in Hong Kong was lower than that of students of the same group in other Chinese communities like mainland China and Taiwan. This, in turn, prevented them from gaining a better education in Chinese culture and heritage.

Meanwhile, the English proficiency level of students in the Chinese-medium schools was much lower than that in the English-medium schools, which might put the former group of students at a disadvantage in society, in spite of the fact that they might have attained comparable or even higher academic standards. As observed in Yu (1986b), in any case, it was socially divisive to have two school systems when one of them clearly led to fewer social and economic opportunities.

Thus, while bilingualism in English and Chinese was supposed to be the goal of language education in Hong Kong, the reality was far from satisfactory. Many proposals were raised to redress the undesirable situation surrounding the use of languages in secondary schools. It was suggested that Chinese be stipulated across the board as the medium of instruction in junior secondary forms or senior secondary forms as well. This was rejected by the Hong Kong government on the grounds that schools, students and parents should have the freedom to choose. Instead, the government proposed that the quality of both Chinese and English teaching be improved by providing more and better trained teachers, and a more efficient allocation of other resources. Acknowledging the fact that Chinese was a better medium of instruction for all Chinese students, especially in lower forms, it encouraged schools to move toward greater use of Chinese as the medium of instruction, and at the same time strengthen the teaching of English as a subject to compensate for the consequential reduction of exposure to English which might result in a fall in the standard of English. It adopted what was called a policy of "positive discrimination", which meant that the government should give additional resources to schools which used Chinese as the medium of instruction to strengthen their teaching of English (Wells 1986). The reaction by schools to the policy was lukewarm at best. Up to early 1997, of more than 400 secondary schools in Hong Kong, only 77 employed Chinese as the medium of instruction.

To alleviate the divisive effect of the two types of schools, the government attempted to end the distinction between Anglo-Chinese and Chinese secondary schools through encouraging schools to remove such references from names. From 1986 onward, the language medium indicator was removed from the Hong Kong Certificate of Education Examination result slip and from the certificate.

Investigations showed that, while textbooks were primarily in English in the English-medium schools, what was typically used in class was a mixed code of English and Cantonese, with widely varying ratios which depended on individual teachers and subjects. One study found that overall, 43 per cent of class talking time was in English, 48 per cent in Cantonese and 9 per cent in a mixture (Yu 1986b:6; also cf. Johnson 1998). In a report prepared by the Education Commission in 1990, it was proposed that the mixture of codes should be replaced by a clear and consistent language. Furthermore, since English was the medium of instruction in most universities in Hong Kong, and, in due course, the majority of secondary school graduates would have received education in Chinese, the Education Commission proposed in 1990 that a bridging program of two or three months be taken by students between the end of secondary schooling and the beginning of tertiary education. Both proposals were criticized by local experts in linguistics and language education as theoretically unsound and practically unworkable (LSHK 1991).

The colonial government of Hong Kong, over a long period of time, failed to formulate an effective policy on the medium of instruction in schools that won support from teachers and language experts as well as the wider local community. It was generally felt that, in comparison with the serious attention given to improving the level of English on the part of students, not much had been done to enhance proficiency in Chinese, in spite of the fact that most Chinese teachers were not satisfied with students' competence in both spoken Cantonese and the standard Modern Written Chinese. It was also maintained by a large number of language teachers that *putonghua* should have received more attention, both because it was going to assume a more prominent role after the British colony returned to mainland China, and also because it was the language on which Modern Written Chinese was based. In 1985, *putonghua* was first formally introduced as an optional subject in primary schools, and was later introduced in secondary schools. It was also promoted as an extra-curricular activity throughout the school system. A survey in 1991 showed that 52.7 per cent of primary schools and 37.8 per cent of secondary schools had started *putonghua* classes, mostly one or two periods a week, and a larger number of schools had introduced it as an extra-curricular activity (He 1993).

On the eve of the return of sovereignty to China, the colonial government of Hong Kong finally decided to adopt a more resolute policy on the issue. In March 1997, the Department of Education issued a "firm" directive which instructed that, starting from the fall semester of 1998, secondary schools should generally employ Chinese as the medium of instruction from Year 1 onward, except for the English subject and some other subjects that were exempted from the requirement. Schools that intended to retain English as the medium of instruction would have to apply for special permission to the Head of the Department of Education, and provide evidence of a sufficient level of competence in English on the part of their teaching staff and students. It was estimated that, on full implementation of the policy, more than three quarters of the secondary schools in Hong Kong would adopt Cantonese as the official medium of instruction.

4. Conclusion

For a long period of time, the language policy of the colonial government of Hong Kong served to guarantee the privileged status of English as a High language, and to relegate Chinese, which mainly comprised spoken Cantonese, Mandarin, and Modern Written Chinese, to the status of a Low language in a trilingual and diglossic society.

Unlike the Chinese government in promoting Modern Standard Chinese on the mainland and in Taiwan, the colonial government of Hong Kong did not launch any special campaign to promote English among local Cantonese-speaking residents. Instead, by ensuring that English was the only de jure and de facto official language in the colony for more than a century, it instilled into the local residents the importance of high proficiency in English as a requisite for success in one's career. On the other hand, the Hong Kong government did not adopt a prohibitive attitude toward the indigenous languages, as the colonial government did in Taiwan after the island was ceded to Japan in 1895, and the Nationalist government did after its restoration in 1945. Cantonese was always the language of home in Hong Kong, and was extensively used in all sectors of society. Except for a brief period in the 1960s and 1970s, language was seldom a source of severe conflict in Hong Kong.

Political factors played a pivotal role in the change of language policy in Hong Kong which resulted in the de jure and de facto status of Chinese as one of the two official languages. How various linguistic and extra-linguistic factors interact to determine the status of English, Cantonese and *putonghua* in post-colonial Hong Kong will be the topic of a further research report.

References:

Bacon-Shone, John and Bolton, Kingsley. 1998. Charting multilingualism: language censuses and language surveys in Hong Kong, In: Martha C. Pennington, ed., 45-90.

Bauer, Robert. 1988. Written Chinese of Hong Kong, *Cahiers de Linguistique Asie Orientale* 17 (2): 245-293.

Chen, Ping. 1996. Modern Written Chinese, dialects, and regional identity, *Language Problems and Language Planning* 20(3):223-243.

Chen, Ping. 1999. *Modern Chinese: History and Sociolinguistics*, Cambridge and New York: Cambridge University Press.

Chan, Johannes M. M. 1986. The Chinese language and legal education in Hong Kong, Paper presented at Conference on Language Policy and Language Planning in Hong Kong, 1986.

Ching, Cheung Fai. ed. 1992. *Aomen Yuyan Lunji* [*Papers on Language in Macao*], Aomen Shehui Kexue Xuehui.

Cheung, Yat-shing. 1985. Power, solidarity, and luxury in Hong Kong: A sociolinguistic study, *Anthropological Linguistics* 27(2):190-203.

Fang, Yuanhua. 1991. Zhuisu Yingwen jiaoyu de lishi [On the history of education in English], In: Jing' an He et al., eds., 225-238.

Gibbons, John. 1979. U-gay-wa: A linguistic study of the campus language of students at the University of Hong Kong. In: Robert Lord, ed., 3-43.

He, Guoxiang. et al. 1993. *Putonghua Ke Jiaoshi de Jiben Yaoqiu Yanjiu* [*Language Proficiency Requirements for Teachers of Putonghua*]. Hong Kong: Institute of Language in Education.

He, Jing'an. et al. 1991. *Xianggang Jiaoyu Pouxi* [*An Analysis of Education in Hong Kong*]. Hong Kong: Guangjiaojing Chubanshe.

Hou, Jingyi. 1996. Shilun' 97 hou putonghua zai Xianggang de diwei [On the status of putonghua in Hong Kong after 1997]. *Zhongguo Yuwen* [*Chinese Language and Writing*] 2/1996: 131-134.

Johnson, Robert. 1998. Language and education in Hong Kong. In: Martha C. Pennington, ed., Hong Kong University Press, 265-276.

Liu, Ching-chih. 1986. Bilingual manpower needs for Hong Kong. Paper presented at Conference on Language Policy and Language Planning in Hong Kong, 1986.

Lord, Robert. ed. 1979. *Hong Kong Language Papers*, Hong Kong University Press.

LSHK (Linguistic Society of Hong Kong). 1991. Education Commission Report No. 4: A response, *LSHK Newsletter* 10: 8-16.

Pennington, Martha C. ed. 1998. *Language in Hong Kong at Century's End*. Hong Kong University Press.

Sin, King-kui, et al. 1992. Shuangyu lifa de yixie lilun wenti [Some theoretical issues on legal bilingualism], In: Ching Cheung Fai, ed., 171-172.

So, James. 1986. Promotion of Chinese in government business in Hong Kong. Paper presented at Conference on Language Policy and Language Planning in Hong Kong, 1986.

So, W.-C. 1986. Differential social selection of Chinese middle schools and Anglo-Chinese secondary schools in Hong Kong and its implications for educational language planning—historical and sociolinguistic perspectives. Paper presented at Conference on Language Policy and Language Planning in Hong Kong, 1986.

T'sou, Benjamin K. 1986. Language planning in Hong Kong: quo vadis? Paper presented at Conference on Language Policy and Language Planning in Hong Kong 1986.

T'sou, Benjamin K. et al. 1992. Hanyu, Yueyu yu Xianggang de falü yuyan [Chinese, Cantonese and legal languages in Hong Kong], In: Ching Cheung Fai, ed., 164-170.

Wells, A. R. 1986. Implications of the Education Commission's reports on language in education in Hong Kong. Paper presented at Conference on Language Policy and Language Planning in Hong Kong, 1986.

Yu, Fong-ying. 1986a. Tradition and change in Chinese education in Hong Kong. Paper presented at Conference on Language Policy and Language Planning in Hong Kong, 1986.

Yu, Fong-ying. 1986b. Towards an accommodation model of language education—A perspective from Hong Kong. Paper presented at Conference on Language Policy and Language Planning in Hong Kong, 1986.

香港 1997 年之前的语言政策

提　要　香港的语言情况可以概括为三语两文，三语为英语、粤语和普通话，两文是书面英文和书面中文。1997 年以前香港政府的语言政策可分两个阶段，1974 年以前独尊英语，行政、立法、司法及其他正式场合限用英语，但在学校和社会传媒等其他地方，汉语也是常用语言。1974 年港英政府修改《法定语文条例》，正式规定英语和中文同为香港法定语言，是政府和市民彼此交流时所用语言。1984 年中英关于香港问题的联合声明签署以后，中文的地位得到进一步加强。1985 年 10 月以后，行政和立法会的所有文件都用中英文两种语言发表。1987 年进一步修定《法定语文条例》，规定所有政府条例都用双语颁布。政府内部的日常工作语言仍以英语为主，但鼓励公务员掌握双语能力，包括普通话听说能力。1990 年颁布的《中华人民共和国香港特别行政区基本法》第九条规定香港特别行政区的行政机关、立法机关和司法机关，除使用中文外，还可使用英文，英文也是正式语文。自此以后，中文地位提升较快。1990 年代早期至 1997 年，立法会中本地议员一般使用粤语，这同 1980 年代立法会以英语为主有很大的不同。中小学历来分为英文学校和中文学校两大类，出于实际利益的考虑，选择英语学校的学生人数自 1960 年代起逐年增加，1990 年代是中文学校人数的十倍。

关键词　语言政策　语言规划　三语　双言　香港

(This article was first published in *Language Planning and Language Policy: East Asian Perspectives*, edited by Nanette Gottlieb and Ping Chen, Curzon Press, pp.111-128, in 2001. Permission by Taylor and Francis Group to reprint the article in the present volume is gratefully acknowledged.)

Policy on the selection and implementation of a standard language as a source of conflict in Taiwan

Abstract The design and implementation of policy on a standard language for the community has been fraught with controversies and wrangles over more than 100 years in Taiwan. In the colonial period between 1895 and 1945, language policy served the purpose of alienating the local population from their ancestral and cultural roots in the mainland. In the post-colonial period, it served to integrate the island with the mainland politically, culturally and symbolically. To achieve this goal, a policy of monolingualism was pursued which aimed at replacing the predominant indigenous language with another language. Such a policy inevitably became a source of conflict on the island. With the changes in the political arena since the mid-1980s, more attention has been paid to the acquisition and use of indigenous dialects and languages.
Keywords language policy; promotion of standard language; dialect; Taiwan

1. A sociolinguistic profile of Taiwan

According to the latest census in 1998, Taiwan has a population of 21.9 million. Of the various Chinese dialects and aboriginal languages spoken on the island, the Southern Min dialect, is the largest, with native speakers comprising 72 per cent of the population. 12 per cent of the population speak Hakka, and 14 per cent speak other Chinese dialects as their first language. Aboriginals account for about 2 per cent of the population, speaking more than a dozen Malayo-Polynesian languages. As a result of effective promotion by the government, Modern Standard Chinese based upon Northern Mandarin, called *guoyu* 'national language', is also extensively popularized, with 95 per cent of the population speaking it in varying degrees of proficiency (Chen 1999). Taiwan is thus a bilingual society, as are mainland China and Hong Kong. According to the statistics in Huang (1993), 82.5 per cent of native speakers of Southern Min are bilingual in Southern Min and *guoyu*, and 88 per cent of native speakers of other Chinese dialects and aboriginal languages are bilingual in *guoyu* and their native tongue.

When the Dutch invaded the island in 1624, they found a local population that was comprised of aboriginals and migrants from mainland China, with the former outnumbering the later approximately by four to one (Fang 1965:2). The aboriginals spoke languages belonging to the Austronesian family; migrants from mainland China were mostly speakers of Southern Min and Hakka. The island returned to the sovereignty of mainland China after the Chinese general Zheng Chenggong repelled the Dutch in 1661. In the following years, there was a steady increase of migrants from mainland China, mostly from Southern Min-speaking areas across the Taiwan Strait. As a result, Southern Min became the dominant local dialect.

According to historical records, the promotion of Northern Mandarin in Taiwan started in 1729, in conformity with an edict from the Imperial Court in Beijing. At that time, Northern Mandarin had served as a lingua franca across China for at least 500 years, used extensively by scholars and officials in addition to their native dialects, except in the Guangdong and the Fujian provinces, where Cantonese and Min were predominant not only in everyday life but also on formal occasions. To ensure efficient communication between local residents and the government, the Emperor ordered that language training institutes be set up in the two provinces, where scholars and officials underwent training in Northern Mandarin. Similar institutes were also founded in Taiwan, which was still part of the Fujian province. The efforts were short-lived, and did not achieve many positive results, presumably due to the inefficiency of the local government, and lack of enthusiasm on the part of the general public.

2. Language policy during the period of Japanese occupation (1895-1945)

Taiwan was ceded to Japan in 1895 after China lost the war with the latter in 1894. In the ensuing half century, Japan pursued a policy that aimed to integrate the island into Japan in a comprehensive way—politically, economically, militarily and culturally. Language stood prominently in the process. Unlike the more or less laissez-faire attitude toward the local languages on the part of the British colonial government in Hong Kong over most of the colonial period, the Japanese took the language issue very seriously, as constituting an important part of the overall policy to alienate the local residents from their ancestral and cultural roots on mainland China and assimilate them to Japan. It was during this period that language first became a highly politicized issue on the island.

From the beginning, the goal was to replace the local languages with Japanese not only for formal purposes but for everyday life as well. To attain the goal, a comprehensive set of measures was carefully designed and implemented step by step. Teaching Japanese language to local residents was given top priority from the first year of occupation, for the stated purpose of cultivating the spirit of Japanese nationals in the residents of the new colony. The government set up publicly-funded schools all over the island, which focused on the teaching of the Japanese language and culture. The curriculum was purged of content that might remind the Chinese of their cultural heritage or ethnic identity. While the Chinese language was taught as a subject in the early period, the number of hours was gradually reduced until 1937, when classes were canceled. Repeated petitions from local residents to pay due attention to Chinese language and to use Chinese as a medium of instruction in public schools were ignored by the government. Students who spoke local languages in schools were penalized and sometimes even beaten up.

Private schools run by local Chinese, on the other hand, attached much more importance to teaching the Chinese language and culture. These schools were very popular among local residents, who were generally ill disposed to the colonial language policy that discriminated against Chinese and preferred to send their children to the private Chinese schools rather than public schools. According to Huang (1993:87), there were about 1,822 such private schools in 1902, more than ten times as many as public schools, with an enrollment of nearly 33,592. To reverse the situation, the government brought the private schools under tighter control. While instruction in Japanese in these schools was encouraged through financial subsidy, instruction in and use of Chinese was increasingly subject to discouragement and restriction. In 1903, the government prohibited the import of books from mainland China and urged the private schools to use the same textbooks as adopted by public schools. At the same time, the authorities suspended or closed down private schools, giving a variety of excuses. As a result of the extremely oppressive measures by the colonial government, the private schools were decimated in the following decades. They were forced to close down in large numbers, with only 129 still in operation in 1933. The curriculum in the schools that survived shifted the focus away from Chinese language and culture, and became almost the same as that in the public schools (cf. Fang 1965:16). The last private Chinese school shut down in 1937.

In the early period, newspapers and magazines, while predominantly in Japanese, still carried columns in Chinese. With the language policy becoming increasingly repressive, the Chinese columns finally disappeared from local newspapers in 1937, the year when Japan invaded mainland China on a large scale. In the same year, government employees were instructed to use Japanese on all occasions. The government even aimed to push Japanese into family life, offering incentives to those who spoke Japanese at home in terms of better career prospects and special language allowances.

The strategy to promote Japanese at the expense of local languages in schools, mass media, government institutions and the wider community had succeeded to some extent. While it failed to achieve the goal of eliminating local languages completely in Taiwan, it did result in a bilingual society in which more than half of the population spoke Japanese as their first or second language, and also a diglossic society in which Japanese was the High language and Chinese the Low language. Close to the end of the Japanese occupation in 1944, 71 per cent of the local population had acquired Japanese, mainly via education in the public school system which covered the whole island (cf. Huang 1993:95). Since Japanese was the medium of instruction from primary schools upwards for a large part of the period, and Chinese was not taught even as a subject after 1937, a whole generation was brought up which was much better at Japanese than Chinese. Some still retained their competency in Chinese for informal purposes, and some lost it altogether. When Taiwan was returned to China in 1945, Japanese was the only language in which most educated people on the island could read and express themselves effectively on formal occasions and topics. Local Chinese dialects like Southern Min and Hakka were confined to family and to informal functions in the community. It was observed that at that time no local residents brought up on the island had a functional literacy in Chinese on topics beyond the trivialities of everyday life (Liang 1983:150, Wang 1990).

3. Language policy immediately after the restoration in 1945

Once language has turned into a highly politicized issue, as happened in the era of Japanese occupation, it demands great care and wisdom on the part of the succeeding government to deal with it. There is general consensus among historians and scholars of language policy in Taiwan that, unfortunately, the language issue was handled clumsily by General Chen Yi, the chief executive sent by the Nationalist government on the mainland to Taiwan, when the island was returned to China at the end of World War 2.

Local residents in Taiwan started learning *guoyu* with tremendous enthusiasm in the first few months after the restoration. In reaction to the colonial policy on language, *guoyu* was associated with the identity of being a Chinese and a part of China. Instructors of *guoyu* were able to attract a large group of learners when they set up a blackboard in the bazaar and started teaching there. No language, however, could be acquired overnight. So far as the general public was concerned, it took more time than was realized by the government for *guoyu* to replace Japanese or Southern Min as the working language on the island.

According to the memoir of Wang Yiding (1991), right after Chen Yi arrived in Taiwan in 1945 he issued an order prohibiting the use of Japanese and the local Southern Min in public places. Newspapers in Japanese and radio broadcasting in Japanese and Southern Min were totally banned. While the prohibition of Japanese might be justified on the grounds that it was the language of the former colonizing enemy, the same stringent treatment of Southern Min defies explanation. The heavy-handed measures, although in force for a relatively short period, caused enormous inconvenience among the local residents. Within a very short time, they were deprived of the competence to express their opinions in public or be informed of what was going on around them. Meanwhile, proficiency in *guoyu* weighed as the most important requirement in the recruitment of public servants, which severely disadvantaged local residents. Communication between the government and the local community was greatly impaired, which was a contributing factor to the tragic riot in 1947 in which hundreds of thousands of people were killed. As Wang noted, such prohibitive measures against the local Southern Min on the part of the then government served no conceivable political purpose and only displayed arrogance and ignorance on the part of the administration.

4. Language policy since 1946

The policy on language, fortunately, was soon delegated to educators and experts in language planning. In April, 1946 the *Guoyu Tuixing Weiyuanhui* '*Guoyu* Promotion Committee' was established within the Department of Education of the Provincial Government of Taiwan; this played a pivotal role in the design and implementation of language policy until 1959, when it was incorporated into the Community Education Division of the Department of Education. Its major activities included a survey of the general linguistic situation in Taiwan, compilation of textbooks, dictionaries and other teaching aid materials in *guoyu* promotion, recruiting and training of teachers, promotion and supervision of *guoyu* instruction, and budget preparation. At the same time, a *Guoyu* Promotion Institute which was responsible for the implementation of the plans and strategies drawn up by the Provincial *Guoyu* Promotion Committee was established in each of the major cities and counties on the island.

Founders of the Provincial *Guoyu* Promotion Committee mostly came from the mainland at the invitation of the Taiwan government. Almost all of them had been policy makers and active participants in *guoyu* promotion on the mainland, and what they intended to do was to apply to Taiwan the guiding principles and concrete measures they were familiar with. One year earlier on the mainland, a nation-wide policy on *guoyu* promotion which was based on the program of the *Guoyu Yundong* 'National Language Movement' in the 1920s and 1930s was promulgated by the Ministry of Education of the National Government. The policy was comprised of five major items (cf. Fang 1965, Zhang 1974):

(1) To standardize the pronunciation of Chinese characters. As Chinese uses a logographic writing system, the same character may have different pronunciations in different dialects. Language planning institutions since

the 1910s had decided on the pronunciation of more than 6,000 characters on a case by case basis, which were later codified in *Guoyu Cidian* 'Dictionary of National Language', published in 1937. It was now stipulated that all school children should follow the standard pronunciation when they acquired literacy.

(2) To promote *guoyu* across the country. *Guoyu* should also serve as the standard for learners of Chinese as a second language. It should be taken as a symbol of the unity of the country which features a large number of diverse dialects and languages.

(3) To promote *Zhuyin Guoz*i 'annotated Chinese characters', which were of a new type comprising of characters in juxtaposition with sound-annotating symbols. It was hoped that this new type would facilitate both literacy and promotion of standard pronunciation at the same time.

(4) To promote *Zhuyin Fuhao* 'sound annotating symbols', which were designed to annotate the pronunciation of Chinese characters in a clear, dialect-neutral manner.

(5) To conduct research on the pedagogy of *guoyu* in order to improve the efficiency of its instruction.

Without much knowledge of the actual linguistic situation in Taiwan at that time, the experts from the mainland assumed before they went to the island that the local residents would naturally use their native tongues, Southern Min, Hakka or aboriginal languages, as effective means of communication after Japanese was banned, and that Southern Min was the dominant Chinese dialect on the island. On the basis of these assumptions, it was intended that the above five items should be implemented in Taiwan in the same way as on the mainland. It turned out that these assumptions were largely unwarranted.

After the first few months of the implementation of the language policy in the winter of 1945, it was realized that the linguistic situation in Taiwan differed remarkably from that in other parts of China. While people of the old generation still retained proficiency in Southern Min or Hakka, the Chinese dialects were very rusty among people in middle age, and had been completely lost with a considerable part of the young generation, as a result of the suppression of indigenous languages under colonial rule. Even where Chinese was still used by some people, the spoken and the written forms were heavily influenced by Japanese, full of words and syntactic structures from the latter. When school children learned Chinese characters in schools, they learned them as part of the Japanese writing system and read them with Japanese pronunciation. The agony of the local residents over their linguistic competence was compared to that of a child who was kidnapped and was made dumb. He was extremely excited when returned to his parents, but could not utter a single word in his "mother" tongue (Fang 1975:133).

The local residents at that time were also faced with the practical problem of the lack of an appropriate language as the medium of instruction in the teaching of *guoyu*, as well as for everyday use by all members of the community before they acquired *guoyu*. The obvious solution was to restore the local Chinese dialects, particularly Southern Min. Language planners agreed that the agenda drawn up on the mainland should undergo some modification to accommodate the actual situation in Taiwan. The revised *guoyu* promotion campaign now comprised the following six tasks:

(1) to restore the local Chinese dialects so as to facilitate the learning of *guoyu* through comparison;

(2) to pay great attention to the pronunciation of Chinese

characters, which should be based upon *guoyu*;

(3) to cleanse the Chinese language of syntax and pronunciation from Japanese. Chinese texts should be read in standard national pronunciation—in the way they should have been read;

(4) to conduct contrastive studies of word classes to enrich the content of the Chinese language and build a new *guoyu*;

(5) to make use of *Zhuyin Fuhao* to facilitate communication among all ethnic Chinese groups, which would in turn contribute to an integrated Chinese culture;

(6) to foster the desire to learn Chinese (on the part of local residents), and improve the efficiency of instruction.

From 1946 onward, the above agenda was implemented under the management and supervision of the Provincial *Guoyu* Promotion Committee. In comparison with the period immediately after the restoration, the government now adopted a more tolerant policy toward Southern Min. It was reported that in 1950, the President even issued an order for government employees and the military to learn the local Southern Min (Huang 1993:101), which, however, was not effectively enforced.

The tolerant stance toward non-Mandarin dialects did not last long. In 1956, a *Jiang Guoyu Yundong* 'Speaking *Guoyu* Movement' was launched, which aimed to accelerate the promotion of *guoyu* by dictating that *guoyu* should be used exclusively in schools, government institutions and public places. For the next decades, the official language policy was directed toward the goal that *guoyu* was to become the predominant language of all the residents on the island, while the use of other Chinese dialects and languages was to be reduced to a minimum.

Before 1956, according to Huang (1993), local dialects and *guoyu* were used in a mixed way in schools. After 1956, *guoyu* became the sole medium of instruction while local dialects were totally banned in schools. In a way similar to the colonial period, school children were subject to fines or corporal punishment for speaking dialects other than *guoyu* in schoolyards. Use of local dialects in mass media was also strictly restricted. Out of commercial considerations, TV stations in Taiwan preferred to have more programs in local dialects. In the early 1970s, half of the programs were in Southern Min. With interference from the government, this was reduced to less than 20 per cent in 1972. In 1975, the bill on broadcasting and TV was passed by the legislature, which stipulated that programs in local dialects should be reduced every year. Consequently, time for programs in dialects was reduced to less than 10 per cent on TV, mostly confined to weather broadcasting and news on agriculture and fishing which accommodate an older audience who may not understand *guoyu*.

The language policy adopted by the Nationalist government on Taiwan over more than three decades up to the mid-1980s differed in terms of goals and implementation from that practiced by the same government between the 1920s and 1940s when it was on the mainland. When *guoyu* was promoted as the standard spoken language on the mainland, it was not intended to replace local dialects for informal uses. The goal was a bilingual society in which people acquired proficiency in *guoyu* and in their native dialect. In Taiwan, on the other hand, what was pursued was essentially a policy of monolingualism, with *guoyu* serving as the sole legitimate language in schools, and with the expectation that it would replace local dialects for all occasions in due course. Furthermore, the measures adopted in Taiwan were also more stringent than on the mainland, particularly in relation to the medium of instruction in schools and the use of language in mass media. The Nationalist government while on the mainland before 1949 did not take any administrative measures to enforce the use of *guoyu* as the language of instruction, and school teachers generally used the local dialect in the classroom. *Guoyu* was the sole or dominant language in mass media, not in accordance with government regulations but as a natural choice by media directors who wanted to appeal to the audience nation-wide. The government of the People's Republic of China founded in 1949 has by and large followed the Nationalist government before 1949 in the design and implementation of language policy on Standard Spoken Chinese.

The stringent measures adopted in the implementation of the language policy in Taiwan proved to be effective, resulting in a better rate of acquisition of *guoyu* in Taiwan than on the mainland either before 1949 or after 1949. According to Chen (1999), in the early 1990s, while about 51 per cent of the population in mainland China spoke the Modern Standard Chinese, the percentage was as high as 95 per cent in Taiwan (cf. Tse 1986, Huang 1988, 1993, Kubler 1985, van den Berg 1988).

The high acquisition rate of *guoyu* has been achieved at a cost. The aboriginal languages and some local dialects, like Hakka, have been dying out in some parts of the island, especially among the younger generation. It was reported that many grandparents who do not speak *guoyu* have linguistic difficulty in communicating with their grandchildren, who tend to lose proficiency in the native tongue of their parents and grandparents. Restrictions on time for programs in non-Mandarin dialects in TV and radio broadcasting have also deprived some aboriginals and elderly people who do not understand *guoyu* of full access to news and entertainment from mass media.

In spite of the side effects of the language policy in the local community, dissenting voices were few and weak before the mid-1980s. This is easily understood when viewed in the political context of the island during the period. Before the 1980s, Taiwan was a totalitarian society in which all political rivals of the government, real and perceived, were effectively suppressed. For all the ideological acrimony and military confrontation between mainland China and Taiwan, the government on both sides of the Taiwan Strait adhered to the policy of one China, with each claiming to be the sole legitimate representative of the country. When *guoyu* was promoted on the mainland before 1949 under the Nationalist government, and after 1949 under the Communist government, it was mainly taken as an endeavor toward the linguistic goal of facilitating communication across Chinese dialects, and acquisition of Standard Written Chinese, which is based upon Northern Mandarin for grammar and vocabulary (cf. Chen 1999). This took on a distinctively political dimension in Taiwan. Language policy on the island was formulated and implemented on the assumptions that Taiwan was a province of China and that *guoyu*, as the national language of China, serves as an important symbol of the unity of the country. Consciousness of the regional identity of Taiwan as against other parts of China was suppressed as a sensitive political issue that could challenge the legitimacy of the Nationalist government which removed to the island after its defeat on the mainland by the Chinese Communist Party. In view of the increased use of dialects in Taiwan, Mu Chao, a national legislator, proposed in 1972 that the *Guoyu* Promotion Committee should be restored at the provincial level of Taiwan, and at the municipal level of Taipei, and that more resources be allocated to the endeavor. What was more serious, he suggested that there were communist spies lurking within the government who were sabotaging the promotion of *guoyu*, and called for their identification and prosecution. He also suspected that there were communists behind many joint venture manufacturers who advertised in electronic mass media in local dialects, which, as he saw it, was a conspiracy aiming at political division (Zhang 1974:214-5). This represented the height of politicization of linguistic issues in Taiwan since the 1950s. Under the martial law then in force on the island, any of these charges could spell disaster for the person accused.

The first systemic critical review of the language policy was published in 1979 by Professor Robert Cheng, a resident native who was teaching at the University of Hawaii. In Cheng (1979:569-573), he elaborated on the main side effects of the language policy as follows:

(1) It brought incalculable advantages to Mandarin speakers and those who had acquired the language before, and disadvantages to the Southern Min and Hakka speakers in almost all aspects of life—economic, political, social, and educational;

(2) It widened the generational gap in Southern Min and Hakka families and communities between parents who had received schooling in Japanese and their children educated in Mandarin;

(3) School education would have been more effective if conducted in the native tongues of children instead of in *guoyu* exclusively.

As is evident from the more open discussions on the issue in Taiwan later on in the 1980s and 1990s, his views are shared by a considerable number of local residents, particularly those of indigenous origin as opposed to settlers who came from the mainland after 1945.

Taiwan suffered further international isolation after the USA established a formal diplomatic relationship with the PRC in 1979 and withdrew its recognition of Taiwan as a sovereign state. To marshal support from its own citizens, the government accelerated the process of democratization and localization, adopting a policy that was more responsive to the demands of the indigenous population as distinct from settlers since 1945. The largest opposition party, the Democratic Progress Party (DPP), founded in 1987, was composed mainly of people of indigenous origin. Language policy became one of the key issues around which the DPP solicited support in its challenge to the government. Calls were increasing for the abolition of the restrictions on the use of dialects. Meanwhile, the Ministry of Education drafted a *Yuwen Fa* 'Act on Language' in 1985, which attempted to further consolidate the primacy of *guoyu* for use for all public functions, in schools, and in mass media, with dialects being subjected to more severe restriction than before. Unlike the situation in the previous decades, the draft aroused strong resistance in the legislature and the broader community. It was aborted in the same year, marking a turning point in official language policy in Taiwan.

Huang (1993:111) provides a succinct summary of the demands that have arisen since the 1980s for changes to the official language policy when he proposes: "We may approve a policy on *guoyu* as the national language. However, the policy must be more magnanimous toward other languages or dialects. If we do not go as far as granting dialects the status of official language along with *guoyu*, we should at least have them as a language of instruction, and promote bilingual education. Meanwhile, restrictions on the dialects in broadcasting and TV should be abolished, leaving the market to decide on the demands for programs in dialects. Otherwise, language will also be an issue of political protest."

What the Nationalist government has done since the mid-1980s is gradually conceding to the above demands. In 1987, the education authorities issued a formal notice, prohibiting any fine or corporal punishment for school children who spoke dialects in class or schoolyards. In the same year, with approval from the government, the three TV stations on the island started a daily 20-minute news program in Southern Min, and in 1989, the first TV program in Hakka was broadcast daily.

At the same time, in defiance of the regulations by the nationalist government, some schools started using dialects as the medium of instruction in 1987, first in cities with a DPP government, then extending gradually to other places. In 1993, the Ministry of Education decided to introduce mother-tongue instruction into the regular curriculum. In the same year, the government abolished the restriction on the use of dialects in the mass media imposed by the Law of Radio and TV Broadcasting.

Meanwhile, there has been significant increased use of local dialects, particularly Southern Min, in society, which was inspired by, and contributed to, a heightened awareness of local identity in contrast to mainland China. Pro-independence activists in particular, who are against the traditional establishment of the Nationalist government, lashed out at the *guoyu* promotion campaign as part of a conspiracy by mainlanders against the local residents. As a matter of principle, and also to highlight their differentiation from mainlanders, they use Southern Min on all occasions, including congress debates, election campaigns and daily administration. Members of the ruling party of government also use Southern Min increasingly to appeal to the local population for support in administration and elections. In current society at large, meanwhile, those who do not speak fluent Southern Min find it increasingly difficult to find a good job, particularly in private businesses, and in cities and towns other than Taipei. While it is still too early to claim that the *guoyu* promotion campaign is all but dead, it has certainly lost the political support it enjoyed before. *Guoyu* still is, and will remain for a long time to come, a most important language on the island, learned by school children and used by a large part of the local population, particularly on formal occasions and as a lingua franca across dialects. It is most probable that they do so out of pragmatic considerations, rather than under political coercion.

5. Conclusion

Taiwan over the past century provides a textbook case that illustrates how political motivations can far outweigh linguistic factors in the design and implementation of policy on a standard language for the community (cf. Kaplan and Baldauf 1997:30). In the colonial period between 1895 and 1945, language policy served the purpose of alienating the local population from their ancestral and cultural roots in mainland China. In the post-colonial period, it served to integrate Taiwan with mainland China politically, culturally and symbolically, and, in so doing, to assert the legitimacy of the government removed from the mainland. To achieve these goals, a policy of monolingualism was pursued which aimed at replacing the predominant indigenous language with another language. Such a policy inevitably became a source of conflict on the island. With the changes in the political arena since the mid-1980s that feature a transfer of power from mainlanders who came after 1945 to those who had been living on the island before 1945, more attention is being paid to the acquisition and use of indigenous dialects and languages. It can be anticipated that language in Taiwan will henceforth be less of a source of conflict than before.

References:

Chen, Ping. 1999. *Modern Chinese: History and Sociolinguistics*. Cambridge and New York: Cambridge University Press.

Cheng, Robert L. 1979. Language unification in Taiwan: Present and future. In: William C. McCormack and Steven A. Wurm, eds., *Language and Society: Anthropological Issues*, The Hague: Mouton, 541-578.

Fang, Shiduo. 1965. *Wushi Nian Lai Zhongguo Guoyu Yundongshi* [*History of the National Language Movement in China during the Past 50 Years*]. 2nd ed. Taipei: Guoyu Ribao She.

Figueroa, Esther. 1988. Evaluating language policy in Taiwan—Some questions. In: Robert L. Cheng and Shuanfan Huang, eds., 285-298.

Huang, Shuanfan. 1988. A sociolinguistic profile of Taipei (1), In: Robert L. Cheng and Shuanfan Huang, eds., 301-333.

Huang, Shuanfan. 1993. *Yuyan, Shehui Yu Zuqun Yishi* [*Language, Society and Group Consciousness*], Taipei: Wenhe Chuban Youxian Gongsi.

Kaplan, Robert B. and Richard B. Baldauf Jr. 1997. *Language Planning: From Practice to Theory*, Clevedon, Avon: Multilingual Matters.

Kubler, Cornelius C. 1985. *The Development of Mandarin in Taiwan: A Case Study of Language Contact*. Taipei: Student Book Co.

Liang, Rongruo. 1983. Guangfu yilai Taiwan guoyu guowen jiaoyu gaiguan (1945-1981) [An outline of instruction in National Language in Taiwan since the Restoration (1945-1981)], *Yuwen Xiandaihua* [*Language Modernization*], Vol. 1:150-153.

McCormack, William C. and Steven. eds. 1979. *Language and Society: Anthropological Issues*. The Hague: Mouton.

Tse, John Kwock-ping. 1986. Standardization of Chinese in Taiwan, *International Journal of the Sociology of Language* 59:25-32.

van den Berg, Marinus E. 1988. Taiwan's sociolinguistic setting, In: Robert L. Cheng and Shuanfan Huang, eds., 243-261.

Wang, Yiding. 1991. Zou guo guanjian niandai [Through the critical period], *Zhongyang Ribao* (Guoji Ban) [*Central Daily* (International Edition)], October 17, 1991.

Zhang, Boyu. 1974. *Taiwan Diqu Guoyu Yundong Shiliao* [*Historical Documents on the National Language Movement in Taiwan*], Taipei: Shangwu Yinshuguan.

台湾地区语言标准的选择和推行政策及其争议

提　要　标准语的确立是台湾地区 100 多年来充满纷争的问题。1895—1945 年台湾为日本所占，日本殖民政府采取的语言政策，旨在极力使台湾本土民众脱离中国大陆的历史和文化根源，强制推行日语，公立学校以日语教育为主，1937 年以后完全取消汉语课程，同时逐步关闭民间中文学校，取消报刊的汉语专栏。政府机构所有场合使用日语，并且将日语推行到民众家庭生活中去。抗战胜利前，人口一半以上以日语为第一语言或第二语言。1945 年国民政府收复台湾，当即禁用日语和本地闽南方言，虽然时间不长，但造成政府和民众沟通障碍，给战后恢复带来困难。1956 年以后，推行国语为标准语的同时，中小学校园禁用方言，违者体罚，类似做法也带来很多争议。对于台湾地区确立标准语过程中的主要考虑因素及采取的措施，本文做了详细的分析。

关键词　语言政策　推广标准语　方言　台湾

(This article was first published in *Language Planning and Language Policy: East Asian Perspectives* edited by Nanette Gottlieb and Ping Chen, Curzon Press, pp.95-110, in 2001. Permission by Taylor and Francis Group to reprint the article in the present volume is gratefully acknowledged.)

人名索引

E

F

G

H

J

主题索引

J

K

L

T

U

V

后　记

文选收录的三十篇论文围绕现代汉语研究的各个方面展开，涉及现代汉语的语法和语义、汉语研究的理论与方法，以及同说汉语、学汉语的人相关的其他语言问题。文选共分三卷，标题分别为《汉语的形式、意义与功能》《引进·结合·创新——现代语言学理论与中国语言学研究》和《语言与中国的现代化进程》。

《汉语的形式、意义与功能》收录十二篇论文，研究对象是汉语句法、语义、语用和话语分析中具有较大理论意义的课题，从形式、意义和功能的角度对相关汉语现象作详尽的实证分析和深入的理论探讨，旨在揭示汉语句法、语义、语用和话语篇章的主要特点，并阐发有关汉语现象在普通语言学层面上的理论意义。

中国传统语言研究领域是文字、音韵和训诂。现代语言学着重关注的音系、句法、语义、语用等研究领域，所用的主要理论、概念和方法大都起源于西方语言研究。20世纪初以来中国语言学家所做的主要工作，是利用外来的理论、概念和方法分析本土材料，并以此为基础对前者进行补充、修正，进而提出描写和解释能力更为周延的新理论、新概念和新方法。要做好本土语言研究，两个前提条件必不可少：一是对语料全面、准确地掌握，二是对语言学理论和方法的深刻理解。《引进·结合·创新——现代语言学理论与中国语言学研究》收录十篇论文，主要内容是笔者就普通语言学和汉语研究两者关系所做的思考，以及对普通语言学主要理论、概念及方法的研究体会。

1898年出版的《马氏文通》开创了中国现代语言学研究的历史。《马氏文通》研究的是古代汉语。中国现代汉语研究的初创之年，可以定于

1917年。那一年白话文运动与《国语研究会》的代表人物双潮合一，整合19世纪下半叶中国开始步入现代化进程以来，社会有识之士提出的“我手写我口”“汉语拼音化”“文字改革”“言文一致”“国语统一”等语言文字改革思想，首次为现代汉语口语和书面语标准形式的属性拟定具体要求，为其发展提出可行路径。现代汉语语音、词汇、语法以及文字改革从此成为汉语研究的重点领域。《语言与中国的现代化进程》收录八篇论文，着重探讨汉语语言文字在中国现代化进程中所起的作用以及自身所经历的变化，并从社会发展的角度观察颇具中国特色的语言规划问题。

三十篇论文均曾刊于海内外学术期刊和文集。2016年夏，徐赳赳教授和尚新教授分别向我建议，从历年发表的论文中选取较具代表性的编为文集出版，免去读者翻检搜寻之劳。该建议得到商务印书馆总编辑周洪波博士的大力支持，并委任何瑛博士担任文选的责任编辑。何瑛博士在时间紧、工作量大的情况下加班加点，高质量地完成了文选的编辑工作。徐赳赳教授也参与了文选英文论文的部分编辑工作。我在此向徐赳赳教授、尚新教授、周洪波博士和何瑛博士表示诚挚的谢意。

多年学术生涯中有幸得到很多师友的指教，文章中的许多思想都是在同他们的切磋辩难之中生发和成熟的，在此一并致谢。这些论文的完成还得益于我所工作的中国、美国和澳大利亚大学和研究机构提供的良好研究条件，得益于安宁的家庭氛围。妻子朱静、爱女Fay和Laura是我人生中最为珍惜的部分，她们对我的支持和关爱，我永远感激不尽。

整理文稿的过程中，时时浮现恩师吕叔湘先生的面容。写作也是对话，吕先生指引我走上汉语语言学研究的道路，也是我自中国社科院语言所学生年代起撰写论文时心目中的主要对话人。文选收录的文章，有好几篇初稿写成后，第一位读者便是先生，并且总能得到先生的悉心指教。先生离去后，我动笔开篇时，往往心目中的第一读者还是先生，只是初稿完成后寄送无由，再也无从聆听老人家的教诲了。

陈平

2017年5月

澳大利亚昆士兰大学

Epilogue

The thirty papers in the present three-volume anthology center around Modern Chinese, covering themes such as its grammar and semantics, theories and methodologies of Chinese language studies, and other language-related subjects concerning speakers and learners of Chinese. The respective titles of the three volumes are *The Chinese Language: Form, Meaning and Function*, *Introduction, Integration and Innovation: The Relationship between General Linguistics and Chinese Language Studies*, and *Language in a Modernizing China*.

The twelve papers in *The Chinese Language: Form, Meaning and Function* focus on subjects with theoretical impact in the areas of Chinese syntax, semantics, pragmatics and discourse analysis. They present findings from empirical and theoretical investigations into the form, meaning and function of the Chinese language, which aim to identify characteristic features of the Chinese language, and explore implications of the findings for issues of more general interest in modern linguistics.

Traditional Chinese language studies focus on script, historical phonology, and critical interpretation of ancient texts (*xungu*). Major theories, concepts and methodologies in the studies of phonology, syntax, semantics, pragmatics and other areas of modern linguistics have emerged and developed mainly on the basis of studies of Western languages. Since the beginning of the twentieth century Chinese linguists have undertaken to apply theories, concepts and methodologies originating in the West to the analysis of the Chinese language, and at the same time have endeavoured to revise and innovate based on findings from Chinese. Two pre-conditions must be met if one expects to conduct proper and meaningful studies of Chinese and other indigenous languages. One is a comprehensive collection of relevant language data, and the other is in-depth understanding of theoretical and methodological apparatuses related to the analysis of the data in question. The ten papers in *Introduction, Integration and Innovation: The Relationship between General Linguistics and Chinese Language Studies* present my reflections on the relationship between general linguistics and Chinese language studies, and investigations into some of the most influential theories, concepts and methodologies of modern linguistics.

The start of research on the Chinese language from a modern linguistic perspective is marked by the publication of *Grammar* by Ma Jianzhong in 1898. However, the subject of study in *Grammar* is Classical Chinese. 1917 was the year when studies on Modern Chinese began to take shape. Major proponents of the Vernacular Written Chinese Movement and members of the National Language Studies Association joined forces in that year to delineate the features of Standard Modern Spoken and Written Chinese, and propose how Modern Chinese should be developed in a way that incorporated major thought and initiatives in language and script reform since the second half of the nineteenth century such as "I write what I speak", phonetization of Chinese, script reform, consistency of speech and writing, and unification of the National Language. Starting from that year, the phonetics and phonology, vocabulary, grammar and script of Modern Chinese fast became major areas of linguistic study in China. The eight papers in

Language in a Modernizing China examine the role of language in a modernizing China, and explore how the Chinese language and script developed in the process partially as an outcome of language planning efforts.

All of the thirty papers have previously been published in scholarly outlets in China and overseas. Professor Xu Jiujiu and Professor Shang Xin proposed in 2016 that I select from my writings in Chinese linguistics for the publication of an anthology to provide easier assess to my work. The proposal received firm support from Dr Zhou Hongbo, Editor-in-Chief of the Commercial Press in Beijing, arguably the most prestigious academic publisher in the Chinese language world, who entrusted the editing of the anthology to Dr He Ying, an experienced editor at the Commercial Press. Putting in a large amount of time and effort, Dr He completed the editing work against a tight time frame with admirable efficiency and exactitude. Professor Xu Jiujiu also helped with the editing of the papers in English in the anthology. I am grateful to all four for their support and kind help, which have resulted in the present three-volume anthology.

I thank all of my friends who have inspired and helped me in the development of many of the ideas in the thirty papers. I have benefited from the stimulating academic environments where I have been working in China, the USA and Australia over the past decades, and also from the tranquility of family life. What I treasure most in my life are my wife Jean, and two daughters, Fay and Laura. I am always grateful to them for their love and support.

Professor Lü Shuxiang, my mentor since I embarked on my career as a Chinese linguist, often appeared in my mind as I was editing the thirty papers for publication in the anthology. Writing is also dialogue. It is Professor Lü who first guided me to the work that I love, and who was also a primary addressee I have kept in mind when writing research papers since my student years at the Institute of Linguistics of the Chinese Academy of Social Sciences. As a matter of fact, Professor Lü was the first reader of several papers in the present collection, and was always kind enough to promptly offer his feedback and advice. Long after his passing away, he is still often the first reader I visualize when writing, and I regret that I can no longer send drafts for his feedback.

Chen Ping

May 2017

The University of Queensland, Australia